THE GUERRILLA AND THE JOURNALIST

THE **GUERRILLA** AND THE **JOURNALIST**

Exploring the Murderous Legacy of
Jonas Savimbi

Fred Bridgland

DELTA BOOKS
JOHANNESBURG · CAPE TOWN

First published in South Africa in 2022 by
DELTA BOOKS
An imprint of Jonathan Ball Publishers
A division of Media24 (Pty) Ltd
PO Box 33977
Jeppestown
2043

ISBN 978-1-92824-812-5
ebook ISBN 978-1-92824-813-2

*Every effort has been made to trace the copyright holders and to obtain their
permission for the use of copyright material. The publishers apologise for any
errors or omissions and would be grateful to be notified of any corrections that
should be incorporated in future editions of this book.*

www.jonathanball.co.za
www.twitter.com/JonathanBallPub
www.facebook.com/JonathanBallPublishers

Cover by Ayanda Phasha
Design and typesetting by Martine Barker
Set in Lato/Arno Pro

*For the Chingunji family especially, but also
for all the people of Angola.*

CONTENTS

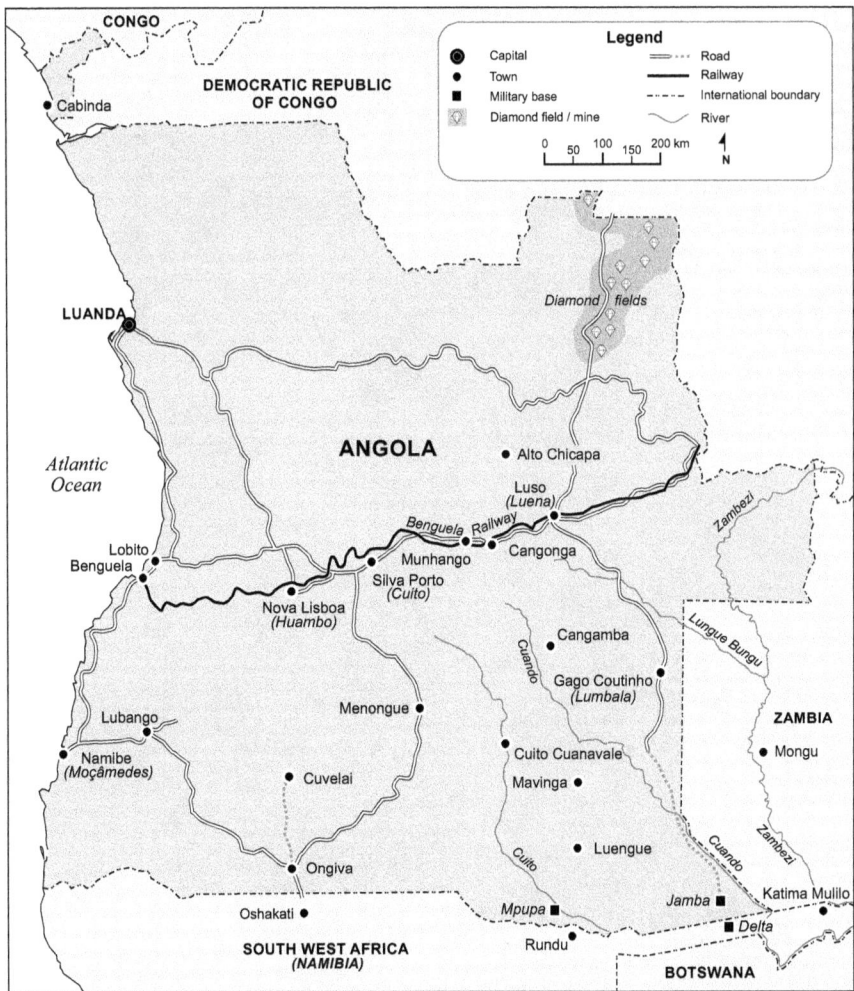

CONGO

DEMOCRATIC REPUBLIC
OF CONGO

Cabinda

Legend

Capital	Road
Town	Railway
Military base	International boundary
Diamond field / mine	River

0   50   100   150   200 km

N

LUANDA

Atlantic
Ocean

ANGOLA

Diamond fields

Alto Chicapa

Luso
(Luena)

Benguela Railway

Lobito
Benguela

Munhango   Cangonga

Silva Porto
(Cuito)

Nova Lisboa
(Huambo)

Cangamba

Cuando

Gago Coutinho
(Lumbala)

Zambezi

Lungue Bungu

ZAMBIA

Menongue

Lubango

Mongu

Namibe
(Moçâmedes)

Cuvelai

Cuito Cuanavale

Mavinga

Cuito

Luengue

Cuando

Zambezi

Ongiva

Oshakati

SOUTH WEST AFRICA
(NAMIBIA)

Mpupa

Rundu

Jamba

Delta

Katima Mulilo

BOTSWANA

Map of Savimbi's Angola.

PROLOGUE
Cuban blitzkrieg (January–February 1976)

I watched the fleeing guerrillas assembling in a small settlement, Gago Coutinho, near a tributary of the mighty Zambezi River and about 50 kilometres from the border with Zambia.

The exhausted UNITA fighters' war to take power in Angola, a newly independent former colony of Portugal, was over. A Soviet-backed Cuban military blitzkrieg was approaching from the west. There was no way the lightly armed Africans could resist the war-planes, tanks, armoured cars and heavy artillery of Fidel Castro's advancing warriors.

The Cubans had begun arriving in Angola, potentially the richest country in Africa, by sea and air from Havana in August 1975 in support of another liberation group, the Marxist-Leninist MPLA.[1]

Both UNITA (the National Union for the Total Independence of Angola) and the MPLA (the People's Movement for the Liberation of Angola) had waged war for decades against the Portuguese, who quit their five-centuries-old colony in early 1975. An agreement to hold pre-independence multi-party elections collapsed and quickly descended into civil war.

On 30 April 1975, as the last American helicopter left Vietnam, an irresistible new window of opportunity had opened in Angola for the Soviet Union in tandem with its ally, Cuba. One year earlier, on 25 April 1974, there had been a coup in Portugal which overthrew 50 years of right-wing dictatorship.[2] Young left-wing Portuguese officers quickly proclaimed the right of Angola to independence.

With the US crippled by the Vietnam debacle and President Richard Nixon's resignation over the Watergate scandal, Moscow saw and seized the opportunity for a further international gain in an assets-rich country strategically placed immediately to the north of the South African-ruled territory of South West Africa and apartheid-ruled South Africa itself. Moscow supplied the MPLA with US$6 million worth of Soviet weapons in one four-month period following the Portuguese coup: hundreds of millions more followed.

I was Reuters' Central Africa correspondent, based in Zambia with my young family, at the time. I had flown into Gago Coutinho from Zambia on 7 February 1976 aboard a battered old twin-engine Fokker Friendship to chronicle the defeated guerrilla army's final days. It was my fourth reporting journey in five months into guerrilla territory. This flight was hair-raising. Cuban warplanes were in action and the lumbering Fokker was an easy target. It was meant to be the last plane out of Angola for the leaders of UNITA before their followers were crushed by the Cubans. Another Fokker, bringing weapons from Zaire, had recently been destroyed on the ground by four Cuban MiG-21 fighter jets.

Some 4000 fighters in battledress milled around the Gago Coutinho landing strip as reports poured in of columns of Cuban tanks and armoured cars, supported by MPLA infantry, advancing from the north and west.

I watched as Jorge Sangumba, UNITA's efficient and articulate foreign secretary, who had flown with me from Zambia, fell into conversation with Jonas Savimbi, UNITA's leader. Savimbi was a charismatic, swaggering 41-year-old, trained militarily and ideologically in Mao Zedong's China. He had led his guerrillas since 1966 in the fight against the Portuguese. Savimbi had a legendary reputation among the tribespeople of central and southern Angola. He was the only liberation leader to have based himself personally inside the country to fight the colonial rulers.

Sangumba staggered away from the Savimbi powwow with his head buried in his hands, muttering, 'Oh my country, it is in trouble.' Town after town in Angola, he told me, was falling to thousands of MPLA and Cuban soldiers, whose heavy weaponry included helicopter gunships and Soviet-supplied Katyusha 'Stalin Organs', a multiple-launch rocket system that terrified the guerrillas and civilians. Hundreds of UNITA fighters were dying in a forlorn defence of Nova Lisboa/ Huambo, Angola's second-largest city, some 500 kilometres to the west of Gago Coutinho. Messengers were arriving with reports of guerrillas facing Cuban armour and being crushed beneath tank tracks. At a mission hospital, Vouga, Red Cross workers watched Cuban forces roll by from the north for two entire days. UNITA guerrillas, retreating fast, executed some Cuban prisoners. Nearer Gago Coutinho, sappers were blowing up road bridges to slow the Cuban advance.

With Savimbi in Gago Coutinho, was the head of his personal bodyguard, 20-year-old Tito Chingunji,[3] who spoke near-perfect American-accented English, self-taught by watching American TV soap operas, from books in front of a mirror, and from Canadian Protestant missionary schoolteachers. He had a calm and relaxed demeanour and was easy to talk with. In the months beforehand, he had briefed me frequently on the state of the conflict and on UNITA's history. The liberation movement had been co-founded by Savimbi and Tito's father, Jonatão, a schoolteacher and devout Christian. Tito's loyalty to UNITA and Savimbi was absolute. Eduardo Chingunji, Tito's nephew, assured me years later in one of many interviews that, 'I can unequivocally say that if an attempt had been made against Savimbi's life Tito, who was usually in front of the president shielding him, would have been the first to die.'

A young Tito Chingunji (middle, left) with his school mates in Namibe. (Source: Eduardo Chingunji)

Jonas Savimbi (centre) and Tito Chingunji (immediately to Savimbi's left). (Source: Eduardo Chingunji)

Tito, in previous weeks, had been leading a raiding company behind MPLA lines. He described to me how his men became entrapped by a larger enemy force and how he had hidden submerged in a swamp, breathing through a hollow reed to escape detection. He said he and his men escaped with the help of a village *ocimbanda* (traditional priest, or witch doctor), who volunteered to make himself invisible and walk through the MPLA front lines to summon help. I laughed patronisingly. Tito smiled indulgently: 'You don't believe in African magic, Mr Bridgland?'

Well, not really. 'It's very real to our people,' Tito replied. 'People in the villages believe Savimbi can fly.' I shrugged as noncommittally as possible and let Tito finish. He said the *ocimbanda* walked towards the enemy and disappeared from view. Later, a UNITA rescue group broke through, allowing Tito and his men to live to tell the tale.[4]

There would come a time when African magic was no longer a laughing matter to me.

As Fidel Castro's forces drew near, I got ready to fly out of Gago Coutinho to safety on UNITA's surviving Fokker with Sangumba, a few wounded guerrillas, some old and sick people and, I anticipated, Savimbi and some of his inner circle.

I asked Tito where he, Savimbi and other leaders of the defeated movement intended going to live in exile. It was a reasonable question. With the Cubans sweeping everything before them, the war was obviously finished. At that point in history, there had nowhere in the world been a successful resistance to Soviet-backed takeovers. The lesson of Hungarian, Czechoslovak and Polish attempts to throw off Soviet-loyal rulers was clear. Resistance by a little-known band of badly equipped Africans would clearly be futile, doomed to failure and annihilation.

To my astonishment, Tito said Savimbi intended leading his remaining forces on a Mao-style 'Long March' back to their old forest bases in the interior, from where they had fought the Portuguese, to regroup and begin a new liberation war against the Cubans, the Soviets and the MPLA.[5] Tito said he would go with them.

'We might all die,' he said. 'That might be our fate. But if we survive the world might begin to change and offer new opportunities.' He said the Cubans and Soviets were foreigners. They did not know the terrain or the rural people, their languages or their customs.

Tito spoke loyally of Savimbi. He had been an inspiration.

'He told us we have to fight first on our own, and only then will people in the outside world want to get in touch again. Foreigners who had helped UNITA will think we cannot resist, that we are finished. We will have to rely on our own efforts, support from our own people, our existing small weapons stocks and what guns we can capture. No help will come from outside before we and the people fight for ourselves.

'Savimbi said we should not accept capitulation, but he tried to put us in the picture about the great courage and the suffering involved in a guerrilla war. So, we are starting a new kind of life. It will be hard, and Savimbi says it's impossible to know how many people will be willing to continue the fight six months from now.'

With guerrilla columns already streaming into the forests, the Long March was beginning even as I boarded the last plane to the outside world on 9 February 1976. Tito came to the foot of the aircraft steps to say goodbye.

'If we survive,' he said, 'maybe one day you will write a book about us?'

I shook his hand and said a hollow 'okay'.

I never expected to see him again. Ever.

Four years later, in February 1980, I was working in Britain, after two years in Zambia, when the phone rang at my home and an operator asked if I would accept a reverse-charges telephone call from Morocco.

I did not know anyone in that country and the operator gave no name. I was deeply puzzled but agreed to take the mystery call despite the expense.

'Hello Mr Bridgland. How are you? I hope you remember me. It is Tito and I have survived.'

So, he said, had Savimbi and the movement after their Long March through the forests and savannah plains of central and southern Angola that had lasted many months and had resulted in many deaths and adventures. They were fighting a new war. And, Tito asked, did I remember the promise about a book? He and Savimbi would like to meet me again. They would provide a return air ticket if I agreed to meet them in Morocco.

Morocco? What on earth did Morocco have to do with the Angola conflict, I wondered.

Despite my young family's alarm, I flew to Casablanca from where I was whisked off by Moroccan secret service agents to a rambling old villa in Rabat in the palace grounds of the country's monarch, King Hassan II. It was all somewhat surreal. Tito and Savimbi were sitting there with many of the other guerrilla leaders I had known in Angola. Not only had they survived, said Tito, but they had begun fighting back and outsiders were again helping, as Savimbi had predicted.

It was unclear to me what was going on and who exactly was involved. Some kind of African Great Game was being played, not unlike the political and diplomatic confrontation between the British and Russian empires in the 19th century. It would take me many more years to work out how and why the United States, France, Saudi Arabia and others were channelling arms and money through Morocco to UNITA to support its struggle in Angola. The Saudis contributed an initial US$50 million.[6] Everything was clandestine, masked by lies, subterfuge and disinformation.

Among the Great Game players backing Savimbi were the

Moroccan monarch and President Leopold Senghor of Senegal, re-garded by many as one of the leading African intellectuals of the 20th century. Senghor gave UNITA's representatives Senegalese passports so that they could travel the world. Senghor then introduced Savimbi to Hassan. Both saw Soviet adventurism as a great threat to black Africa, a view not universally shared by many African leaders.

King Hassan allowed 500 UNITA soldiers at a time to be trained by French Army and Central Intelligence Agency (CIA) instructors at the Ben Guerir military base near Marrakesh in the Atlas Mountains. The instruction was in basic infantry techniques, radio and explosives skills, anti-tank warfare, commando reconnaissance, logistics and intelligence and communications. For the best UNITA personnel, the commando training included parachute drops over the moun-tains. Morocco itself began supplying UNITA with weapons and other equipment, including ten thousand military uniforms.

Saudi Arabia and the Gulf States opened bank accounts for Savimbi and funded a right-wing public relations agency, Black, Mana-fort, Stone and Kelly, in Washington, DC, to support him. One partner in particular, Roger Stone, was notorious for taking no prisoners. He worked on the presidential campaigns of Richard Nixon, Ronald Reagan, George W Bush and later Donald Trump. One of Stone's battle cries was, 'Admit nothing, deny everything. Launch counterattack.'

Arms were delivered by Savimbi's backers through Angola's back door via various transit points, including Zaire (since renamed the Democratic Republic of Congo). There was one early delivery of 600 tonnes of rifles, mortars, cannons and anti-aircraft guns from the People's Republic of China, courtesy of Mao Zedong, who was an admirer of Savimbi and had trained him and his top guerrilla officers at Nanking Military Academy.[7]

The MPLA played into the hands of its enemies by refusing to hold the promised independence elections, by declaring a one-party state and signing a 20-year Friendship Treaty with Moscow. East Germany sent to Angola, in support of the MPLA, a paramilitary unit of the Felix Dzerzhinsky Regiment, named after the stony-faced Bolshevik who founded the Soviet state security police. The MPLA announced a sweeping purge of dissidents.

'The aim is to eliminate all elements disagreeing with the party's Marxist line,' said top Commissar Mendes de Carvalho, who paradoxically had been a friend of Tito's father when they were imprisoned together by the Portuguese in the Cape Verde Islands.

Tito said he and Savimbi would cooperate with me in every way possible if I honoured my pledge about a book. My original 'promise' had not been even half-hearted. Such a book about guerrillas whose future looked extremely perilous would be a difficult challenge. But I was sorely tempted – the vibrancy of Angola had got under my skin – and agreed. Journalistic instincts hardened. The lure of adventures crossing some of the least-known, most remote and wildest parts of Africa with Maoist guerrillas was too enticing to turn down. I knew that a tangled web was being weaved.

What I did not know then was just how immensely twisted and complex it would all be and how it would come to dominate my life. Nor how many profound experiences Tito and I would share, how many hundreds of kilometres I would trek across Angola following guerrillas as they went into battle, or how close my friendship with Tito Chingunji would grow.

1

How it began (1975–1976)

I suppose it all began in the 1970s when I was posted by Reuters from India, from where I had reported for four years, to become the international news agency's Central Africa correspondent based in the capital of Zambia.

Lusaka then was home to nearly every African liberation movement. It was a young foreign correspondent's dream, a moralist's theme park and a magnet for every kind of unscrupulous adventurer. Down-at-heel men who would become their countries' presidents and ministers sat in the lounge of my house on the road to Malawi, feeding me just enough stories to keep my Johnnie Walker whisky and Drambuie flowing into their glasses into the early morning hours.

I had been a member of the Anti-Apartheid Movement, a campaigner against sports and economic ties with South Africa, and now I fantasised about liberating white-ruled South Africa and Rhodesia with the power of my pen. In those days, many young British idealists espoused black liberation almost as a substitute for religion. The faith was fundamentalist, the doctrine clear: black southern Africans were oppressed and needed freedom; white southern Africans were oppressors and deserved comeuppance. It was an uncomplicated, single-issue creed. We, the true believers, were leftist or liberal and sanctimonious. We felt very pleased with ourselves.

For me and many others, the ending of apartheid had such transcendent importance that other issues seemed diversionary. There was no greater litmus test of one's liberal or revolutionary credentials than being an opponent of South Africa's Afrikaner and British-origin white rulers.

In truth, my faith had been dented a little while in India as I witnessed Indira Gandhi's corrupt 'socialist' practices, which culminated in her suspension of constitutional democracy and which ultimately led to her assassination. It was also challenged in early 1975 when factional strife broke out, as soon as I arrived in Lusaka, within the exiled Zimbabwe African National Union (ZANU), one of the exiled Rhodesian movements I was so eager to write about. For my first few days in Africa, I earned my living in a distressing way, reporting the daily body count in Lusaka's hospital morgues from ZANU's internal bloodletting, not understanding one little bit the genesis of this internal mayhem.[1]

Angola, on Zambia's western border, took me rather by surprise. Desultory civil war had broken out there in August 1975 after Portugal's spluttering dictatorship collapsed in April 1974 and announced that the country would depart from its 500-year-old resource-rich colony, the jewel in Lisbon's imperial crown, in size nearly the entire area of Germany, France and Spain together.

There were three contesting Angolan liberation movements, and I was asked by my editors in London to find out something about Savimbi's little-known Maoist faction in a country much bigger and richer than Zambia.[2]

To get to Savimbi's territory for the first time, on 22 September 1975, I was taken by Jorge Sangumba, UNITA's foreign secretary and chief spokesman, into the top security area of Lusaka airport where a

Learjet was being prepared for departure. The leather-seated executive plane was owned by the British trading company Lonrho, whose boss, the German-born merchant adventurer Roland 'Tiny' Rowland, was a close friend and an enthusiastic backer of Zambia's President Kenneth Kaunda. Rowland, who was giving funds to Savimbi at Kaunda's request, had close links with Britain's MI6.[3]

'You can call us MI5 and a half,' said one of the two pilots, perhaps only half-jokingly, as we flew for hours towards Angola across apparently endless savannah, forests and winding rivers. It was thrilling.

We landed at Silva Porto, an exquisite gem of a small railway town whose wide streets were lined by crimson flame of the forest and mauve-flowered jacaranda trees. Pink and white Mediterranean-style villas with ochre roof tiles were swathed in bougainvillea. Silva Porto[4] was a perfect setting for a Graham Greene novel.

Stepping from the Learjet, I was escorted by guerrillas wearing Mao caps adorned with red metal stars to the sumptuous official residence of the recently departed Portuguese provincial governor, where I was served at table by the grandee's servants on his silverware and delicate bone china. I did not realise it at the time, but Tito's father, Jonatāo, was now living in the residence as governor following his release from prison by the Portuguese.

Of the many paintings in the residence, one remains the most stunning I have ever seen. The large canvas was of an open-sided Angolan African *django* (meeting hut) at night, with people gathered on their haunches around a blazing central wood fire. The artist had painted the exquisitely beautiful scene with great skill, using only red and black oil paints. With warfare increasing, I coveted it and pondered how I might 'liberate' the painting and smuggle it out of the country. Circumstances and a small dose of conscience put paid to the daydream. To this day I wonder what happened to that wonderful work of art. Did someone else liberate and save it, or was it destroyed in the looming conflagration?

3

Slogans painted on Silva Porto walls read, *'Deus no Ceu: Savimbi em Angola'* (God in Heaven: Savimbi in Angola).

What God wanted for Angola was hard to judge, but UNITA's control of the town high on the central Angola plateau was obvious.

The next day, I was driven to Savimbi's headquarters in a requisitioned former Portuguese secondary school. Runny red paint on a big cardboard sign identified the building as the 'Quarters of the Dragons of Death'. Young guards draped in belts of bullets for their machine-guns ushered me into Jonas Savimbi's office, studded with large maps of Angola and bookshelves lined with the works of Chairman Mao. There I was greeted by one of Africa's most remarkable and controversial men.

Jonas Malheiro Savimbi, then aged 41, was in prime physical shape, having recently emerged from his forest base after a decade of guerrilla war against the departing Portuguese. He wore commando camouflage uniform, brightly polished boots and a green beret studded with a general's three gold stars.

Savimbi's smile was broad and warm, and his big eyes glistened. His handshake was firm, and his élan, energy and magnetism were immediately apparent. His manner was courteous and open, and his voice deep and rich. To my surprise, he spoke fluent English, despite the fact that he had never lived in an English-speaking country. I was impressed. I was reminded later of John Laputa, the African revolutionary in John Buchan's novel *Prester John* who mesmerised the Scottish adventurer John Crawfurd.

Savimbi told me he had given up hope that elections, promised by the Portuguese, would be held. Fighting had broken out six weeks earlier between UNITA and the MPLA, which had proclaimed itself the only legitimate Angolan liberation movement and installed itself in Luanda as the post-independence government. Supplied with arms by the Soviet Union and Moscow's other East European allies,

MPLA forces were probing UNITA's defences in central and southern Angola with armoured cars. Angola, which many Europeans and Americans would have found difficult to place on a map, was on its way to becoming the hot epicentre of the wider Cold War.

Before the skirmishes began, Savimbi had played a leading role in securing an agreement[5] that elections would take place in advance of independence on 11 November 1975, now just seven weeks away. Although those elections now looked highly unlikely, Savimbi was nevertheless strangely optimistic about the future. He told me he did not believe the world would stand idly by without reacting to an uncontested takeover of Africa's potential El Dorado by a Soviet client.

Angola had been blessed by God with every kind of natural resource – oil, diamonds, nickel, gold and other minerals, prolific sea fisheries, fine harbours, rich soils, great rivers and abundant rains, magnificent scenery, teeming wildlife, vibrant people. All the Great Powers wanted for themselves a slice of Angola's wealth.

As I talked with Savimbi, I had only the thinnest grasp that Angola was becoming a hot adjunct to the Cold War – of all unlikely places, it had become a cockpit of the wider international ideological struggle. I had no immediate insight into the fact that the civil war that was beginning would last for a quarter century.

Savimbi, in that first meeting, said – so casually that I hardly noticed – that Cuba had entered the conflict. There were Cuban Army commanders and instructors with the MPLA forces. Referring to his rival, Agostinho Neto, the Marxist poet who led the MPLA, Savimbi told me: 'Neto always used to say he wanted to build here a sort of Cuba. But we don't think we have anything in common with Cuba. The cultural background is so different.'

But the Cubans kept coming in ever larger numbers. And warriors came from other countries too.

I asked Savimbi from where he would obtain a flow of arms to pursue his fight. He said weaponry was arriving, but he declined to say from where. It was all a mystery to me at the time, but arms were in fact arriving by air and land. As well as weapons from China, US supplies were being organised by CIA case officers, including propaganda experts based in the American Embassy in Lusaka.

It was that day that I first met Tito. He stood behind Savimbi. Tall and slim with fine facial features, Tito had soft, intelligent eyes and wore a military beret set at a jaunty angle. Despite his guerrilla fatigues, he exuded laid-back calm. Women thought Tito Chingunji was beautiful. It was true.

Tito, then aged 20, introduced himself. And so began what became a close and intense relationship.

Tito was commander of the Dragons of Death, Savimbi's 50-strong bodyguard. He had not risen so high and fast entirely on merit. He was the scion of a family that matched Savimbi's importance in the resistance movement. Tito's father, Jonatão Chingunji, had co-founded UNITA with Savimbi. Jonatão was a descendant of clan kings who had ruled in central Angola back into the mists of time. There were 22 clans among the Ovimbundu, Angola's biggest tribe, each with its own royal ruler. Oral histories have it that one branch of the Ovimbundu arrived from the Horn of Africa, possibly accounting for a wide variety of skin complexions and a remarkable number of people with aquiline features more typical of the Ethiopian region.

'My father was a devout Christian,' Tito told me in one of our many conversations over the years in Angola, London, Edinburgh, Brussels, Rabat and Washington, DC.

The family had to pray at every meal and before bed. His father felt the Chingunjis had to be an example to people by the honest way they lived. But he was also a nationalist who was incredibly knowledgeable about Ovimbundu history and that of the Chingunji family. He was

outspokenly critical of the way the people regarded American missionaries as gods, addressing them as *senhor*.

While Savimbi led the guerrillas in the forests, Jonatão, a church
pastor and schoolteacher, organised the first UNITA underground
cells in Portuguese-controlled small towns and villages along the
Benguela Railway. The line is one of the most dramatic and romantic
in the world, running nearly 2 000 kilometres from west to east and
effectively dividing Angola into northern and southern halves. Beginning at Lobito Bay, a magnificent natural harbour on the Atlantic coast
of Angola, it rises 2 000 metres in tight loops through steep mountains
to the fertile Central Plateau before crossing into the Congo and northern Zambia. It was built from 1903 onwards under a Scottish engineer,
Sir Robert Williams. Historically, it was the shortest route to haul
copper from what had been the Belgian Congo and Northern Rhodesia
to Lobito and from there by sea to Europe. Its massive steam engines,
built in British factories, were wood-fired from eucalyptus trees grown
on railway plantations. The railway's influence on economic growth
was powerful: it employed thousands and was lined by agricultural
settlements, grain mills, sawmills and paper mills. As well as hauling
minerals, its trains carried maize, wheat, cotton, sugar and cattle.

Jonatão began recruiting men in 1965 to fight alongside Savimbi.
He gathered intelligence, food, medicine and boots for the guerrillas,
and established escape routes from the country for Angolans threatened by the ruthless PIDE political police, guardians of the Portuguese
dictatorship.[6] Tito, the eighth-born of Jonatão's children, as a small boy
from the age of ten, visited UNITA's supporters with his twin sister,
Helena, to deliver secret messages and collect money for the movement, carrying a basket in which small sums of money were placed and
covered with food.

Tito's two oldest brothers, Samuel and David, were among the
first guerrilla recruits. With Savimbi, David accepted an invitation

from Mao Zedong to train at China's Nanking Military Academy in 1965. Both Samuel and David were killed during the war against the Portuguese.

Jonatão was arrested by the Portuguese in March 1969, convicted of terrorism by a military court and sent to a hard-labour prison in the Cape Verde Islands. Tito's mother, Violeta, Tito himself, at the age of only 14, and one of his younger brothers, Paulo, were also detained. The boys were released, though not their mother at this time, but the family home had disintegrated, and they lived as street kids in Luanda, Angola's capital, foraging on rubbish tips, begging from foreign sailors and doing odd jobs in Portuguese houses.

Tito, as the son of a 'dangerous revolutionary', was re-arrested in 1972 and imprisoned with his mother at the notoriously harsh São Nicolau penal colony in the remote coastal desert of southwestern Angola. There was extensive torture and there were extra-judicial killings in São Nicolau, where inmates laboured in coastal salt pans. For one six-month period, Tito was kept in solitary confinement in total darkness, living among his own waste. He lost track of time. Food was delivered through a narrow slot in the cell door on to a small shelf.

'I used to grope for the plate,' he told me. 'But I was weak, and I could see nothing. Often, I knocked the plate from the shelf, but I was so hungry I would kneel and lick the food from the floor. When they released me from solitary I couldn't see for days. I was blind. But I was more frightened when I began to see again. My black skin had turned grey.'

With the war in its infancy, I moved on from Silva Porto to Nova Lisboa. It was September 1975, during my first trip into Angola, soon after I had met Savimbi and Tito for the first time. I witnessed some of the most pitiful death throes of Portugal's empire. The imperium was not ending with dignified ceremony but with a rush to the airports. Nearly all of Angola's 500 000 Portuguese settlers were fleeing the country.

After Luanda, Nova Lisboa, a handsome city once planned by the Portuguese to be Angola's capital, was the main point of escape for departing families. Thousands, who were about to become refugees, were waiting for special international evacuation flights. Some had been at Nova Lisboa's airport for many days, sleeping on aircraft hangar floors. Some family groups comprised three generations, the children clutching dolls and teddy bears. Toilets, no longer serviced by staff, were in unspeakable states. A black African nun dressed in white was comforting families.

As the airlift went on, more and more Portuguese kept arriving in trucks and cars from across central Angola. As they abandoned their vehicles, the Portuguese retained their car keys or, in many cases, dropped them down drains. Enterprising Africans hot-wired the vehicles and drove them away.

The Portuguese abdication I was witnessing was near complete. Their villas were emptying. Banks had closed, factories had stopped production and only a handful of shops, with fast-diminishing stocks, remained open. All government doctors in the city's hospitals had left. There were ten Portuguese Red Cross doctors looking after the refugees and feeding some 3 000 Africans who had entered the city to escape fighting to the north. Otherwise, the only doctor in the whole of the territory controlled by UNITA was George Burgess, a Canadian missionary with the Protestant United Church of Christ at a hospital in Dondi, a mission institute where Savimbi had attended school in the early 1950s and one of the places where Tito's father had taught.

I later visited Dondi on a day when Savimbi was scheduled to speak in a nearby forest glade. Several thousand singing and dancing villagers gathered to hear the UNITA leader speak. Savimbi advanced over a path strewn with palm leaves and white, sweet-smelling frangipani flowers. He wore a gold-coloured toga in the style of traditional African chieftains, with one shoulder bared. It was in homage to a hero of Savimbi's youth, Kwame Nkrumah, the Ghanaian pan-African nationalist, who also liked to wear togas. On Savimbi's right wrist was a yellow bead bangle and on his left a yellow gold watch. It was vibrant and impressive theatre.

Tito interpreted for me as Savimbi spoke to the crowd in Umbundu, the language of the Ovimbundu tribe. His charisma was apparent as he used proverbs, irony and traditional jokes to make his points.

'We've lost everything there was to lose,' he told his ecstatic audience. 'Now the time has come for the MPLA to start losing. The MPLA controls the capital, but in Luanda they produce only sand. Here we produce food. The MPLA started this criminal war. All we can do is fight back and hope for a just peace. The MPLA talks of peace and democracy when it means dictatorship.'

I kept telling Tito there was no point in me hanging around in UNITA's strongholds. My company wanted me to report the growing fighting. He said he would try to get me to scenes of the conflict, but nothing happened. After nearly three weeks I decided to return to Lusaka. However, I first watched an old four-engine propeller-driven DC-4, the kind that had served in the Second World War and the 1948–1949 Berlin Airlift, make several landings at Silva Porto and disgorge cargoes of small arms. No one would say where the plane had flown from, though with hindsight I learned that it had come from a military air base at Kamina in southern Zaire, where there was a United States CIA base. The pilot and co-pilot spoke in British and German accents, but they moved away when I asked questions. However, a colleague of theirs, who I knew only as 'Skip', was a little more approachable. He introduced himself as an American journalist who had once served with the US Marine Corps in Vietnam, but he did not stay at the former governor's palace where I was housed. I did not know it at the time, but Skip was the CIA's resident liaison man with Savimbi, guiding a series of American military experts, most of them hardened former Special Forces operatives in Vietnam, into UNITA's bosom.

A Man of God had landed in Silva Porto before I first arrived. He wore black shirt and trousers, moustache, sideburns, heavy sunglasses. A big silver cross swung across his chest on a long black chain, and he was the newly appointed chief of the entire CIA Task Force in Angola. His name was John Stockwell, and he had come to brief Savimbi on US$14 million worth of military aid covertly committed to him by US President Gerald Ford at a National Security Council meeting in Washington on 27 June 1975.

'I found a different kind of revolutionary,' said Stockwell. 'Savimbi had spent the entire time in Angola – 20 years. He had led the guerrilla fighting himself.'[7]

A month later, on 29 July, a giant US Air Force C-141 Starlifter transport plane, the first of many, landed at Kamina, loaded with weapons for transfer to UNITA in Angola in a series of Fokker F27 flights, also financed by the CIA. Israel provided shoulder-fired surface-to-air missiles for the deliveries in exchange for the delivery of modern state-of-the-art American military equipment to Tel Aviv.[8]

The CIA priest attended a UNITA congress where he noted that Savimbi's skin was very black, his beard full and shiny, his eyes wide, prominent and flashing, and that he was a spellbinding orator. 'As Savimbi began to speak,' Stockwell wrote later,[9] 'the assembly stilled to hear a master of a speaking style once popular in our own society but now as rare as the deep-throated belly laugh and the bar-room brawl.'

Dr Henry Kissinger, the US Secretary of State, had tasked the CIA with establishing air bridges from Zambia and Zaire to deliver arms clandestinely to UNITA. There was little public appetite in America for their military getting sucked into another foreign conflict so soon after the Vietnam debacle. Stockwell recalled, 'They (Kissinger and the US Government) took me down to Washington three months to the day after we left Saigon as North Vietnamese forces overran South Vietnam's capital. The CIA had been ordered by Kissinger to stop the Soviets (in Angola). Because of the political situation, the US Army couldn't do it. It was one of the most sensitive, one of the biggest, operations in CIA history.'[10]

Pondering what he described as the cynicism and joylessness of a CIA case officer's job, Stockwell added, 'For a moment I resented him (Savimbi), with his clear objectives and clean conscience. He was that rare coincidence of history, a throwback to the great tribal leaders of Africa – Shaka Zulu, Msiri and Jomo Kenyatta – a far cry from the conflicting values and goals of America, and of the CIA in its middle-aged mediocrity.'

I saw some of Skip's military so-called experts. They hardly made efforts to make themselves unrecognisable or inconspicuous. There was yet another American Man of God who wore a large wooden cross around his neck and assured me he was a missionary just checking on the fates of his Angolan parishioners. Another, in his late twenties or early thirties, was straight out of an American nightmare: black Texan cowboy hat, raised-heel Wild West cowboy boots, studded jeans, a mean swagger and a tight unsmiling, surly, gum-chewing face.

When I returned to Silva Porto airport to fly back to Lusaka early in October 1975, a massive camouflage-painted C-130 transport plane bearing the insignia of a Caribbean state was on the tarmac. It was heavily guarded by UNITA soldiers. Weapons were being unloaded, and Skip was there supervising the operation, possibly unaware that the 'little war' in which his masters were getting involved would become a huge conflict that would lay waste to Angola and its people.

By now, CIA and MI6 operatives and their counterparts from France, West Germany, Israel, Italy, Spain and other countries regularly met UNITA officials inside Angola to ensure they were not duplicating each other's efforts. The CIA and MI6 Lusaka stations liaised routinely between Zambia and UNITA. On one occasion I saw an entire planeload of Western intelligence agents disembark from an aircraft on the tarmac at Nova Lisboa airport. I spotted a British agent I had got to know in Lusaka. His first and only reaction was, 'You haven't seen me here.'

2
Jonas Savimbi

Tito, his mother and father, two of his brothers and 1 200 other political prisoners were freed from imprisonment in Cape Verde and São Nicolau after Lisbon's new rulers decided in April 1974 to abandon Portugal's colony. The family returned to their home in Silva Porto and resumed contact with Savimbi and the UNITA movement as Angola began its descent into civil war. Jonatão, who greatly admired Savimbi and regarded him as a surrogate son, was filled with pride when the guerrilla chieftain asked Tito to join his bodyguard as its commanding officer.

Savimbi promised Jonatão that he would protect and mentor Tito as though he was his own young brother. Both Jonatão and Tito responded enthusiastically. From then onwards Tito was frequently seen at Savimbi's side.

What I did not know until many years later, was that Britain's then Labour government under Prime Minister James Callaghan had brought Tito and other young UNITA activists to Portsmouth, England, in late 1974 for a military intelligence training course.

On his first visit to London, soon after we had met in Rabat in January 1980, Tito suggested that the story of UNITA's struggle could be best told in the form of a biography of Savimbi, the man both he and his father followed and greatly admired. It made sense. Savimbi exuded charisma, charm and intelligence. His was an exceptionally colourful story. Tito said he would give me extensive help.

Tito's nephew Eduardo Chingunji, however, told me years later, that a Savimbi myth was being created as part of UNITA's strategy to counteract the publicity being given to the MPLA's Neto. Many illiterate young boys were coming into the movement who were ignorant of the pre-independence struggle. Savimbi, a magnificent speaker who knew classical Ovimbundu and all the proverbs, exploited the myth. He told the people he'd travelled everywhere and read everything.

Jonas Malheiro Savimbi was born on 3 August 1934 in Munhango on the Benguela Railway. As Tito told it, Savimbi's father, Loth Savimbi, was a man of strong and independent mind who became the first black stationmaster on the railway. Loth was aware that four million Angolans had been exported as slaves to the Americas by the Portuguese. It has been estimated that some nine million black Angolans died during the slaves' marches to the coast and while waiting to be herded on to ships, after first being forcibly baptised by Roman Catholic clerics.

Loth had defied his own father, Sakaita, a traditional animist, to become a devout Christian. He established small churches everywhere he was posted along the railway. However, he told Jonas that he had to think of the Portuguese as oppressors and that he must never tolerate humiliation at their hands. Savimbi told Tito that by the time he was six, the idea had already formed in his head that one day he would fight the Portuguese for liberation from colonial rule.

Jonas, after a mission education, arrived in Lisbon in 1958 to study medicine. He had been sent there by a Brazilian Roman Catholic priest and teacher, Father Armando Cordeiro, who recognised Savimbi as an exceptionally brilliant pupil, for whom he had arranged a scholarship to study in Portugal.

'Father Cordeiro reminded me all the time that I should prepare myself to serve my people,' Savimbi told me during one of many discussions. 'He used to point to the trucks packed with forced labourers going north (from the Ovimbundu tribal areas of central and southern Angola) to the coffee plantations of the north and say they were like slaves. Although I was now being treated like a Portuguese, I should never forget that I belonged to the people of Angola. Father Cordeiro said that if I became a doctor and never did anything for my people, my life would have been a waste of time.'

By the time Savimbi stepped off the ship in Lisbon, he had been reading books on Marxism and was burning with desire to join a liberation movement. Savimbi saw in Lisbon the trappings of the capital of a great European empire: triumphal arches, palaces, wide boulevards, statues and warehouses of colonial trading companies. It was wealth based substantially on the sweat of cheap labour in Angola and in Portugal's other African territories, Mozambique and Guinea-Bissau. The riches were concentrated in the hands of a narrow elite; the people of Portugal were the poorest in Western Europe.

Portugal's ruling dictator, Dr Antonio de Oliveira Salazar, was aware of his country's economic dependence on Angola and the other African colonies, as well as on East Timor, Goa and Macau in Asia. Salazar was supported by the dictator of neighbouring Spain, General Francisco Franco, who intended holding on to his own small African colonies of Rio Muni, Fernando Po and Spanish Sahara. While Salazar and Franco continued to rule, there was no prospect that Lisbon would relinquish its overseas possessions.

Savimbi began to distribute Marxist pamphlets around the University of Lisbon. He was impressed by clandestine Communist Party activists who seemed to be the only ones resisting the regime. His

commitment was reinforced when the party denounced the Portuguese Army after it cracked down in August 1958 on striking dock-
workers in Guinea-Bissau, in West Africa, and shot dead fifty dockers.

Savimbi managed to pursue both his studies and his politics until
April 1959, when he was summoned to the offices of the PIDE and
shown letters he had received from a friend in Angola, 22-year-old Arao
Kunga, and which the PIDE had intercepted. Savimbi said he managed
to avoid choking when he read one sentence which went, 'Look, you
must open your eyes and see what these people are. We are going to fix
them.'

'So which people are you going to fix?' asked the PIDE interro-
gator. 'The Portuguese?' No, replied Savimbi. Kunga was referring to
foreign missionaries who had taught both of them.

'We are all Portuguese, unless you are thinking that because we are
black, we are not Portuguese?'

They let Savimbi go. He immediately wrote to Kunga and told him
to drop controversial subjects. A short time afterwards Kunga was
arrested. He died, aged 24, in Mombaka Prison, in the Angolan port of
Lobito, on 14 April 1961 after a series of beatings.

Savimbi himself was beaten in June 1959 after he heard that Kwame
Nkrumah, the President of independent Ghana, planned a transit stop
at Lisbon airport on his way to the United Nations in New York. The
impending presence of the man who symbolised pan-African freedom
was not announced, but word nevertheless spread among the city's
African student community. Savimbi joined the throng at the airport
and was arrested soon afterwards by the PIDE, who demanded that
he become an informer. Realising that it was now impossible to live in
Portugal and continue his studies, Savimbi was smuggled out of Portugal in the boot of a car, across Spain and into France, where he was
sheltered by members of the French Communist Party who at the time
were heavily involved in Algeria's struggle against French colonial rule.

Resisting advice by the French communists to travel to Moscow to study there, Savimbi headed for Switzerland where a missionary society had awarded him a scholarship to resume his medicine studies at the University of Fribourg in the Swiss Alps. However, Savimbi threw himself so heavily into founding a new liberation movement with fellow Angolan and law student at Fribourg, Tony Fernandes, that he abandoned his course and registered to study international politics and law at Lausanne University under Professor Henri Rieben.

Savimbi and Fernandes went to a hotel at Champay, in the Swiss Alps, at Christmas 1964. There they decided, over three days, the new party's name, UNITA, and drew up a constitution. The name symbolised the unity the two men believed was necessary among all Angola's peoples if there was to be any hope of ending Portuguese rule.

'We were very young,' Fernandes recalled. 'Savimbi was a hundred per cent a Maoist and told me he did not believe in a God. I was demonstrating at the university against American involvement in the Vietnam War. Savimbi argued that in the struggle between East and West, the Chinese example was one we had to follow. I said that if that serves the struggle, fine, but I am a Christian and will remain so.

'I and other Angolan students nevertheless liked the way Savimbi argued about the future of Angola and its people. We were impressed and I was a close confidant. I liked the idea of UNITA basing itself inside Angola, relying, like Mao, on rural peasants, not the urban workers. I accepted it. I thought the theory was basically correct.'[1]

Professor Rieben, one of the architects of the European Coal and Steel Community, the forerunner of the European Union, was impressed by his new African student's qualities which he summed up, in an interview with me, as 'charisma, intelligence, courage and honesty'. The professor told me, 'I was amazed and excited by Savimbi's examination papers. He showed remarkable insight and a grasp of the geopolitical scene which was very rare indeed.'[2]

Savimbi never completed his studies under Rieben. He was spending alternate three-month periods in Lausanne and three months touring Africa and the communist world in his attempt to get his new liberation movement off the ground. Despite graduating with only an ordinary degree, let alone a PhD, he would later insist on being addressed as Dr Savimbi.

Now Savimbi and Fernandes faced the problem of beginning to fight the Portuguese on Angolan soil. Among contacts they made were with Chairman Mao's Chinese government. First, they were given US$1 000 by the Chinese ambassador in Congo-Brazzaville and then established close contact with Co Liang, a top Chinese clandestine agent in Africa, who was working undercover as a Xinhua News Agency correspondent in Ghana. Co Liang gave Savimbi the complete works of Mao Zedong and invited him to train as a guerrilla fighter at Nanking Military Academy.

Savimbi arrived in Nanking in July 1965 to begin a four-month course.[3] While there he was told he could send eleven more recruits to be trained as the core fighters of the new movement. The eleven were instructed and drilled in Nanking for ten months. They included one of Tito's older brothers, David Samwimbila Chingunji, who became a legendary UNITA hero before he was killed in 1970 in mysterious circumstances. The 'UNITA Eleven', who became known as the 'Black Chinese', were joined by eleven Rhodesian African nationalists of the ZANU movement, led by Josiah Tongogara, later to become commander of Robert Mugabe's guerrillas fighting the white Rhodesian government of Ian Smith. Tongogara himself would die in mysterious circumstances in December 1979, just as Zimbabwe was about to become independent.

Before going to Nanking, Savimbi had met, in 1964, Che Guevara, the Argentina-born Cuban revolutionary and international cult figure beloved by youthful leftists. Savimbi claimed that he and Guevara exchanged views for five hours at both a conference of international liberation movements and afterwards, at the Cuban embassy in Dar es Salaam. Savimbi told me, 'I argued (to Guevara) that the leadership of any liberation movement has to go inside the country it is trying to liberate and live with the people, even if it means risking death. People would rally around the cause if they saw their leaders suffering alongside them.'

Guevara told Savimbi he had met Agostinho Neto, when the MPLA leader was based outside Angola, and, by Savimbi's account, had dismissed him as 'just a bourgeois.' Guevara said Savimbi's belief in the need for political leaders to fight alongside the people chimed with his own concepts that he was developing concerning the liberation of Latin American countries beyond Cuba. Che died before the end of the decade while putting into practice the ideas he discussed with Savimbi. He chose Bolivia as the Latin American country in which to launch his revolution, fighting and living alongside the peasantry. Bolivian troops, armed and trained by US Special Forces and CIA operatives, trapped Guevara in a forested ravine in October 1967. There he was riddled by bullets and fell dead.

Ten of the Chinese Eleven were smuggled from Tanzania, across Zambia (hostile to Savimbi at the time, but not later), into Angola from September 1966 onwards. On 26 October, Savimbi himself crossed into Angola, setting foot on his native soil for the first time since he left for Portugal eight years earlier.

To take on 50 000 Portuguese soldiers in Angola, Savimbi and his Eleven had between them only knives, pangas, bows and arrows, an Italian submachine gun and one Soviet Tokarev pistol. The pistol was a personal gift to Savimbi by the leader of another liberation movement, Sam Nujoma of the South West Africa People's Organisation

(SWAPO). Nujoma was trying to launch guerrilla war to free the South African-ruled territory immediately to the south of Angola, later to become Namibia.

Savimbi solved the problem of lack of weaponry by sending a UNITA recruit to the Congo to buy some rifles. The envoy returned with ten standard NATO 7.62mm FN rifles.

By March 1967, UNITA had achieved a few minor military successes. So Savimbi left Angola to raise more arms and more money, first visiting Gamal Abdel Nasser in Cairo. The Egyptian President gave Savimbi arms and promised money. From Cairo, Savimbi flew to Kunming, in southwest China, where he met Mao Zedong for the first time. Mao gave Savimbi yet more money and said China was ready to ship arms to UNITA. Mao said he knew Tanzania's President Julius Nyerere well. He was sure Nyerere would allow the arms through the port of Dar es Salaam, and he said he further hoped President Kenneth Kaunda would eventually allow them to be transported freely across Zambia.

On his return to Angola, Savimbi appointed Samuel Kafundanga Chingunji, Tito's oldest brother, who had trained militarily in the Portuguese Army, as chief of staff of the guerrilla movement. Kafundanga's role, until his death in 1974, was to move between Tanzania, Zambia and Angola smuggling the Chinese weapons, money and other supplies across Zambia into the guerrillas' Angolan bases. 'Kafundanga' was Samuel Chingunji's *nom de guerre*. It translates as 'Man of Gunpowder' because he had manufactured a grenade his guerrilla fighters used against the Portuguese.

While fighting the Portuguese, UNITA identified closely with Black Power organisations and Pan-African socialist movements in the United States. One of its military units was named the Black Panthers.

By early 1973, Savimbi was confident enough in UNITA's resistance to invite a *Washington Post* journalist to travel through the movement's liberated areas. Leon Dash, a Pulitzer Prize winner and founder of the US National Association of Black Journalists, spent nearly three months with the guerrillas, walking some 1 300 kilometres across virtually trackless savannahs and plains after entering clandestinely through vast border swamps into Angola from Zambia. Vivid accounts by Dash,[4] then aged 29, were the first real indication to the outside world that Savimbi's people were an effective fighting force.

Dash attended a week-long UNITA conference in a reed-walled amphitheatre where he was served slices of roast antelope and chicken washed down with *ovingundo*, a beer made from wild honey and maize. About 150 huts had been built to house delegates from several tribal groups. During the conference, a courier arrived from a distant area to say that UNITA's Switzerland-based representative, Francisco Talanga, had been killed in a helicopter attack by an elite Portuguese airborne commando unit. Delegates observed a minute's silence.

Dash noted Savimbi's charisma and an almost mystical allegiance to him by the peasant people of central and southern Angola.

'Savimbi seemed the epitome of a new kind of African visionary, one who was tough enough to prevail yet idealistic enough to truly favor pluralistic politics and democratic government,' Dash commented.

Savimbi told the conference, 'Many of us will fall before this war is over.' That was prescient. The war would last another three decades, and many hundreds of thousands would die.

3

A military coup in Portugal (1974–1975)

Following the April 1974 coup, the latest Portuguese autocrat, Marcello Caetano, who had ruled for six years, was sent into exile, first in Madeira and then Brazil, where he died in 1980.

The coup was triggered by rising unpopularity in Portugal with the country's colonial wars. In the previous decade, some 11 000 Portuguese soldiers had been killed in the conflicts in Africa and, to a lesser extent, in East Timor, and at least 30 000 more wounded and disabled. The coup ended almost half a century of fascist-style nationalism. Many military commanders were arrested, and government radio and television stations were seized by the new leftist Junta of National Salvation.

Only four people died in the coup. Red carnations stuck by civilians into the rifle barrels of patrolling soldiers and pinned on their uniforms became the symbol of the successful rebellion.

The significance of the coup, which was all over in a single day, was not immediately clear in Angola, which, paradoxically, was enjoying an economic boom. Coffee and iron ore exports had achieved new record levels, but they had been recently surpassed for the first time by oil, from new fields offshore from the northern enclave of Cabinda, giving

Angola a record trade surplus for 1973 of US$235 million. Portugal's new rulers were nonetheless determined to end the country's colonial responsibilities. In early May, the new president, General Francisco Costa Gomes, flew into Angola and announced that the country's nationalist guerrilla groups – UNITA, the MPLA and the smaller FNLA (National Liberation Front of Angola) – would be accepted as legitimate political parties as soon as they stopped fighting. All military operations by the Portuguese military occupation force were suspended in the hope that a ceasefire could be achieved.

After months of negotiation, the three liberation movements and the Lisbon government signed an agreement on 15 January 1975 at Alvor, a small village on Portugal's Algarve coast. The Alvor Accords set 11 November 1975 as the date for Angola's independence after the holding of elections in October for a Constituent Assembly. Until 11 November, power would be vested in a Portuguese High Commissioner and a transitional government. UNITA, the MPLA and the FNLA would each have three ministerial posts in the transitional administration, and each would hold the premiership on a rotating basis. Portuguese troops would steadily return home.

Angolans were euphoric when the transitional government was inaugurated in Luanda. The path to independence in a multi-party democracy looked smooth. Intensive campaigns for the pre-independence election began. But even before the Alvor Accords were signed, events were happening that would ensure that independent Angola would be born in blood and chaos.[1]

Moscow resumed arms aid to its long-standing MPLA client from August 1974 onwards, precisely at the time when the struggle against the Portuguese was over and preparations were being made to create an independent democratic Angola. At much the same time, America's CIA began making payments to its then (pre-UNITA) client, the

FNLA, which was supported also by the Zairean dictator, Mobutu Sese Seko.

The inauguration of the transitional government in Luanda on 31 January 1975 was the high point of Portugal's efforts to guide the territory peacefully towards independence.

It was downhill all the way from then onwards.

China now gave Savimbi 70 tonnes of arms. Presidents Nyerere of Tanzania and Marien Ngouabi of Congo-Brazzaville also sent weapons to the UNITA leader. Nyerere accepted 120 UNITA soldiers on a nine-month officer training course in Tanzania.

From March 1975, there were frequent bloody skirmishes between MPLA and FNLA soldiers. The flow of Soviet arms to the MPLA, in Soviet, Greek and Yugoslav ships, escalated in parallel with the growing fighting. Rumours grew that Cuban military instructors were training MPLA soldiers in Massangao camp, near Luanda. Kenneth Kaunda visited Washington, where he warned President Gerald Ford and Secretary of State Henry Kissinger that the Soviet Union intended implanting the MPLA as the sole ruling party in Angola. Kaunda, by now a convert to Savimbi's cause, encouraged them to react effectively and give assistance to UNITA.[2]

By 9 July 1975, the transitional government had collapsed, and on 4 August UNITA entered the war after MPLA soldiers turned on UNITA and killed 30 of its troops in Lucusse, a small central Angola town. All hope for a peaceful solution was gone.

Nearly thirty years of civil war followed.

4

Some surprise help for UNITA (1975)

With Independence Day only ten days away, I flew back to Angola from my home in Zambia on 1 November 1975. Reports were emerging that UNITA was making dramatic military advances, including laying siege to the spectacular Atlantic port of Lobito, at the western terminal of the Benguela Railway. I was again aboard one of Tiny Rowland's executive jets loaned to Savimbi, this time a Hawker Siddeley 125.

I was surprised by what I saw as I stepped on to the tarmac at Silva Porto. Two trucks crossed the apron towing spick-and-span armoured cars decked in camouflage but with the word UNITA and a crowing cock, UNITA's emblem, adorning the sides in red paint that had trickled like a waterfall. Tito had told me UNITA expected to obtain armoured vehicles. They seemed to be arriving.

The trucks halted, so I wandered across to one of the armoured cars. A slight, sunburned teenager with a wispy beard sat in the driving compartment. I assumed he was Portuguese. As Portugal began leaving Angola, some of its soldiers deserted and gave their services to the different liberation movements. I thought he must be one of them. But a greeting, *bom dia*, provoked only a blank look. So I asked him in English what language he spoke.

'I speak Inger-lish,' he replied. Astonished by his thick guttural accent, I asked where he was from, and he replied grudgingly: 'I am from Inger-land.'

I realised at that precise moment the secret behind Savimbi's spectacular advances. What were these Afrikaners in armoured cars doing some 650 kilometres deep inside Angola from South Africa-ruled South West Africa? By luck, I had begun to suss exclusively a secret South African, Western-encouraged, military invasion of Angola. It was a moment of personal triumph for someone who had arrived on the African continent wishing primarily to undermine apartheid South Africa by the power of his pen. And, of course, it was exhilarating to know immediately that I had the makings of a world scoop.

I sauntered in a kind of unreal haze to the second armoured car in which another young white man occupied the driving compartment. He looked at me suspiciously, and when I asked him where he had come from, he said, 'I am a mercenary.'

Okay, but from which country?

'I cannot say,' he replied. However, the accent spoke for him – it had obviously been shaped at his mother's knee somewhere far south of the Orange and Limpopo rivers. How long had he been in Angola?

'Two or three weeks.'

In the trucks sat three more whites. A polite 'good morning' produced from one of them a heavily Afrikaans-accented 'good morning' reply.

Before I could ask more questions, a fawn-coloured Range Rover raced across the tarmac and out stepped Skip, accompanied by a tall blond-haired man in a blue sports shirt and khaki shorts. The newcomer issued orders in Portuguese to a couple of UNITA soldiers. Then, switching to English – again South African-accented but smoother than that of the armoured-car occupants – he courteously ushered me to the Range Rover, and I was driven off to the comforts of the former Portuguese Governor's residence. Only fourteen years later did I learn this man's name – Willem van der Waals – and what the exact nature had been of his role in Angola. He invited me to Pretoria in 1989 and, with the same civility he had exhibited that day in Silva Porto, he gave me a signed copy of his book *Portugal's War in Angola*.[1]

Van der Waals, a fluent Portuguese speaker, had trained as a South African Defence Force (SADF) paratrooper and in military intelligence. He was, by 1975, the SADF liaison officer, with the rank of colonel (later brigadier), with Savimbi. Among other responsibilities, he was in charge of 25 fellow South African soldiers training Savimbi's fighters in great secrecy in a camp near Silva Porto with the purpose of ensuring that UNITA's central Angola strongholds would not fall to the MPLA.

Two armoured cars whose nameless drivers declined to confess they were South African soldiers was insufficient evidence as yet to substantiate a story of an invasion of another country by the South African Army. Patience, persistence, guile and a big slice of luck would be needed to pin down the truth sufficiently firmly before I could write an account that would meet Reuters' exacting standards for breaking highly controversial exclusive news stories.

South Africa, it eventually became clear, was committing soldiers to the Angolan war at a time when black majority unrest over white minority rule was growing in the Republic itself and when insurgency was growing in South West Africa by the SWAPO guerrilla movement. SWAPO had numerous bases in Angola, from where it launched raids across the border into South Africa-ruled South West Africa. The white South African government had resolved that SWAPO would never come to power in its colony by force, although it had already accepted that at some point it would inevitably become independent with a new name, Namibia. The South African government had also resolved that any transition to majority rule in South Africa itself would be achieved by negotiation, not conflict. It saw support for UNITA's resistance as one way of making life more difficult for the Cuban-Soviet-MPLA-SWAPO axis which had ambitions for triumphs beyond Angola against South Africa.

At the time, total victory for the MPLA in Angola, together with its allies from Havana, Moscow and East Berlin, looked probable. This might be followed by the possible fall of South African rule in South West Africa and even in the Republic itself. In South Africa's green fertile valleys in Natal, next to the Indian Ocean, veteran white men in the Commando forces, the equivalent of Britain's World War II Home Guard, prepared ancient armoured cars and polished old rifles to be ready to give invading columns of cigar-chomping Cuban soldiers a hard time before they took the land and collectivised it.[2]

I waited, after my encounter with the South Africans in Silva Porto, and concentrated on gathering material for more routine accounts of the approach to independence as seen from UNITA's territory.

In those days, it was impossible to file any stories directly from UNITA-land. There were no phone communications to the outside world and the era of the mobile phone was a distant dream. I had to fly back to Lusaka to send my pre-Independence Day stories to London by telex from my office, which was attached to my house, and which was overshadowed by clouds of fragrant purple flowers of a magnificent jacaranda tree. On board the flight on 9 November, I met a friend, British ITN journalist Michael Nicholson, who had just made his first short venture into Angola and who also had to return to Lusaka to put film on a plane to London.

We agreed to meet up the next day, 10 November, to return to Savimbi's territory so that we would be there on Independence Day, 11 November.

Mike[3] was a genial, generous, breezy and occasionally wild soul, the kind of colleague I liked and trusted and was happy to share insights with. So, on the flight to Lusaka I told him of my encounter with mysterious South Africans claiming to be Englishmen. He was as gobsmacked as I had been. While I went home to my wife and then two small daughters who were living with me in Lusaka, Mike, away from his home in southern England, struck up a friendship over drinks into the small hours at his hotel with the pilots of Savimbi's Lonrho jets. The pilots liked Mike – inevitably – and so they suggested when they flew back to Angola the next day that he and I remain aboard for a mystery trip after they had delivered some supplies for UNITA in Nova Lisboa.

There was no jet fuel in Nova Lisboa, so the pilots said they would head 'somewhere else' to refuel Rowland's aircraft. They would show us something that would greatly interest us. There were conditions: we were not to report the flight or anything we would see to our news organisations, and we were not to ask questions. But one of them assured us, 'What you will see will help you understand what's happening here.'

Before we could set off into the unknown, we were told to persuade a well-known *Newsweek* correspondent, Andrew Jaffe, who had flown with us from Lusaka, that it was essential for him to get UNITA press accreditation in Nova Lisboa before he could begin reporting. It was completely unnecessary, but 'helpfully' we told him where to go and who to see. I am sure he knew we were lying, but as soon as he had gone, we were on our way.

The plane flew due south. We had flown some 650 kilometres over the immense bush and forests of southern Angola before the executive jet began to descend. Now the trees were more stunted, and their crowns no longer overlapped, revealing expanses of sandy soil.

One of the MI5 and a half pilots beckoned me to the flight deck and pointed to a silver river snaking through the thin dry woodland. The radio crackled into life and the conversation revealed that we were crossing the Kavango River, which formed the international border between Angola and South West Africa. A woman spoke in the same obvious South African English as the young men in the armoured cars at Silva Porto. She was ground control at the airfield at Rundu, on the Kavango's south bank, where the Republic of South Africa maintained a forward military headquarters base against SWAPO insurgents.

We touched down on a runway lined by machine-gun emplacements. Mike and I crouched on the floor of the plane. We had been told to keep our heads down and stay away from the exit door until we were back in the air. The plane taxied towards an area surrounded by a wall of sandbags some six metres high. It passed through a narrow entrance into a vast tarmacadam area, and there we saw the pot of gold at the end of Jonas Savimbi's rainbow.

Like kids in a *Hardy Boys* adventure, we kneeled and peeped over the bottom edge of the plane's small oval windows as the pilots talked on the apron to South African Army and Air Force officers while mechanics refuelled the plane. It was obvious that we were at the hub of what could only be Pretoria's staging post for its military incursion into Angola.

There were lines of Panhard armoured cars of the UNITA kind I had seen at Silva Porto airport, and there were whites in the gunnery and driving positions as though preparing to leave without delay. They began moving into Hercules C-130 and Transall C-160 transport planes painted in black and green camouflage and with all registration and other identification marks obliterated. Next stop for the planes and their cargoes surely had to be Angola.

Soon we were flying back to Nova Lisboa. Neither Mike nor I could quite believe what we had witnessed. Or how Savimbi's plane was able to land, apparently routinely, at what we knew was South Africa's most sensitive military base, giving us a glimpse into the heart of its secret war in Angola. It felt surreal, but it was real. The pilots, for some reason best known to themselves, and which I never subsequently discovered, had guided us directly to concrete evidence of South Africa's embroilment in the Angolan tragedy.

We joined up on return to Nova Lisboa with Mike's cameraman and soundman and, once again, with Andrew Jaffe, seething because he discovered there was no accreditation requirement. He demanded, unsuccessfully, to know where we had been.

We now flew by a Beechcraft light plane to the coastal city of Benguela and neighbouring Lobito to do some eve-of-independence reporting. As we landed at Benguela, we saw some 30 or so young fair-haired white men, stripped to their waists in khaki shorts, try to slide out of sight into a hangar. Then, as we stepped into the terminal, a Hercules C-130, painted in exactly the same colours as those we had seen a few hours earlier in Rundu, touched down. As we asked questions, UNITA soldiers hustled us into a minibus. But driving away we passed a Panhard armoured car guarding the narrow approach to the airport. Its camouflage paint was identical to that I had seen on Panhards at Rundu and earlier in Silva Porto. The Benguela Panhard was surrounded by young whites in shorts relaxing in the sun.

Mike's immediate problem was how to obtain film evidence of this South African presence without the white soldiers realising they were being filmed. Such footage was certain to be confiscated, otherwise the secrecy of their country's actions – known to its masterminds, in liaison with the CIA, as Operation Savannah – would be blown on international TV.

Preparing on the return bus ride from Lobito to Benguela, Mike's cameraman took a seat and rested his camera casually on his shoulder, but with his eye turned away from the viewfinder. He had set the camera at an angle he thought, with luck, would frame the teenage soldiers and the Panhard. As the minibus passed the armoured car, we all waved to the lounging troops while the cameraman casually squeezed the record trigger.

We flew to Nova Lisboa for UNITA's celebration, on 11 November, of Angolan Independence Day from Portugal. More than 300 000 Portuguese were leaving Angola, mainly on military and chartered commercial flights, but also aboard two Portuguese ships from Luanda. While press colleagues more than 500 kilometres to the north in Luanda filed independence celebration stories to the world and described how the Portuguese were scuttling ships as they completed their departure, we remained unable to contact our editorial headquarters. All communication systems to the outside world had either broken down or been cut off.

Water supplies to our once-comfortable hotel in Nova Lisboa had collapsed, as much of the infrastructure had due to the war. The stench was awful, and I worried about infection. A lot of time reporting wars involves waiting. Mike relieved the tedium by asking a UNITA soldier if he could fire a couple of shots with his FN rifle. He shot at a street-lamp. We were plunged into pitch darkness as every light in the street and in the hotel went out, and probably remained out for the rest of the civil war.

We caught up with Savimbi on 13 November, two days after independence, in an abandoned hotel in Lobito after he had addressed a rally of 50 000 people. Mike and I put to him a 'suspicion' by 'some people in Luanda' that South African soldiers were maybe the secret behind his forces' spectacular northward advances in recent weeks. Of course, we did not tell him that we had gathered our own clinching evidence aboard his own plane or that Mike's cameraman had filmed South African soldiers in Benguela.

Savimbi's reply was ambiguous but revealing.

'There are no South African troops committed by the South African government here,' Savimbi lied to us. 'I agree that we have some white troops – not soldiers, but technicians – working for us here, doing things that we don't know how to do. I need people to fight with armoured cars that we cannot operate ourselves. The MPLA had the Russians with them. We had to address ourselves to people who could match them.'

As the handful of other journalists, including Andrew Jaffe, picked up the thread of our questioning they too joined in. Jaffe asked whether the whites 'allegedly' fighting alongside UNITA were mercenaries. It angered Savimbi, who said the MPLA was using mercenaries in the shape of thousands of Cuban soldiers. 'So, in my mind, if I have to get support from anyone, I will do it without any heavy conscience … I am doing it to save the fate of my country.'

Afterwards, as we left for Lobito airport, Savimbi, so recently (and still) a Maoist, stung by the pointed questions about South Africa, grabbed Jaffe's arm and said passionately, 'You journalists from Western countries, you say you want to oppose communism, but you are the ones who just help communism by the way you act. Why? You are weakening your democracy and giving a chance to the East to come up. We could not accept that the communists will come here, but we knew that the MPLA was building a strong army.

'In 1974 I went to see every embassy of the Western countries in Lusaka. I told them, "The danger is this one, the danger is this one" … but they did not act until the MPLA got us.'

The refusal of the West to respond openly to the Soviet-Cuban build-up was at the heart of UNITA's dilemma. Savimbi felt he had been left with no choice other than to sup from the West's gift of a poisoned chalice and accept help from black Africa's sworn enemy, apartheid South Africa. Dodging and ducking that day in Lobito, he related a parable which effectively told the truth.

'If you are a drowning man in a crocodile-filled river and you've just gone under for the third time, you don't question who is pulling you to the bank until you are safely on it.'

In the snake pit that Angola was becoming, taking help from South Africa was a matter of sheer survival against forces backed by Fidel Castro, Moscow's Leonid Brezhnev and East Germany's Erich Honecker. But in a ruthless struggle, and in the wake of passions aroused by the recently ended Vietnam War, it was infinitely more acceptable and respectable to be a Brezhnev puppet than a pawn of South Africa's then Prime Minister John Vorster.

Savimbi had pleaded for open help from the Western democracies, who had given limited clandestine help, only to be told by them, in a ruthless exercise of realpolitik, to take Pretoria's hand on condition that he – and the South Africans – denied, if necessary, knowledge of everything.[4]

The cynicism was immense, and my friend the Lusaka-based journalist Trevor Grundy summed it up this way: the Western powers – aware they could never publicly acknowledge support for South Africa's Angola adventure – stood collectively on the South West Africa–Angola border, their left arm raised with open palm indicating stop as they chanted 'Get back, you filthy racist South Africans', while their right arm waved and signalled the direction north towards Luanda as they added, 'The Soviets and the Cubans are that way.'

5

International scoop (November 1975)

I wrote by hand my scoop about South Africa's military invasion as we returned to Zambia aboard the Lonrho jet on the evening of Angola's Independence Day, 14 November 1975. We landed after dark in Lusaka, where the twice-weekly British Airways flight to London was preparing to leave. Mike sprinted from the Hawker Siddeley to the VC10 airliner and tossed the bag containing his precious film through the still open front door of the plane with shouted instructions to stewardesses to phone ITN's studios in London to say an important package had arrived. The door closed, but as the plane began taxiing towards the runway it reopened slightly and someone tossed the bag out, presumably for security reasons. Mike stood dumbfounded on the tarmac apron, and as the plane moved away he shook his fist in impotent rage and shouted, 'I hope you crash, you bastards!'

Mike's misfortune was a godsend for me. It gave me more time to flesh out the invasion narrative before I telexed a long story to Reuters just before midnight. My account became front-page news around the world long before Mike's film eventually arrived in London.

But my story was not published anywhere in South Africa, where it was ruthlessly censored. The South African public were not told that their young soldiers were fighting a war in a foreign country.

Reuters' editors were nervous that my exclusive dispatch said categorically that the South African Defence Force was secretly invading Angola – they found it difficult to believe. Because of my promise to the Lonrho pilots, I could not tell my employer that I had been flown clandestinely into the heart of the South Africans' invasion base. My action would anyway, I suspect, have been deemed highly reckless, irresponsible and unsafe by my bosses in London. Two years earlier, I had been severely reprimanded by Reuters' international editor when I was detained in Damascus at the height of the 1973 Israel-Arab Yom Kippur/Ramadan War. I had broken out of the Syrian capital, against the Damascus government's orders, to try to reach the heavy fighting on the Golan Heights. I was arrested, detained and interrogated by Syrian intelligence and subsequently expelled, leaving my agency without coverage from Damascus.

Editors in London worked on my South African invasion scoop and changed it so that its international subscribers received an account that began, 'Columns of armoured vehicles manned by white personnel are slicing across great tracts of Angola through the defences of the Marxist-oriented MPLA, informed sources said. The major unanswered question is the origin of the white soldiers.'

It was a question to which I knew, and had comprehensively supplied, the answer.

For days afterwards, the story was reworked as I pleaded that the South Africans should be named. Almost a week later, my entreaties bore fruit and the story, now identifying the South Africans unequivocally, appeared in the *Washington Post* and hundreds of newspapers and on broadcasting stations around the world.

Prominent Marxist philosopher Jean Ziegler, Professor of Sociology at the Sorbonne in Paris and the University of Geneva, said the *Post* report impelled the most powerful country in black Africa to change sides from UNITA to support for the MPLA.

'On 22 November 1975, Fred Bridgland published an unambiguous report about the presence of South African troops on Angolan territory. Nigeria, the leading political power of black Africa and supplier of petrol to the United States, changed camp, rejected UNITA, and gave an immediate grant of US$20 million to the government of (MPLA leader) Agostinho Neto.'[1]

The CIA's John Stockwell later wrote that my story fatally weakened his agency's covert support for Savimbi, as well as undermining the South African effort in Angola.

'The propaganda and political war was lost in that stroke,' said Stockwell. 'There was nothing the Lusaka station (of the CIA) could invent that would be as damaging to the other side as our alliance with the hated South Africans was to our cause.'[2]

The volte-face by Nigeria triggered a stampede by other waverers to recognise the MPLA as the legitimate government of Angola. Fearful as the Nigerians were about the adventurers from Havana and Moscow, there was no way they could support a liberation force bolstered by South Africa. Almost overnight, UNITA was transformed from a legitimate contender for power into a pariah rebel movement which had supped from Pretoria's cup.

6

South Africa and the US pull back (1976)

Following my exposé of the South African invasion, the United States Congress for a while cut off even covert aid to UNITA. I was besieged in Lusaka by journalists wanting advice on how to get into Angola to see South Africans for themselves.

There was mayhem in Zambia. President Kenneth Kaunda had permitted some South African Army units to penetrate Angola through southwestern Zambia. It was in that area of the country that Kaunda had allowed the SWAPO liberation movement to establish guerrilla bases for attacks against the South Africans in South West Africa. To square this circle, Kaunda now told SWAPO leader Sam Nujoma to confine his guerrillas to their bases.

Here was one of the many incongruities in this spillover of the Cold War into Africa. Zambia was supporting SWAPO in its guerrilla struggle against South African rule in South West Africa, but, along with the intelligence services of every major Western nation, it was also abetting, albeit deniably, the South African military in Angola. Kaunda told Nujoma that fighting communism in Angola took priority over the liberation of South West Africa. Nujoma ordered his guerrillas to suspend operations.

Unsurprisingly, the guerrillas felt they had been sold out. There was a revolt in the SWAPO camps, from where a South West African Wat Tyler's army of about a thousand men marched on Lusaka. They were intercepted by Zambian soldiers and interned in a prison camp in northern Zambia, where many died. Some escaped, and I interviewed them in their attic hiding place in a Finnish diplomat's home in Lusaka.[1]

Southern Africa was getting less simple. It was more difficult to decide who were the righteous and who were the villains.

South Africa's leaders, outraged and embittered by what they saw as an American and more general Western betrayal, began a military withdrawal from Angola that was completed on 26 March 1976. Some countries – Britain, France and Zambia, for example – got off the bandwagon so comprehensively that they recognised the MPLA and condemned Pretoria for the very SADF activities in Angola they had once slyly encouraged.

Before switching support from UNITA to the MPLA, Zambia's President Kenneth Kaunda had pleaded with Brand Fourie, the top civil servant in Pretoria's foreign ministry, and with Hilgard Muller, South Africa's then foreign minister, who Kaunda frequently hosted at his luxury game lodge in the South Luangwa National Park, to ensure that the SADF continued pressing forward in Angola.

The South African prime minister John Vorster wearily told *Newsweek* magazine that Henry Kissinger had urged South Africa's military incursion into Angola and then declined to provide the necessary back-up. The US and other Western states could not be seen to be supporting apartheid South Africa in an invasion of a black African country.

South Africa's defence minister, PW Botha, who later became his country's executive president, fulminated in the whites-only

Parliament in Cape Town. 'If the West does not want to contribute its share for the sake of itself and the free world, it cannot expect South Africa to do it. South Africa is not prepared to fight the West's battle against communist penetration on its own.[2]

'Furthermore, South Africa will defend with determination its own borders and those interests and borders we are responsible for.'

Botha said South Africa's military had crossed into Angola 'with the approval and knowledge of the Americans ... The story must be told of how we went in there with their knowledge, how they encouraged us to act and, when we had nearly reached the climax, we were ruthlessly left in the lurch.'

The ebullient Pik Botha, who became South Africa's foreign minister in 1977, asserted that, 'The United States, at the highest level, requested assistance, or rather requested South Africa to go in and assist UNITA.'[3]

As the South African withdrawal went on, to be completed by March 1976, and as Jonas Savimbi's guerrillas and my friend Tito crept away into apparent oblivion, a top British journalist, Max Hastings, published a lament. 'In any internal power struggle in Africa the personal risks for those involved of execution or exile have always been high. So, when entering a struggle the message of Angola is that it pays to be on the side the Russians are on. They win. Whatever amiable mutterings the American ambassador whispers into receptive ears, when it comes to the crunch he cannot deliver the cash, votes or guns from Washington to back them. And so now in Angola the Russians can confidently prepare to rake in their huge winnings, staked successfully on the resounding apathy of the West.'[4]

And Chester Crocker, the US Assistant Secretary of State for Africa, observed some years later that, 'The South Africans, who had become central players in a war they did not start, were left holding the can as Washington became reluctant even to acknowledge the obvious close links among all players in the Western-African coalition. Pretoria blasted what it saw to be Western flakiness, if not perfidy, and pulled out of Angola.'[5]

7

The young Cuban who never fired a shot (1976)

The Organization of African Unity (OAU) had, in the wake of Angola's independence, been divided 22–22 in support for UNITA and the MPLA. Following my report, UNITA's supporters, critically Nigeria and Tanzania, switched their allegiance to the MPLA. The Nigerian and Tanzanian decisions, in particular, made inevitable Savimbi's diplomatic downfall among black African states.

The South Africans, having been found out, did agree to hold some of the territory they had gained pending the outcome of an extraordinary OAU summit meeting on Angola on 12 January 1976 in Addis Ababa. There, the OAU, which had previously argued for a government of national unity, recognised the MPLA as the sole legitimate government of independent Angola. Savimbi reacted by saying that only free elections, as promised in the Alvor Accords, could determine which liberation movement commanded majority support.

'The four million people who support us will continue to hope that UNITA will come back one day,' he added.

Among UNITA's dwindling band of black African sympathisers, there were pleas for the South Africans to hold the ring for just a bit longer. Mark Chona, the bright and wily special adviser to Kenneth

Kaunda, became known as 'Zambia's Kissinger' because of the similar Machiavellian role he played in the conduct of his country's foreign policy to that played by Dr Henry Kissinger in the United States. Chona, a thin, bespectacled man with an enigmatic smile, was militantly anti-Soviet on Angola. He confronted me at a reception in Lusaka just before Christmas Day 1975 and said, 'The Soviet Union made elections impossible in Angola. It was the first foreign power to interfere, and now there are more troops from Cuba in Angola than from any other power … The origin of the Angolan conflict does not lie in South Africa. The South African presence is an effect of the civil war, not a fundamental cause.

'Why now that Angola is independent should the Russians supply SAM-7s (Soviet shoulder-launched surface-to-air missiles) for blacks to kill blacks when they did not provide such sophisticated weapons before? The people running from their battered homes in Angola are blacks.'

South Africa's withdrawal from Angola was slow but precise. If ever it could have been persuaded to stay despite condemnation across Africa, the possibility ended on 5 January 1976 when three of its soldiers were captured by the Cubans and publicly paraded and displayed.

I was banned from re-entering UNITA territory after I reported the South African invasion on 14 November 1975. But as the situation for Savimbi became more and more disastrous, Tito delivered a message to me in Lusaka in January 1976. UNITA, he said, would lift its ban on me if I was willing to return to its territory. There I would be shown something that would interest me as a foreign correspondent.

And so, I made the long journey again aboard the Lonrho jet on 5 January 1976. My ban had lasted just over seven weeks. This time Savimbi wanted to show the world that he had Cuban Army prisoners. He intended taking three of them to the extraordinary OAU summit to demonstrate what UNITA was up against. The three, wrists bound, clad in grey prison uniforms and shoes without laces, were paraded outside the small Portuguese jail in Silva Porto. One of them was Private Samuel Ducentes Rodriguez, a thin, white, very frightened 17-year-old, who was to become indelibly engraved in my memory. He had been conscripted in Havana, sent to Angola and taken prisoner before he fired a shot in combat. Travelling south from Luanda by taxi to join his unit, he was sitting in a coffee shop when UNITA guerrillas walked in and captured him.

Rodriguez had a big wound on the left side of his face on which new scar tissue was forming. Through a translator, he said 'some mothers' had stoned him after he was captured. Rodriguez, however, won the affection of the guerrillas because of his cheeriness and his efforts to learn Umbundu. He became a kind of mascot, and Savimbi gave him a promise that he would not be executed.

Savimbi was prevented by the Ethiopian government from taking his Cuban prisoners to the Addis Ababa OAU summit. The MPLA, however, turned up with two young white South African soldiers who became the propaganda hit of the meeting when they were paraded before the international press corps.

Having got back into UNITA territory, I remained there for three weeks with a handful of other foreign correspondents.

In Silva Porto, I glimpsed two middle-aged whites in khaki shirts being whisked through the town in a Land Rover. UNITA officials refused to admit that the two men were present, let alone say who they were or what they were doing. But a Portuguese journalist[1] close to Savimbi said they were South African and American generals carrying out a joint analysis of the military situation.

Tito organised a magical 150-kilometre trip for four of us from Nova Lisboa eastwards along the Benguela Railway and promised it would take us near to the front line. A big and beautiful double-tender steam locomotive built in Glasgow more than fifty years earlier pulled a column of freight cars filled with UNITA soldiers destined for the front. At the back, we reclined in an ornate, teak-lined VIP passenger carriage with shiny brass and velvet fittings and a rear open-air viewing platform of the kind on which, in my childhood memories, 'goodies' and 'baddies' desperately fought in Hollywood Western movies. In one grandiose delusional moment, I could almost have imagined myself as John Wayne.

It was a trip divorced from the reality of Angola's rising tragedy. I stood on the platform and gazed across the great African plateau in a semblance of peace and wonder as the sun set in the west in breathtaking fiery redness. At that moment, there was nowhere else I would rather have been. And I was being paid for this.

We laughed when the sombre, humourless *Wall Street Journal* man, newly arrived from his London base to have a look at the Angolan conflict, was unmoved by the glories of the sinking sun. Instead, he moaned: 'What a goddamn country. You can't get a single statistic. No figures on coffee production, no banana tonnages …' There was one production statistic I should perhaps have shared with him. Before independence Angola produced more than 200 000 tonnes of coffee annually, but now, by best estimates, it was down to 1 000 tonnes.

Through the night, red-hot embers flew past from the furnace of the wood-burning engine. It was one of the most memorable train journeys of my life. The locomotive's spotlight lit up the bush for hundreds of metres ahead. At every little station where the train halted, hissing steam, soldiers stood over fires cooking their maize porridge. There was lots of loud laughter and chatter because everybody seemed to know everybody at each station. It was as though these young UNITA followers, most of them impoverished and poorly educated village youths, had no understanding of the fates bearing down upon them.

I realise, with hindsight, that it was by the time of that journey that

I had begun falling in love with this benighted land and with many of the people I moved among. The Angolans had brio, warmth, vivacity and exceptional charm – uniquely their own, but with a Latin patina added under Portuguese rule. Most reporters fell under the Angolans' spell, no matter which side of the conflict they reported from. I had also realised it was inadequate to understand Angola only in terms of outside interference.

Angola was never a simplistic battleground between right and wrong, between light and darkness. Its politics were a complex weave of tribalism, self-interest, ideology and racial conflict. And as for the MPLA's 'communism', many of its leaders were more familiar with Mercedes-Benz owners' manuals than with Marx's Manifesto. It is a country with a long history and unresolved differences that existed before the Soviets, Cubans, South Africans, Britons, Americans and others arrived and would persist after they all left. There were clear divisions between the coast and the interior, between town and country, between north and south, between the capital and the hinterland.

There were also fundamental divisions between different tribal groups. By some estimates there are more than a hundred distinct ethnic groups and 46 different languages, with Angola Radio broadcasting in 14 of them.

The critical divide is between the Kimbundu and the Ovimbundu, as different from one another as, perhaps, English people and Scots. The Kimbundu, concentrated around Luanda on the coast in the north, comprise about 25 per cent of the population and they were the core ethnic supporters of the MPLA. Their language is Kimbundu. The Ovimbundu mainly live high on the great African plateau in the centre and south of the country and make up about 35 per cent of the overall population. Their language is Umbundu.

The Kimbundu had been in close contact for five centuries with the Portuguese, whose live-and-let-live attitude towards the races had created a big *mestiço* (mixed race) population in the Luanda region. The Portuguese scarcely bothered to settle the interior until the early 20th century. Ovimbundu society, with its networks of royal kings and chiefs, had therefore, to some extent, been left undisturbed. It also meant there was far less miscegenation, and the Ovimbundu derided the heavy *mestiço* influence on Kimbundu culture and politics. The Ovimbundu took pride in ancient tradition, encapsulated by the proverb *Etu tua tunga vovipembe viovopakula* – 'We have roots in the fields of our ancestors'.

The Ovimbundu were singled out by the Portuguese for forced labour on the coffee plantations of the far north. The annual press-ganging by the Portuguese of fit males provoked constant Ovimbundu emigration to the neighbouring Belgian Congo and British-ruled Northern Rhodesia. Describing the historic antipathy between the two tribal groups, novelist Sousa Jamba wrote, 'The Ovimbundu believe the Kimbundu to be a tribe of house servants for the Portuguese. The Kimbundu, on their part, believe the Ovimbundu are a tribe of flea-infested peasants.'[2] The Ovimbundu also used to say of the Luanda *mestiços* that their stomachs were in Angola and their hearts in Portugal.

There was another key generalised difference. Portugal's and the Catholic Church's neglect of the interior left an opening for Protestant missionaries from North America to establish primary schools there. African Christian converts were therefore largely Catholic in the Kimbundu/MPLA coastal heartland and mainly Protestant in the Ovimbundu/UNITA interior. During the final struggle against the Portuguese the MPLA, led by urban intellectuals, many of them *mestiços*, adopted Moscow as its liberation patron. UNITA, with its rural peasant base, looked towards Beijing, thus widening the chasm between the capital and the interior.[3]

These and other vital differences between the combatants were virtually ignored as the world saw and interpreted the Angolan conflict in over-simplistic terms of racist South Africans versus communist Cubans. Many Angolan realities were scarcely acknowledged.

Our splendid steam train arrived the next morning at the small town of Luso, where we left our luxury compartment and also the *Wall Street Journal* man – who set off elsewhere in search of some reliable statistics! – and were packed aboard a small diesel rail-inspection car to travel further eastward towards the fighting. We were joined by a *Panorama* BBC-TV camera crew and a German TV team who had both arrived to try to film South African soldiers. They failed.[4]

Some 100 kilometres east of Luso the rail car approached what appeared from a distance to be the twisted wreckage of a bridge across a river. The driver, a young Portuguese, did not slow down as he got near the bridge – indeed, he accelerated. His British and German passengers, brainwashed in the virtues of the stiff upper lip, said nothing. At the last moment the driver slammed on his brakes. It was far too late. The rail car skidded on at great speed. We reached the destroyed bridge and plunged down the broken hanging rails towards the river-bed. We were halted in mid-dive towards oblivion by a twisted girder that blocked the line, leaving us hanging precariously above the water. We clambered out one by one and climbed back up the ladder-like dangling line towards safety.

The rail car could not be recovered, and we lived for several days in an abandoned house with no electricity or running water, being served glutinous rice and boiled goat at every meal, before Tito was able to send a train, pulled by yet another Glasgow-manufactured engine, to rescue us.

It was one of several smashes I experienced within a short time, which led me and others to dub UNITA's territory 'The Land With No Brakes'.

The weirdest of these crashes happened as we travelled in a UNITA convoy of largely brakeless cars and Land Rovers along a forest-lined road littered with elephant dung. After zooming over the brow of one hill, we were confronted on the downslope by a burnt-out truck blocking the road. The one vehicle with working brakes, in which I was a passenger, drew up beyond the wrecked truck. We then watched the other brakeless vehicles cascade over the hilltop and either swerve off into the forest undergrowth or snake around the truck to come to rest about a kilometre further down the road.

One of two French journalists travelling with us was missing when all the vehicles had finally halted. Fearing our French colleague might have been badly injured, we trudged back up the slope and found him lying unconscious in the thick roadside vegetation.

His pal explained that they had arrived in Angola from Zaire, where they had both been aboard a military helicopter hovering at about five metres when the pilot and co-pilot dashed through and jumped out of the open side door without explanation. The helicopter crashed. The other passengers survived with only slight concussion, but our unconscious Frenchman had obviously not recovered from his Zairean trauma. On coming over that Angolan hilltop road and spotting the wrecked truck, he had run through the back of the Land Rover, opened the rear door and leapt out in fear for his life at something like 80 kilometres per hour.

I seriously feared he might die as he lay groaning on the ground. Fortunately, he had nothing worse than another severe concussion.

The UNITA guerrillas had no first-aid equipment other than an old-fashioned inflatable sphygmomanometer, with which one of them measured the Frenchman's blood pressure. We were hundreds of kilometres from the nearest town, and all clinics were far beyond reach. As our journey and assorted small crashes continued, he gradually recovered. I never discovered his ultimate fate, but I suspect that from then onwards he gave both Zaire and Angola a big miss.

I left UNITA's territory on 27 January 1976 and returned once again on 7 February at the invitation of Jorge Sangumba. As Cuban forces approached Gago Countinho (see Prologue), I picked up fragments of information for a farewell story on 9 February. Tito, as well as suggesting that day that I might write a book about UNITA if the movement survived, also told me sappers were blowing up every road and rail bridge as the guerrillas retreated before the Cuban onslaught. Elsewhere, the South African military, which had become crucial for the UNITA resistance, continued a retreat that was completed by March 1976.

What Tito did not tell me, and which I learned only later, was that UNITA had executed, in Silva Porto, all of its Cuban prisoners of war. They included Samuel Rodriguez, the 17-year-old Cuban soldier who never fired a shot in combat and who had been assured by Savimbi he would never be killed. I had also interviewed another two of the Cubans whose lives were snuffed out: Lieutenant Selso Caldez, 22, from La Sierrita in southeast Cuba, and 21-year-old Private José Durudi, from Guantanamo, near the site of the US Navy installation enclave in eastern Cuba. Durudi had told me he wanted his wife and baby daughter to know he was safe. A UNITA communiqué, reported by Reuters on 11 March 1976, said the firing squad that killed the Cubans was composed entirely of women. 'The Cubans were shot with their own guns,' said the communiqué.

Knowledge of Rodriguez's death and the betrayal by Savimbi of his pledge greatly depressed me. I suppose it crystallised all the futility of the war that should have been avoided. My wife, Kathryn, too was deeply upset. Although she had never met Rodriguez, I had told her about him when I was home in Lusaka and about how impressed I was by his geniality. She wrote a poem that captured the pathos and significance of his death and those of all the other unsung or anonymous casualties of the war.

Rodriguez

By Kathryn Bridgland-Kane

The green time has come
The rains
Invade

Smitten earth yields dust
comes lush
alive

Streamlets form columns
surround
'high ground'

Earth redoubt crumbles
into
fresh moat

The citadel's laid bare

Ribcage whitely gleams
through flood-force rising
a one-man Mary-Rose

The listing masthead
tilts and tilts again
surrend'ring eighteen years

Heeling beneath mud
final arms laid down
rebuke life's brevity

No dry dust remains
Nor sign
Nor shallow mound

Angola's reclaimed

Unsung
The boy from Cuba dies again

8
The Long March (1976)

Following my surprise reunion with Tito in Morocco in 1980, he was sent later that year by Savimbi to London to be the movement's Europe representative. We met frequently at my homes in Edinburgh and London, in his London flat, provided to UNITA by the owners of the Benguela Railway, and later in Brussels when I was posted there as Europe correspondent of *The Scotsman*.

I listened as Tito described his version of the UNITA story for the book I'd promised to write. I told him that at some point I would need to return to Angola and travel with the guerrillas. But first he related what had happened on the Long March into the interior after what I thought had been our final goodbye four years earlier in Gago Coutinho on 9 February 1976.

The purpose of the march had been to escape the better-armed Cubans and MPLA, and to retreat to former bases in the war against the Portuguese so that they could regroup and reorganise for a new war. He said the March had lasted seven months. There was much suffering along the way.

Some 4 000 guerrillas and civilians had gathered at Gago Coutinho as Cuban military convoys were advancing throughout central Angola.

Soon after they began moving out of the small settlement on 9 February 1976, the straggling UNITA column was strafed by Cuban and MPLA warplanes and several guerrillas were killed. Those attacks triggered a withdrawal by 20 French mercenaries who had been attached to UNITA by the French intelligence agency, the General Directorate for External Security (DGSE), and the CIA, which paid nearly half a million dollars to fund the French fighters. Tito said the French commander, an army colonel, told him that he and his men were leaving because UNITA's cause was hopeless. He said Tito, Savimbi and all UNITA's leaders would be dead within two months. The French left by truck for an airstrip some 80 kilometres to the south where they were picked up by a South African aircraft and whisked out of Angola.

UNITA took with it three trucks and five cars as its Long March began. As Cuban and MPLA MiG-21s attacked, the drivers of the vehicles kept their doors open so that they could leap out easily when they heard warplanes approaching. They moved slowly forward and drove into the shade of the forest whenever they heard aircraft noise. After the warplanes returned to base the drivers pushed forward again, their vehicles crudely camouflaged with tree branches to gain distance before the next attack. All the vehicles were abandoned when they ran out of fuel.

Cuban helicopter gunships began traversing the forests and patrolling the rivers in search of the retreating forces. Savimbi took a leaf from his mentor Mao Zedong, who on the Chinese Communists' Long March in 1934 broke his force into several columns that took varying paths to confuse the enemy. Savimbi dispersed his own guerrillas under senior commanders to different parts of central and southern Angola, leaving him with a personal column some 1 000 strong, comprising 600 guerrillas, including Tito, and about 400 civilians, including women, several Protestant pastors and three Catholic priests.

Tito said the column entered a Chokwe tribal area of long-standing

UNITA support. Villagers helped to carry baggage but also demanded that Savimbi explain how he had managed to lose the war. 'But they were also the kind of people who were not easily shaken once they had pledged their loyalty,' Tito told me. 'Once these people were with you, they were really strong. They wouldn't give a secret away or betray you.'

A month later, the column reached an old UNITA base, from the years of the fight against the Portuguese, in the valley of a meandering river called the Lungue Bungu, the largest tributary of the Upper Zambezi, densely populated by hippos and crocodiles in its multiple channels and oxbow lakes. There Savimbi, Tito and others organised a conference that proved one of the turning points in the struggle for survival. They were joined by about 2 000 guerrillas who had been left behind in other areas during the Cubans' February advance. Tito recalled one village elder telling the conference, 'I have only my arrow and axe, but these will be enough to fight the Cubans. These people did not come from here. Who planted these trees under which we are talking? Not the Cubans.'

Savimbi ordered yet another dispersal of his forces. He encouraged his commanders by emphasising Angola's vastness, which the Portuguese had never been able to control completely during their 500-year rule.

Savimbi's own column included members of his elite bodyguard, commanded by Tito, who said they did not stop moving, day or night, except for very brief rests. Many women in the column found it difficult to keep up. Bela Malaquias, a young woman from a leading UNITA family, said Tito continually encouraged the women to keep going, to not be left behind and to follow him closely even though they were perplexed, tired and hungry. Ominously, he told them that some stragglers who could no longer walk had been shot by security personnel so they could not be captured and made to talk.

Tito said that at each rest point Savimbi moved up and down the column explaining what they must do.

First, they had to walk at great speed, faster than the pursuing enemy could imagine was possible.

Second, they were not to leave a trail that could easily be picked up by MPLA trackers. Every effort had to be made to confuse their pursuers. For ten to fifteen minutes after most halts the column doubled back in the direction from which it had come to lay misleading tracks. Then, as the column turned again to head in the right direction, everybody would spread out over a broad front for a few kilometres before joining up again in a single column.

At one point, said Tito, a herd of about 60 cattle joined the column to provide food on the hoof. Savimbi instructed the drover to use the cattle to cover the guerrillas' tracks. Weaving and circling through the forests, the UNITA column often recrossed its own earlier tracks and crossed those of its pursuers.

I was fascinated as Tito sat in my homes recalling deep into the nights his memories of the Long March, during which he said Savimbi displayed brilliance, courage and the fruits of his training in China.

Third, said Tito, Savimbi ordered everyone to be quiet as possible. There were children, including babies, in the column. At first, the babies cried often. But the tension was so great that eventually even they fell permanently silent.

Fourth, Savimbi said they had to camouflage themselves and discard ever more of their possessions. Everybody wore a shroud of leaves and twigs over their heads and shoulders, and women had to abandon bright dresses.

Fifth, tight discipline was essential. Things that were discarded were buried in deep pits which were covered by a thickly woven framework of logs and branches which in turn was covered with earth and sand. By June and July of 1976, the winter nights in southern Angola had turned cold, frequently dipping below freezing. Exhausted men were dying of exposure after they got soaked in river crossings. Fires were necessary at night. Officers had to ensure that all traces of ash were eliminated in the morning and that every scrap of unused food and paper was buried.

A new challenge arose. Hunger and growing starvation. Meat supplies ran out as the cattle were slaughtered and the rate of progress slowed to a crawl because people were weak with hunger. At one halt traditional Chokwe hunters killed a bush pig. The fleeing people ate its skin and bones, as well as the meat, Tito told me. The bones were boiled, and the thin soup was drunk, then the softened bones were crushed and devoured. For a while the only other source of nourishment was red-coloured, wild *kumussequele,* also known as Bushmen beans, which were gathered and boiled. Once soft, the skins were peeled, and the poison flesh discarded. The skins were boiled again with leaves from a tree. It was food of a sort, but the resulting soup left the emaciated diners weak and bloated.

One guerrilla collected honey from a wild bees' nest high in a tree. Savimbi's wife, Vinona, was an expert on edible forest fungi and she collected some for the pot. But five soldiers died of poisoning after they gathered and ate fungi without consulting Vinona.

Tito said he became so thin and hungry that he believed he would die. Savimbi, he said, urged his soldiers not to surrender to death because people were waiting for them to make an effective fight against the Cubans and the MPLA.

'That was a really shocking and frightening moment,' he told me, 'because some of the soldiers just didn't have the physical ability to respond to his call, although you could see they wanted to. Most did manage to stand and say they would fight on, but several collapsed moments later.

'The group grew weaker and weaker because of lack of food. We sprawled on the forest floor and after a few days many were unable to drag themselves to their feet. Eventually, a patrol brought life-saving news: they had discovered a village 15 kilometres away, and the villagers were long-standing UNITA supporters.'

Savimbi, Tito, Vinona and other members of the column staggered through the forest and over a hill towards the village. 'Villagers came out to meet us and help bring the column to their huts,' said Tito. 'They did not have big stocks of food, but they gave us maize, cassava and antelope meat. Savimbi, drawing on his medical training in Portugal, ordered us not to take solid food straightaway. Solids following a long period of starvation could result in stomach spasms, resulting in death, he said.'

The maize was first ground to make a thin gruel and was the only food eaten for two days. Nevertheless, it caused severe cramps on the empty stomachs. After that, a little meat was eaten.

The village was very isolated. No Cuban or MPLA patrol had ever reached it, but after about five days, by when most of the party was taking solid food again, a Cuban helicopter flew high overhead. Although the Cubans could not know that Savimbi's column was below, Tito said they would inevitably plot the village on their maps and return with ground patrols. Savimbi ordered the guerrillas to split up yet again and to disperse and travel lightly and as fast as possible.

Tito buried three thick notebooks, probably outside the village, in which he had been keeping a record of events on the Long March – all the participants' names, their special skills, their illnesses and their deaths. Superfluous possessions were being discarded. If captured, Tito would not have wanted the MPLA to have access to his thoughts and experiences.

For 36 hours, Savimbi's dwindling party walked non-stop. 'On halting, he reminded us that we no longer had any active allies,' said Tito. 'All of our friends would think we were incapable of resisting, that we were finished. We would have to rely entirely on our own efforts, on support from the people and on existing stocks of weapons and captured guns. First, we had to fight and then we would discover that people in the outside would want to get in touch with us again.

'He said the Cubans had clear advantages over us, but they were also at a disadvantage compared with our knowledge of the forests and countryside, of the people and their languages. He said we resembled ants: once we get into the elephant's trunk, we'll be able to bring him down.'

Savimbi finally halted the Long March on 28 August 1976 in Cuelei, an old UNITA base in the fight against the Portuguese, after seven months and a winding journey of more than 3 000 kilometres from Gago Coutinho.

Cuelei was in deep forest hundreds of kilometres south of the Benguela Railway line. Following the numerous splits in the columns and many deaths, there were now only 79 people with Savimbi, including nine women.

'The march had been the most profound experience of my life,' Tito told me. 'You felt you needed to love your brother as yourself. Alone, you couldn't survive. When comrades died, you truly felt diminished. Something of oneself died with them. During this time we were completely alone in terms of help from the outside. Nobody was prepared to help us. We had to concentrate purely on survival. But all of us who were on the march believed by the end of it that the war really could be won.'

Tito recalled tuning-in his small radio and hearing a speech by Henry Kissinger, who was on a diplomatic safari through southern Africa. Kissinger outlined a programme for black majority rule in Rhodesia and a timetable for South West African independence and warned that racial discrimination must end in South Africa.

'At the time I was suffering from exhaustion and starvation, and I had watched some friends starve to death. So I was shocked that Kissinger had nothing to say about Angola. I realised then that few people in the outside world cared about us. We had only ourselves to rely upon. We had to look after ourselves because none of the Big Powers would. Steel entered my soul that day.'

9

All external support for Savimbi collapses (1976)

For a while, after his UNITA friends had vanished into Angola's depths, Zambia's President Kenneth Kaunda continued to speak out on behalf of Savimbi and his followers. Kaunda argued that the people of Africa had barely begun to understand the consequences of events in Angola. 'Independence is impossible with Big Brother hanging over your shoulder,' he told me in an interview in March 1976 at State House in Lusaka. 'He is overbearing and will overpower you. It's a real puzzle to me how people can talk of independence when they are unable to govern a country without Cuban and Russian soldiers.'

Much as Kaunda knew where his heart lay, he obeyed what his head told him. Zambia, on 15 April 1976, announced its official recognition of the MPLA as the legitimate government of Angola. It came in the form of a one-sentence government statement, with no elaboration: 'The Minister of Foreign Affairs Mr Rupiah Banda today announced Zambia's recognition of the People's Republic of Angola.'

A few days later, Banda, who was close to Savimbi and who'd been one of the staunchest advocates of UNITA in Kaunda's government, was dismissed. All anti-MPLA rhetoric ceased. Realpolitik reigned. Banda had to go if relations were to be repaired with the MPLA.

Kaunda had appealed to US President Gerald Ford just a few weeks earlier to reverse 'a tide sweeping the MPLA to victory'. He had cooperated with the CIA and the South Africans to save Savimbi, whose intelligence and courage he admired, from annihilation.[1] Declaring a state of emergency, after the South Africans had begun their withdrawal from Angola, Kaunda made what became a famous allusion to Moscow's and Havana's intervention in Angola.

'We have witnessed imperialism at work in all its manifestations,' he said in a television and radio address. 'Africa has fought and driven out the ravenous wolves of colonialism, racism and fascism from Angola through the front door. But a plundering Tiger (the Soviet Union), with its deadly cubs (Cuba), is now coming through the back door.'

Rupiah Banda said, 'After they have killed the South Africans in Angola, who will the Cubans and Russians be remaining there to fight? The Soviet Union knows very well that it is not in Angola because of the South Africans. If they're supposed to be in Angola to help us (black Africans), why don't they go and fight in South Africa and Namibia? Haven't they heard of Cape Town?'[2]

Despite Kaunda's switch of allegiance, Savimbi continued to speak highly of the Zambian president.

'He is my friend and I respect him,' he said. 'I don't believe that Kaunda is with the MPLA. He is forced to. He cannot help me, but I believe his heart is with me … He's a good man. He is the one who has backed UNITA, and we lost, so he has to join with them (the MPLA).'[3]

10
Fighting back (1976–1980)

For UNITA, the initial strategy after completing the Long March was mere survival.

'The longer we survived the more the situation would change around us to UNITA's advantage,' Tito told me. 'But survival did not mean passivity. It meant preparation, training in guerrilla warfare and linking up again with scattered groups of our own fighters. Savimbi said we would have to test ourselves against the MPLA, the Cubans and the Russians and study their thinking.

'There could be no all-out large offensives. We were far too weak. There would be pinprick attacks designed to confuse the enemy and let us understand their tactics. We aimed to damage the economy, blowing up bridges, laying ambushes to make roads unsafe for travel and stopping transport along the Benguela Railway.'

The early assessments showed that several UNITA groups had continued to struggle on independently, hoping their leader had survived and would eventually make contact. Three particularly interesting young organisers of this self-reliant resistance were Demóstenes Chilingutila, Geraldo Sachipengo Nunda and Ben-Ben Arlindo Pena, destined eventually to become some of Savimbi's most outstanding senior officers. Chilingutila was leading a small band of guerrillas in the difficult open country of the coastal province of Benguela. Nunda headed a group in the immediate country around Nova Lisboa, now renamed Huambo, and Pena was at the head of a group with bases in the forested hills further to the south of Nova Lisboa/Huambo.

'Until we managed to link up again with Savimbi in 1977, the future looked pretty dark,' Ben-Ben told me in Angola in 1983. Much earlier, back in May 1974, Ben-Ben had pulled down the Portuguese flag and burned it in Nova Lisboa.

Chilingutila, Nunda and Pena represented a new trend. They were young and had not fought with Savimbi against the Portuguese. They were high-school graduates, products of educational opportunities that had expanded rapidly in the 1960s under the Portuguese. All three had been conscripted into the Portuguese Army, rising to become sergeants, the highest rank permitted to blacks. They joined UNITA as the war developed in 1975–1976. Others like them continued to be recruited through the late 1970s.

Marvine Howe of *The New York Times*, reporting from Nova Lisboa/Huambo, said that in April and May 1976, UNITA guerrillas destroyed three locomotives and derailed another on the Benguela Railway and cut the line in several places.[1] The attacks were carried out by groups acting independently of Savimbi.

An event that helped end UNITA's isolation from the outside world began on 8 March 1977 when several thousand Zairean Katangese gendarmes exiled in MPLA areas of northern Angola crossed the border into Zaire. These tough fighters, organised by the Cubans, pressed hard towards Kolwezi, a major copper-mining town some 350 kilometres inside Zaire in Shaba Province.

Zairean President Mobutu Sese Seko's numerically superior but ill-disciplined, disintegrating army fled, but Moroccan paratroopers, led by French military instructors, airlifted by French Air Force transport planes and supplied with American, Belgian and Chinese weaponry, turned the tide after twelve weeks of intense fighting during which up to 100 000 people were estimated to have been killed.[2] Mobutu, despite his wholesale corruption and general misrule, was strategically and economically important to the West because of Zaire's immense mineral wealth and other natural resources.

Immediately after the Katangese invasion of Zaire, Tito explained to me that countries which had discounted UNITA realised that the Cubans were not only a threat to UNITA but potentially to the whole region.

'We began receiving messages from several African governments who asked to see Savimbi and hear about our resistance. Until then, there had been little interest. The problem was how to get out from the areas where we were fighting to the outside world. Savimbi sent an envoy to ask the South Africans if they would be willing to give him safe passage through South West Africa and onwards to black Africa.'

The South Africans agreed to Savimbi's request and also provided a small rear base, called Delta, for UNITA just inside South West Africa. In September 1977, Savimbi flew from the South African military base at Rundu to Kinshasa, Zaire's capital. He briefed President Mobutu on UNITA's resistance. The Zairean leader gave Savimbi luxury accommodation for two months and arranged for him to make clandestine trips across Africa to meet leaders worried about Fidel Castro's plans for the continent.

One of Savimbi's first trips was to Dakar to meet Senegal's President Leopold Senghor, who had openly supported UNITA in 1975–1976. It was then that he told Savimbi that UNITA representatives would be given Senegalese passports and identities to enable them to travel freely around the world. It was then also that Senghor contacted King Hassan of Morocco and asked him to meet Savimbi.

Savimbi arrived in Morocco in October 1977.

'His meeting with Hassan changed the situation for UNITA completely because the king agreed to orchestrate our diplomatic struggle,' said Tito. 'From that point onwards, UNITA was no longer isolated. King Hassan made his friends our friends, and we had a secure external headquarters in Rabat from which to conduct diplomacy. Visitors wanting to meet us passed quickly through VIP channels.'

It was there in Rabat, in February 1980, that I had again met Tito after an interval of four years.[3]

What were King Hassan's motives for helping Savimbi and UNITA?

He was conducting his own war against the Polisario Front. The Front, not dissimilar to UNITA, had been fighting Morocco's security forces since early 1976 in a struggle for the independence of the former Spanish colonial territory of Western Sahara. King Hassan had annexed Western Sahara into Morocco after Spain's withdrawal in early 1976. The United Nations supported the Polisario Front because the majority of Sahrawis wanted self-determination and complete independence. Polisario fought fiercely, with the backing of neighbouring Algeria, which provided the Sahrawis with a secure base and sanctuary at Tindouf in Western Algeria. Polisario was also supported with Soviet arms.[4]

King Hassan therefore saw the Soviets as a major threat to his interests. Consequently, the Soviets and their close allies, the Cubans, were to be opposed in all possible regions where they had intervened in Africa.

Tito told me, 'I had no illusions that we were anything but pawns in a very big international game in Africa. While we were being used, we were also working out how to use what was on offer to our advantage. To defeat one beast in what we were learning was a ruthless world, we knew we had to ally ourselves with other beasts.'

Savimbi needed a route into Angola for arms and materiel from Morocco. South Africa willingly re-entered the Angolan fray to oblige.

Its bases in the north of South West Africa became transit points for arms deliveries. SWAPO, following its humiliation by Kenneth Kaunda, had moved from Zambia to new bases in Angola, where Soviet, Cuban and East German trainers were making it a more effective guerrilla force. South Africa preferred to fight SWAPO on Angolan rather than South West African soil while at the same time bolstering the West's strategy to counter the plans of Leonid Brezhnev and Fidel Castro.

The South Africans appointed a young military intelligence officer, Lieutenant Colonel Philip du Preez, who was fluent in Portuguese, to the role of liaison officer with UNITA. The project was code-named Operation Silver. The official UNITA propaganda was that it received no help from South Africa at this time other than transit facilities. However, John Marcum, Professor of Politics at the University of California and widely regarded as the leading expert on the revolution in Angola against colonial rule, said the instructors helping UNITA included officers of the South African crack commando 32 Battalion, also known as the Buffalo Battalion.[5] Supplies were being flown at night into Angola by South African Air Force Puma helicopters. South Africa began taking seriously wounded UNITA soldiers into military hospitals in South West Africa for treatment.

The French Secret Service arranged for several young UNITA women to travel to Paris for two-year secretarial and language-training courses. I had met some of these teenage women in Silva Porto in 1975. They were a gleeful, friendly bunch who laughed a lot and dressed flamboyantly in bright colours. One of the most elegant and high-spirited of them was particularly beautiful. Her name was Ana Isabel Paulino. She

UNITA recruits drill at an Operation Silver training camp.

and Tito were close friends, became lovers and planned to marry when the conflict ended, or, if necessary, even earlier.

Several science graduates of the Portuguese *liceu* (high school) system in Angola were sent by Savimbi to medical schools in France, Switzerland and Portugal and to agricultural universities in the United States. They only began to return to UNITA territory as qualified doctors and agricultural scientists from 1984 onwards.

Meanwhile, there was an influx of highly qualified nurses to UNITA from MPLA-held areas of central Angola. They helped make up for the guerrillas' total lack of doctors, with the exception of one, Adelino Manassas, kidnapped from the MPLA and held permanent hostage.

By September 1978, South Africa was moving brand-new Mercedes trucks, diesel fuel, ammunition and tinned and dried food across the border to the guerrillas, who had set up a new central base in southeast Angola in a vast wilderness area, teeming with wildlife and laced with pristine rivers and swamps, which the Portuguese knew as *a terra do fim do mundo* – 'The Land at the End of the World'. The sprawling base, spread over some 100 square kilometres of virgin bush, was christened Jamba – 'Place of the Elephants' – after the great herds of elephants that moved through and around it.

The Chinese continued to deliver more weapons for new battalions being trained under UNITA officers returning from courses in Morocco. The weaponry included rifles, mortars, 70mm cannons and anti-aircraft guns. American journalist Edward Girardet, who followed the Angola story closely, wrote that the Chinese supplies were channeled into Angola via South West Africa.[6]

American press reports said that Dr Zbigniew Brzezinski, President Jimmy Carter's hawkish National Security Advisor, had asked the Chinese, during a visit to China in May 1978, to supply arms and equipment for Savimbi's fight with the MPLA and Cubans. During a trip to the Great Wall, reporters on the Brzezinski visit said they heard him joking with Chinese officials as to whether he or they would be the first to keep the Russians out of various parts of Africa.[7] Brzezinski also said Washington would not open diplomatic relations with the MPLA as long as Cuban troops remained in Angola.[8]

It was a logical way for the Carter administration, deeply concerned by events in Angola and Zaire, to get around the Clark Amendment, an amendment to the Arms Export Control Act of 1976, and which banned all future US covert military aid to movements in Angola. In the spring of 1978, Senator Dick Clark, author of the amendment and chairman of the Senate's Africa sub-committee, had accused Carter of sending secret supplies to Savimbi.

This linkage between Brzezinski, China and South Africa was especially ironic and interesting since the US at that time was committed to the Clark Amendment and a policy, in public at least, that involved the withdrawal of South Africa from South West Africa and the creation of an independent state there, to be called Namibia. The gaps between rhetoric and reality illustrated the whole game of smoke and mirrors being carried out by the international community over Angola and its neighbours.

(The Clark Amendment was later repealed by the US Congress in July 1985 under the presidency of Ronald Reagan).

By this time, 1979, there were more Cuban soldiers – possibly 19 000 – in the country than at independence to help the MPLA to counter UNITA. Tito reacted with quiet amusement when *The New York Times* foreign affairs commentator Jonathan Power described MPLA supporters as '*the* Angolan people'.

Here, he later wrote to me, emphatically underlining some words, was a paradox. 'What right does Jonathan Power have to dictate *which* Angolans have the right of being nationals of *their* own country? Are there *right* and *wrong* Angolans? The MPLA has never been elected and therefore has no right to speak on behalf of *all* Angolans. The traditional African way of solving problems is by dialogue, and we think we are being deprived of that. We are saying that Power is wrong to say the MPLA are the *right* ones because the promised ballot was never held.'

I began researching and writing *Jonas Savimbi: A Key to Africa* with Tito when he was posted to London in 1980. He had spent most of 1979 and the early months of 1980 based in Morocco, liaising with Hassan and Senghor, and with Brzezinski's clandestine envoys. He suggested that the best way of telling the UNITA story was by making the book a semi-biography of Savimbi.

He initially had few London contacts other than with Tiny Rowland and some MI6 operatives. For predictable reasons he was welcomed by the right and rejected by the left. It would become a major part of his strategy to reach out beyond the mainstream right to liberals and, if possible, some leftists. It was easy to smear UNITA as a mere puppet of South Africa and he was determined somehow to shake off that image. I could never help thinking of Tito's suffering and his father's incarceration in Portuguese prisons with Angolans of all political persuasions. In our conversations, he pondered endlessly why it was that that the cry for one man, one vote and the holding of multi-party elections for Angola was as rarely heard from the lips of anti-apartheid campaigners as their demand for such freedoms in South Africa and South West Africa. He said the call for Angolan multi-party elections would be the central plank of his diplomacy.

Tito operated in central London out of a poky Mayfair office, registered under the name of a front company, Scarbray, provided by Tanzania Concessions Limited, the British majority-owning company of the Benguela Railway. He travelled regularly to my Edinburgh home, where I lived in the early 1980s before I was posted to Brussels in 1983. Those were times of special value and tranquillity. It was then and there that I began to appreciate fully his qualities of intelligence, of curiosity, of fundamental kindness, of apparent calm and of deep concern for his troubled people. He always brought gifts for my wife, Kathryn, and soft toys for my daughters. He was particularly fond of two-year-old Rebecca Esmé. He gave her teddy bears and in the evenings, as he relaxed in an armchair and spoke about religion and family life, Rebecca would stand behind him and gently touch his hair. Tito handled it with placid wisdom, just continuing his conversation with Kathryn and me and keeping his head still, letting Rebecca feel natural, warm and loved. Sometimes she climbed on to his knees and snuggled down in his lap.

Tito and I worked together for hours in Edinburgh on the narrative, using Savimbi as the peg on which to hang the UNITA story. But afterwards, over dinner and around the living-room fire, he revealed to me and Kathryn his other profound concerns, preferring to discuss anything other than war or politics.

He told how he wished one day to train as a teacher rather than

71

become a politician. Education, he said, had to be top priority once Angola was at peace. He dreamed of going to university to study economics. He read books on political theory voraciously, but he gravitated more and more towards works on political economy. Without economic development, he had concluded, all the political theory in the world was useless. One of his major concerns had become how Angolans were to be lifted out of poverty – how to generate growth, jobs and prosperity. One United Nations survey said that about 60 per cent of Angola's children were dying before the age of five. Of those who did survive, fewer than half were receiving any form of schooling. Angola had become a wasteland of wandering refugees. The UN survey proclaimed it 'as the worst place in the world for a child to grow up in'. Tito said he had come to recognise that people could not eat slogans, nor could problems be solved with rhetorical clichés.

Tito's upbringing and his war experiences also stirred his interest in the life of the spirit. He wondered where our spirits went when we die.

'Water doesn't disappear when it evaporates – it becomes a cloud. Do we do something like that?'

Justified though he considered his movement's fight, he sought desperately for some meaning which transcended UNITA's particular struggle. Although he was a very private person, he confided to me and Kathryn his attempts to resolve the contradiction between his own Christian faith and the violence of war in which he was a committed soldier. He told Kathryn, a devout Roman Catholic, that he wanted passionately to be a truly good man, but he said the politics of war and international intrigue clashed harshly with this desire. He longed for an ordinary family life but worried about how a just peace could be established to allow Angola's children to grow up in some kind of normality.

He described how, while serving briefly at the war front, he had stumbled across the body of a young MPLA soldier on the battlefield. He searched for some identity and found a diary soaked in the blood of the dead youth's wounds. Entries made just before his death spoke about his anxieties about having to fight. There were emotional passages about his mother. Tito said he found himself overwhelmed with sorrow. He had prayed silently for God to receive the youth's soul. He promised himself and the dead enemy fighter that he would do everything possible to end Angola's disastrous war, and that when it was all over he would seek out the young man's mother and hand her the diary.

Tito was gentle and thoughtful even at his lowest. Always soft-spoken, he had impeccable manners. He was also an immaculate, though not flashy, dresser. And I saw how tidy he kept his work surfaces in London and later in Washington. I do not know how he managed it, but there was never anything on them, not a single paperclip or piece of paper.

He confided his feelings of cosmic loneliness, bad stomach problems and an inability to keep food down. He told me he felt ill-prepared for the difficult task assigned to him by Savimbi, lamenting, 'We've been left entirely on our own.'

He described how his initial personal isolation, in a British society very different from his own, physically and culturally, was actually causing him great stress. Added to that was the strain of conducting vital diplomacy in sophisticated democracies. It was causing him sleepless nights that he knew was affecting his health.

Kathryn, always generous-minded, was wonderful with Tito. She cosseted and cared for him as though he was her own son and helped him to begin to eat more healthily. In a later personal memoir, she wrote, 'That he eventually came to perform his task extremely well, both in Europe and then in the United States, points to the ability, courage, integrity and perseverance which had at our first meeting been veiled by his shy though charming manner … He was slim, quite tall and good-looking. With his gentle manner, he was good with children. I discussed with him for many hours his interests in philosophy, religion, politics and African culture. Fred and I at first could not know just how much mutual affection, empathy and respect would grow between us down the years.'

I teased Tito frequently about his use of the totalitarian word 'masses'. I used to say it was Vladimir Lenin-speak for 'people', for 'human beings'. Tito used to just laugh.

He was stressed and ashen on one occasion when I collected him at Edinburgh's Waverley Station after the 650-kilometre rail journey from London. He had terrible news. His parents, Jonatão and Violeta, had been killed. They had not retreated before the Cubans in 1976 with the main UNITA column. Instead, they fled to a group of friendly villages where years earlier Jonatão had established a bush primary school. Savimbi, he said, had sent a message saying his parents had been shot dead during a surprise MPLA attack. Few details were known.

Tito was devastated by the news. He had often told me his love and respect for his father was immense. Jonatão, born in 1910, had been a strict but fair parent, compassionate but unbending in upholding the highest standards. As Tito described his father, I envisaged him as one of those 'old school' Christians one bumps into through much of Africa – serious, humble, kind, dignified, often at ease with both their faith in Christ and with traditional African beliefs in a multiplicity of good and bad spirits. These spirits, I slowly learned, are real, lodging in house rafters and under beds, among the stones of the fields, in the animals of the grassland and the trees of the forest. Unlike Western societies, traditional African communities don't necessarily separate the visible and invisible world. There is no sharp demarcation between the physical and the spiritual.

There was grace before every meal in Jonatão's home, and a roster of household chores for the children before they went to school. Jonatão, who first taught at a school run by Canadian Protestant missionaries, made his children study hard. He was one of the first black Africans to receive an education in Angola. He believed education was the Europeans' strongest weapon, said Tito, and that Africans could only free themselves by also acquiring knowledge.

Jonatão established the first cooperative for black peasant farmers on the Central Plateau, cutting out Portuguese middlemen. But it was as a preacher that he commanded most respect. Tito said congregations were so big when his father preached that people had to stand outside the church and listen through open windows. Occasionally, Jonatão would go on a retreat to meditate and pray, fasting for days at a time, consuming only water. 'At every meal the family had to pray and also before we went to bed,' said Tito. As Christians and as descendants of the Ovimbundu kings, Jonatão said his family should live lives that would be an example to others.

Jonatão clung for a long time to his Christian conviction that the hearts of the Portuguese could be changed, that there could be reconciliation between the different cultures and races. He preached to his congregations that they should live good, restrained lives and that they should conduct amicable relations with all levels of Angolan society, including the Portuguese. 'He believed that all people were equal before God, and he passed that belief on to me,' said Tito.

But Jonatão gradually despaired. One event helped tip him over into radicalism. His two youngest sons, Tito and Estevão, as small boys, attended a primary school a few kilometres outside Silva Porto. They travelled by country bus. But one day the bus broke down and the boys had to walk home. On the way, they cut through a Portuguese residential quarter where they were ambushed by white boys who subjected them to a brutal assault, threw rocks at them and called them 'filthy niggers'. Tito said his father was anguished and angry when he saw his sons' bloody wounds and bruises.

'He had taught us that all men were equal and that we must

be proud. He used to say there were good Portuguese, but I think something snapped that day.

'Anyway, he said that from now on we would have to fight if we wanted to be free. It saddened him.'

So Jonatão responded positively when he was approached by Jonas Savimbi's father, Loth, the first black stationmaster on the Benguela Railway, to help the then-exiled Jonas to form a new liberation movement. Savimbi needed Jonatão's influence with the people of the interior. Jonatão had known the young Jonas as a bright, energetic, rebellious youngster who, against enormous odds, had gone on to obtain a university education in Switzerland. He liked Jonas's ideas. While Jonatão respected the MPLA, he knew that the rural people of the interior – the Ovimbundu and the smaller Chokwe, Lunda, Nganguela, Nyaneka-Humbe, Herero and Bushmen groups – were disdained by the MPLA's Kimbundu and *mestiço* leaders clustered in and around Luanda. He liked the UNITA name chosen for the new movement, symbolising the unity he believed was necessary among all Angola's peoples if they were to have any hope of defeating the Portuguese.

Jonatão agreed with Savimbi's criticisms of the MPLA's leader, Agostinho Neto, who lived outside Angola and whose guerrillas had no permanent bases inside the country. Savimbi, heavily influenced by his short friendship with Che Guevara and by Mao Zedong's *Selected Military Writings*, said UNITA's leaders would establish themselves inside the country, swimming like fish in the sea. It meant risking death, but people would rally when they saw their leaders suffering beside them. The peasantry, that 90 per cent of the population that survived on subsistence farming, hunting and trapping, might seem weak and placid to zealous, well-read revolutionaries, but they would stoically endure prolonged suffering once they had been won for a cause.

Tito described the clincher for Jonatão as the respect Savimbi expressed for the traditions and religious beliefs of the peasantry.

Jonatão was appalled by anti-religious trends within the MPLA leadership, most of whom were pro-Soviet Marxist-oriented urban intellectuals. Tito said Savimbi, on the other hand, had asserted that, 'The African believes in a Higher Being, whatever his name may be or whatever the place where he is worshipped. There is an ancestral force which transcends man.' (Savimbi, however, privately asserted that he was in fact an atheist.)[9]

Jonatão regarded Savimbi as a son and a potentially great leader. He told his sons and daughters that Savimbi had the qualities of a fine human being and that they should learn from him. When his oldest sons, David, Samuel, Estevão and Paulo, died in the struggle, Tito said his father told relatives, 'My sons have been taken from earth by Almighty God because He needs them more in Heaven for his work than they are needed here on earth.'

Tito told me he loved his father so fondly and deeply that it was natural for him to honour his ideals and those of his elder brothers. With his father now dead, he committed himself to working harder than ever on behalf of the leader whom Jonatão had endorsed.

Savimbi, in July 1980, visited London where he had been invited to give a lecture to the influential International Institute for Strategic Studies, close to the UK's security and intelligence establishments. Savimbi and his delegation, which included Tito – newly arrived as UNITA's London-based Europe representative to liaise with governments and intelligence agencies – were lodged under tight security on the top floor of a hotel owned by Lonrho. In a long address, Savimbi called for an end to apartheid in South Africa, which, he said, 'only makes easier Soviet penetration in Africa'. Savimbi also had meetings at the Carlton Club and Reform Club, favourite haunts of intelligence officials, top politicians and civil servants. The meetings were chaired by Edward du Cann, MP, a Lonrho director and chairman of the ruling Conservative

Party's powerful 1922 Committee.[10] A major West European channel of support for Savimbi was established through a consortium of businessmen based in Paris.[11]

Meanwhile, violence levels were rising in Angola. In Luanda, the MPLA government announced that it had executed sixteen UNITA supporters. Thirteen days later, nine members of a UNITA cell in Huambo were executed by firing squad. UNITA responded by executing fifteen MPLA prisoners.[12]

The MPLA governor of Huambo Province, Commissar Santana Petroff, said there were now so many regular UNITA sabotage acts along the Benguela Railway that there was no longer any prospect of it operating normally again in wartime. He said that twenty-five of thirty diesel engines on the line had been destroyed by guerrilla activity.

UNITA also took its first Soviet prisoners. An Antonov An-26 transport plane was hit on 22 November 1980 soon after take-off from Mpupa, an MPLA post near the border with South West Africa that was under siege by UNITA. The plane crash-landed and its stunned pilot and chief engineer, both members of the Soviet Air Force, were taken prisoner. UNITA claimed that their prized captives demonstrated that the Soviet role in Angola was not confined to advising and training the MPLA. They were also participating in combat missions. I would later meet and interview these Soviets.

11
Mavinga (1981)

'I'm about to return to Angola for talks with the leadership,' said Tito. 'Will you come with me? We will show you something new.'

We were at my parents' home in 1981, on the dreary council estate where I grew up. I had always hungered for adventure and escape from some of the limitations of working-class life. My father, a hard-working print industry machine minder and former Second World War soldier, was not the greatest of conversationalists and, as the first person in my extended family to go to university, I snobbishly cringed as he asked, 'I suppose it's a bit hot where you come from, Tito?'

My nascent middle-class sensibilities were entirely out of order. Tito hugely valued my mother and father because being with them were the only times when 'ordinary' Britons, other than Kathryn and me, had admitted him into their homes and lives. He told me he valued the sheer workaday normality. He felt thankful not to be quizzed about the politics and warfare in Angola, a country about which my folks knew nothing. Tito liked being asked by my father which football team he supported. He enjoyed listening to my nephew talk about British birds. He liked telling me and my folks how he once dreamed of becoming a professional basketball star before events in his country wrecked that ambition. He submitted contentedly to being mothered by my mother, who fussed around him, put her fabulous roast dinners in front of him and made cocoa for him in the evenings before he went to bed. He took pleasure from my father's runner bean crop and from helping to mow the lawn and wash the car. I understood only gradually just how much he rated such things because he wished something not too dissimilar for all the ordinary people of Angola instead of the death and destruction that was enveloping them. He had never been happier in Britain than when staying in my parents' humble home, he later told me.

News reports from Angola at that time were scarce and thin, and when UNITA said its guerrillas had a secure salient more than 320 kilometres deep into southeast Angola, the MPLA and its media sympathisers poured scorn on the claim. There was no war, they said. UNITA had no army; it was a mere handful of *fantoches* ('puppets'). Tito insisted the advance was true, that UNITA had acquired SAM-7 ground-to-air missiles and had captured Soviet airmen and Cuban soldiers.

'You don't believe me? Come and see for yourself. This war is getting hot, and we are making many advances.' It was said with the usual soft smile, the familiar casual shrug.

And so I found myself with Tito in Kinshasa, the capital of Zaire, where UNITA clearly had government support. Before sunrise one morning, we boarded at Kinshasa's N'Djili Airport an oil-stained, overworked, battered old four-engine Viscount aircraft to fly into Angola via the back door on a false flight plan.

Three hours later, while over Zambia, we saw a shimmer on the horizon. We were approaching the Zambezi. We crossed the great river and saw below the endless expanses of forest, marbled by thick veins of savannah grass and winding silver watercourses that are part of the great roadless and untamed wilderness of southeastern Angola, the

Land at the End of the World. It looked perfect territory in which to conceal an army.

Throughout the day, the Portuguese pilot and co-pilot scanned the skies for Angolan government MiG-21 fighters. I wanted badly to get back on the ground.

A thin olive-green ribbon appeared in the forest below. The Viscount dipped and circled, and I could see soldiers, trucks and swaying dancers dressed in bright red and green. The pilot made a perfect landing on the grass-covered sandy airstrip near a river at Luengue, a former Portuguese big-game hunting base 80 kilometres north of UNITA's new headquarters, Jamba, the Place of the Elephants.

I was back in Angola after more than five years away.

The landing strip was maintained well enough to take medium-sized transport planes. If this had been a novel, I might have imagined arriving to the sound of gunfire. Instead, we came in to the sound of music, with the dancers singing in rich African descants and a cappella harmonies which made my spine tingle. The words, in translation, were banal propaganda slogans. But the melodies were sweet.

Savimbi was waiting. Carrying a silver-tipped ebony baton and wearing commando uniform and a green beret studded with a general's three gold stars, he first bear-hugged Tito like a favourite son before welcoming us. Savimbi was all broad smiles and oozing charm, his magnetism and charisma readily apparent.

Another journalist, invited by Tito, had joined the flight from Kinshasa. Dick Harwood was the managing editor of the *Washington Post*. I was more than a little awestruck. In the wake of its exposé of the Watergate scandal, the *Post* had become a journalism legend. Dick was a grizzled Marine Corps veteran of the 1945 Battle of Iwo Jima, during which some 7 000 marines died fighting the Japanese and 20 000 were wounded. Dick himself was shot in the chest but lived to tell the tale after being evacuated. He described it as a lucky break.

Jonas Savimbi addresses a rally at his Jamba HQ.
(Source: Fred Bridgland)

If he had fought on longer he reckoned his chances of dying or being permanently maimed would have been high.

Dick was a deeply experienced reporter who covered the Vietnam War and the Kennedy brothers' presidential campaign trails and supervised the Watergate reporting. I was not surprised to learn later that he had a tough but deeply respected reputation among *Washington Post* staff. With his gruff common sense, old-fashioned integrity and disdain for bullshit, he was a reassuring companion on this hazardous venture. I learned a lot from him that remains permanent. When, twenty years later, Dick died of cancer, the *Post*'s celebrated editor Ben Bradlee said of him, 'Dick was fair as hell, and he tolerated no sacred cows of any kind.'

Night descended soon after we landed. We were shown to our quarters – two double-compartment grass huts under trees. In one section was a raised bed of elephant grass, in the other an elephant grass sofa and a table of rough-hewn logs lashed with strips of tree bark. A small wood fire burned on the floor of the hut. It was the southern African midwinter with night temperatures below zero and thin ice forming on water buckets. It was so cold overnight that I wore thermal underwear, a woollen pullover and a tracksuit as I burrowed into my down sleeping bag under a blanket. Two guerrillas nestling Kalashnikovs sat outside my hut around their own fire. I joined them for a while and shared a meal of hot and tasty rice, potato, onion and tomato soup.

Tito briefed us the next morning. We would be taken to Mavinga, a trading-centre town – though it was small enough to be called a village – some 250 kilometres north of the border with South West Africa. The MPLA said that it controlled Mavinga, that UNITA's claims were the product of the *fantoches'* imagination. Tito said we would see that UNITA's story was the true one. UNITA had captured the town. Its guerrilla army now controlled it and was pushing beyond it north-wards towards the Benguela Railway. What we would see, he asserted, would prove to the outside world that UNITA and the war for Angola were very much alive.

I looked forward to seeing Mavinga again. I had visited it back in 1975. It was a settlement that only a Somerset Maugham or Graham Greene could describe satisfactorily in some colonial melodrama. Mavinga was in the middle of nowhere. Surrounded by forests, it con-sisted of two dirt roads, crossing at right angles, that were lined by big Portuguese colonial villas once lived in by district officials and big-game hunters. Orange trees planted by the Portuguese grew at precise intervals along the sides of the roads. Bougainvillea veiled the houses. I thought it was incredibly beautiful, unique and romantic.

Soon we were thrusting north in a fleet of captured Polish Star and Soviet-manufactured military trucks. The Star was the basic military transport of communist Poland's armed forces. We sat with rifle-toting guerrillas on sacks of dried salt cod at the back of the trucks. The trucks had forged a snaking trail, often barely detectable, along river valleys, over forest ridges and across fords. We traversed magnificent *anhara* savannah grasslands, where great herds of elephant, buffalo, wildebeest, zebra and the occasional giraffe ambled past. Ostriches and their tiny offspring ran ahead for kilometres. For a while, a magnificent herd of roan antelope galloped beside us. Mongoose families flowed across the trail, and over-head, in the clear blue sky, vultures wheeled and soared. Majestic martial eagles lifted from their tree perches. As the light faded a lioness crossed in the headlights. A couple of buck and some guinea fowl were shot for the pot. Conservationists heralded this region, the Cuando Cubango, as one of the last of Africa's great unfenced free-ranging wildlife areas outside proclaimed game reserves.

It was sheer joy to be back in the African wilderness, especially in the evenings by the light of wood fires. I felt privileged to be experienc-ing this 170 000-square-kilometre virtually untouched animal paradise. But not for much longer. Unknown to us, mass slaughter – by interna-tional mafia gangs, with UNITA cooperation – of the area's elephants, rhinos and other game was about to begin.

From the grassland the trucks plunged into forest, along UNITA's Savimbi Trail, the equivalent of the Vietcong's legendary Ho Chi Minh Trail. Avoiding established tracks, long since mined and denied to both sides, the trucks, rarely exceeding 15 kilometres per hour, ricocheted off big trees and ran straight over smaller ones. As we crashed through thickets, trees fell across bonnets and branches enveloped us on the back of the trucks. We had to keep ducking to avoid the falling green-ery. Our arms and faces became criss-crossed with bloody lacerations. We travelled day and night and stopped only when transmissions blew and fanbelts snapped. On the poorly sprung East Bloc vehicles, it was like riding bucking broncos.

It was exhausting.

The guerrillas had fascinating *noms de guerre*: Lonely, Gringo, Red Sun, Angola, Big Rat, Long Journey. Gringo was popular because in Western movies these young men had seen, before independence, the gringos always won the gunfights. We broke down one night and the repairs took many hours. Lonely, Big Rat and others quickly lit fires, produced coffee and protein biscuits and, under God's amazing southern skies, made our beds – raised earthen platforms padded with leaves and covered by groundsheets. In southern Africa's midwinter the heavens are cloudless, the nights freezing and the air crystalline. As Lonely and the others sang and went about their tasks, I lay gazing at the immense canopy of millions of winking stars. Meteors and shooting stars traced sparkling trails in a celestial fireworks display and the moon came up as a huge red disc, as though it had absorbed all the blood that had been shed in Angola's tragic land.

'A beauty to make the heart ache,' Dick accurately described it.

Entering Mavinga on 23 June felt like being on the set of *High Noon*. No one stirred … because no one was there. Dust devils skipped through the empty ghost town. The oranges were ripe, and guerrillas dismounted from our trucks and picked sackloads. Every one of the bungalows, small offices and stores lining the two dirt streets had been destroyed by cannon and mortar fire. Wrecked trucks and tractors littered the place. But the MPLA was certainly not occupying the town, as official communiqués from Luanda were saying.

The UNITA commanding officer for Mavinga, Savimbi's Chief of Staff, Lieutenant Colonel Demóstenes Chilingutila, strode into town and said four battalions totalling about 2 500 fighters had attacked in daylight and swept aside an MPLA brigade of 2 000 men. Chilingutila claimed his men had killed 512 MPLA soldiers in the battle and had captured thirty trucks in working order, all East European (except for a French Berliet mobile vehicle repair workshop), plus a Soviet armoured car, two SAM-7 missile systems and an array of other artillery and thousands of rounds of ammunition.

Mavinga had a useful dirt airstrip to the north of the town. At one end of it were the dirt graves of UNITA and MPLA youths who had died in the fighting. The strip was littered with spent ammunition and a truck was stuck in a crater blown by the landmine it had detonated.

Chilingutila also said his forces, now deeply entrenched near the airstrip, had shot down a Soviet Antonov transport plane. No one had survived. Another Antonov had been shot down earlier further south. Its crew had survived, and we would meet them later, said Chilingutila.

To UNITA, Mavinga, this little-known outpost in the middle of the African wilderness, was a prized treasure, concrete evidence of its ability to attack and defeat an army of MPLA soldiers supported by Cuban troops and Soviet logistics.

We had secured our exclusive story.

Not only was the war definitely on, but UNITA had moved beyond purely hit-and-run guerrilla ambushes and was beginning to function as a semi-conventional force. Tito said Mavinga was UNITA's biggest victory to that date, in terms of the quantity and type of weaponry captured and the hundreds of MPLA soldiers killed. 'The MPLA are still saying in communiqués that they have Mavinga under their control,' he said.

Mavinga was an ideal base from which to extend the Savimbi Trail further north towards the Benguela Railway. 'There are big enemy gaps we can pass through,' Tito said. 'And once we have done that we are going to create havoc because the Cubans and the MPLA are thinly spread.'

We returned on another bone-crunching journey to UNITA's main bases further south. On the trip, Dick and I grew increasingly appreciative of and beholden to the teenage men and women soldiers who looked after us. Honorio and Chimoko were my personal bodyguards and batmen. Annabella, Linette and Elizet mothered us and cooked for us over open fires. Their constant chatter and laughter were delightfully infectious.

Back in Jamba, Dick suggested to Savimbi that the outside world would suspect that South African forces were somehow involved in the Mavinga victory. Denying it, Savimbi however said UNITA and South Africa did cooperate on 'certain matters'. Specifically, he said, the South Africans allowed UNITA to take seriously wounded guerrillas across the border into South West Africa for treatment in military hospitals. The South Africans sold UNITA medicines, trucks and truck engines, petrol and food. They also bought ivory and diamonds from UNITA. But South Africa provided no weapons, he claimed, and it did not engage in joint military operations with UNITA. He added passionately, 'We are not African rabble or savages. We are intelligent and resourceful people who are creating something out here in the bush you cannot imagine is possible from a black guerrilla army.'[1]

Tito took me aside and chided me on South Africa. It would not be the last time.

'This just won't go away, will it?' he said softly. 'You and I have discussed this so much. Yes, I've always said we get help from the South Africans. But it is because of our geography and our political situation.' Many people accused UNITA of being pro-apartheid, he said. 'But how can that be? Look at the colour of my skin, of our skins. It's not possible. Who would we practise apartheid against? Ourselves? I am opposed to apartheid. It is a dead ideology, and I believe things will have to change in South Africa. We say it all the time. But right now, we are fighting for our own very survival against a force which refused to hold guaranteed elections (at independence) and which is backed by three powerful nations (the Soviet Union, Cuba and East Germany). We were alone and had to take help from wherever it was available. Some people seem to feel we should be willingly eradicated by the Cubans and Soviets, but nobody can sincerely tell us it is better to be killed by Cubans than to take help from wherever we can get it.

'We do not want to be an African Hungary or Czechoslovakia. We do not apologise for that. But it makes no sense for anyone to accuse me of believing in apartheid. We only want to live and have our independence. We have no interest in being dead revolutionaries. Why should we not defend ourselves?'

Nevertheless, the truth was that South Africa was providing UNITA with massive logistics support. Unknown to us at the time, the South African Air Force had already begun using the Mavinga airstrip to ferry supplies to UNITA by transport aircraft and helicopters. A few weeks later, the South African Defence Force launched a massive multi-pronged assault, Operation Protea and Operation Daisy, hundreds of kilometres into Angola, mainly attacking SWAPO bases. Following these, the South Africans handed on to UNITA more than 4 000 tonnes of captured Soviet military equipment, and this reinforced Savimbi's ambitious plans to extend the movement's guerrilla activity far to the north.

For the moment, however, Tito guided me towards the secretarial school, being run by its head, Ana Isabel Paulino, after her return from Paris. Ana, wearing a smart but demure Parisian suit and high heels, and Tito were clearly at ease with each other and laughed a lot. I did not know at that time that Tito and Ana had been in love with each other for years.

Dick and I admired the efficiency of Ana's school, run from a large open-sided grass hut. Some thirty women under six instructors were learning to touch-type on ranks of typewriters under Anna's watchful eye and how to write in shorthand and take dictation in Portuguese, French and English. Their course included maths and accounting.

From Ana's school we were taken to the communications centre, where electronic intelligence was being gathered and radio operators were being trained on captured Soviet equipment, and also to a 120-bed hospital, where we watched a self-taught surgeon remove an appendix.

Ana Isabel Paulino, the great love of Tito Chingunji's life.

We moved on to the armoury, where men were repairing UNITA's imposing collection of captured and donated weapons. At the vehicle repair shop a colonel said Savimbi needed more than 500 working trucks to realise his ambitious plan for a push into the heart of Angola.

At the blacksmith and carpentry workshop, a major said he was awaiting the delivery by air of a US$20 000 lathe that would enable his team to rebore worn or damaged gun barrels. We moved on to a teacher-training school, and then to Roman Catholic and Protestant church services where both the Christian Bible and the gospel according to Savimbi were being taught.

But what we most wanted was an interview with the Soviet pilots. Where were they?

12

Soviet prisoners (1981)

The rendezvous with the Soviets happened in a forest clearing several kilometres beyond Jamba.

They arrived surrounded by armed guards on the back of separate Star trucks. They were heavily bearded and had clearly not seen each other for a long time because they exchanged affectionate slaps and conversed hastily after they climbed down from the trucks.

We shook their hands and talked to them, separately, in nearby huts. A junior UNITA officer, Jardo 'Jimmy' Muecalia, translated. A brilliant linguist, Jimmy had learned Russian working with the airmen over seven months. As well as Portuguese and Umbundu, the tribal language of the Ovimbundu, Jimmy also spoke fluent English and French, and passable Spanish.

Mollaeb Kolya was the 39-year-old pilot of an Antonov An-22 military transport plane when it took off eight months earlier from the small town of Mpupa, then held by the MPLA but subsequently taken by UNITA. Kolya, from the Dagestan region of the Soviet Union, said he was flying at about 1 000 metres when a missile hit his right outboard engine. The four-engine An-22 was at that time the world's largest turboprop-powered plane.

The engine caught fire and part of the wing disintegrated. As the plane lost height, Kolya estimated he had a ten-kilometre window before the Antonov would crash-land.

'I passed over some trees and put it down in high grass between the Cuito River and the forest,' he said. Kolya hurt his back in the crash-landing but, expecting an explosion, he managed to run from the burning wreckage. He lay dazed for some time but regained consciousness and went to the river to wash his face and hands. He heard shooting and raised his hands in surrender when he saw soldiers approaching.

Kolya denied he was a member of the Soviet Air Force. He said he was employed by Aeroflot, the Soviet civilian airline, and had been sent to Angola under a contract with the MPLA government to work with the national airline. He said he knew nothing about the war.

'I thought it was a trifle. All I had heard was that there was some tribal unrest.'

But why, we asked, had the plane been transporting nineteen MPLA soldiers between bases as his fellow Soviet captive, Ivan Chernietsky, told us?

'I didn't know who was on the plane or how many there were,' Kolya said. 'I was in the cockpit. I never looked back there. They could have been civilians, or they could have been troops.' At which point UNITA's deputy leader, Miguel N'Zau Puna, accompanying us, exploded in a splutter of rage, 'You see what a liar he is.' Puna, who had trained with Savimbi in guerrilla arts at the Nanking Military Academy, always reminded me in physique and belligerence of a kind of black Nikita Khrushchev.

Chernietsky, a 47-year-old aircraft engineer originally from Kiev in the Ukraine (then still part of the Soviet Union), also professed ignorance about the war or why Cuban troops were in Angola. He too said he was a civilian working for Aeroflot. But his story differed from Kolya's on one important point. Of course they were hauling MPLA

*Soviet Air Force pilot Mollaeb Kolya, taken prisoner by
UNITA in November 1980 after his Antonov An-22 aircraft
was shot down in southern Angola. (Source: Fred Bridgland)*

troops on the Antonov. 'Who else would we be carrying?' he said.
'There is nothing down there (at Mpupa) but military bases.'

Chernietsky said he too fled from the burning plane and lay stunned
for about four hours before he became aware of an armed UNITA
soldier standing over him. He assumed that the MPLA soldiers had got
out of the aircraft and escaped to safety, probably by swimming across
the Cuito River.

Puna insisted both men were liars and that they were military men
'very well-trained in the art of disinformation'.

Within imprisonment limits, Kolya said he was being treated well.
But he was tired of the food – maize or cassava meal porridge every
day – and he had no radio, no books or writing materials, and no one

UNITA's deputy leader, Miguel N'Zau Puna (right),
with Jonas Savimbi and their bodyguards.

to talk to other than Jimmy. He was missing his wife and two children in Moscow. Tears welled in his eyes as he said in a quavering voice, 'If I have to stay here for a long time, I will die. If my government is not trying to help me, I will die.' Asked what he was missing most, he laughed and said, 'Freedom'.[1]

Chernietsky was more stoic than Kolya. He said he had been working for Aeroflot in Angola for two years. Like Kolya, he professed little knowledge of the war and asserted that he did not know why so many Cubans were in Angola. He had seen them walking around Luanda, but he never talked to them, saying, 'They are black like the Angolans.' He said he was well treated by his guards and played cards with them. He kept fit by walking under guard twice a day ten kilometres to and from a nearby river.

We shook hands again and wished them good luck. Their chances of early release looked slim.

'I'm getting sentimental in my dotage,' Dick later wrote. 'As a running dog of capitalism, I went to bed hoping these godless commies would somehow soon get home to their families. But knowing Puna, I wouldn't bet on it.'

We also interviewed some Cuban prisoners, all of them teenage conscripts. They were very frightened and we thought they overdid their denunciations of Fidel Castro. They were probably executed after our departure. It was the standard UNITA practice with all captured Cubans.

13

Our aircraft crashes (1981)

It was time to leave and publish our stories.

We arrived at the Luengue air strip – by Star truck – on the night of 2 July and, well before first light the following morning, walked through the bush to the aircraft that would take us from The Land at the End of the World. The plane was a swish-looking twin-engine Fokker Friendship. We were flying at night to avoid patrolling government MiGs.

Dick was elated and keen to get moving. He calculated he could catch a flight from Kinshasa, our immediate destination, to the United States in just enough time to get to his Delaware beach house to celebrate American Independence Day on 4 July with his wife, sons, daughters and grandchildren. It would be the first time in years they would all manage to get together.

It was not to be.

The take-off was not to be relished. There was no moon. It was pitch black and the runway lighting consisted of just two corned beef tins filled with paraffin-soaked sand with lighted wicks that dimly marked the end of the strip: they were guides to ensure that the pilot rose more than 50 metres to avoid smashing into the blackness of the forest.

Dick, Tito and I buckled up in our seats. Two seriously ill people were brought aboard on stretchers to go to hospital in Kinshasa.

The Portuguese pilot and his co-pilot ran up the engines to full power. The Fokker strained on the brakes, and then surged forward towards the distant paraffin lamps. Then, as the plane accelerated beyond the point of no return, its undercarriage collapsed with an almighty thud. The nose, right propeller and right wing ploughed into the grass and sand runway, but fortunately the aircraft did not cartwheel. On concrete it would certainly have done so. Fuel poured from the right engine but did not ignite.

We crawled out of the plane. Our injuries were no worse than severe whiplash. But the Fokker's wounds were so serious that it would never fly again. A personable UNITA officer made us laugh as he surveyed the wreckage. 'No problem,' said Wilson dos Santos, Tito's brother-in-law. Except that our problem was very serious indeed. We were now stuck in one of the most remote places in Africa with no immediate possibility of a way out. And Dick would no longer be able to make it to his family and beach house for 4 July.

Savimbi sent a message from Jamba assuring us he would secure another aircraft to enable us to leave as soon as possible. But on 4 July, when Dick had intended to be swigging cold beer at his beach house in the bosom of his family, he was mooching around his jungle hut working out what he would write in his accounts of his Angolan adventure for the *Washington Post*.

After supper, Ernesto Mulato, one of Savimbi's senior officers, invited us to a party. Soldiers from the local battalion had gathered around a giant bonfire in a forest clearing. Annabella, who had looked after us on the rough ride to Mavinga, was the mistress of ceremonies. She introduced each song, dance and poetry reading.

And then Mulato stepped forward and read a proclamation in English. It concerned the 4th of July and what it meant to America and the world.

'We regret the circumstances in which you, Mr Richard Harwood, are celebrating this joyous day of yours, far away from your loved ones. But the values and ideals that have made your country the greatest on earth are the same values and ideals that bind us together – the struggle for freedom and liberty. We are therefore gathered here tonight, around this campfire, to share with you some moments of reflection and joy on your national holiday.'

It was a touching gesture that brought tears to the eyes of tough old Dick who, in his speech of thanks, also thanked me, as a 'colonialist Brit', for having made America's 4th of July possible – although I had not been around in 1776 when mad King George III lost Britain's American colonies.

We were stuck for nine days in Luengue, sharing one book between us, Martin Cruz Smith's *Gorky Park*, and with Gringo, Big Rat and Annabella as our carers. When the rescue plane landed late one afternoon it was an overworked DC-4, a model that had gone out of production in 1947. Nevertheless, we thought it the loveliest machine we had ever seen. The gossip was that the plane's owners, Mafia-style Italians whose aircraft spent most of their flying time shuttling illegal ivory, diamonds and cobalt from remote parts of the African bush, had charged Savimbi US$60 000 – twice the normal rate at that time – for our rescue. The money was delivered in wads of crisp new dollar bills in a neat briefcase and counted by the pilots before we were allowed to board the aircraft. We lurched down the pitch-black runway at 3 am into the air and away from The Land at the End of the World.

Approaching Kinshasa's N'Djili Airport, two of the DC-4's four engines stopped working. We landed successfully with two, but the old bucket was pushed to the side of the airport, never to fly again and to join scores of hulks, skeletons and wreckage of other discarded planes. The pilots said their bosses would simply buy another second-hand DC-4 for a few thousand dollars from somewhere around the world and flog that too unto its final death in the Africa trade. There were no regulation maintenance checks on the cowboy fleets that kept the teetering Zaire economy going while simultaneously looting it.

14
Consequences (1981)

Dick and I liked to think we put the Angolan war back on the international journalism map. Dick wrote a seven-part series for the *Washington Post*, and I wrote a big front-page and centre-page article for the London *Sunday Times* and a four-part series for my then employer, *The Scotsman*, Scotland's national newspaper.

Dick wrote, 'UNITA's young guerrillas' capacity to endure, their courage, their ingenuity and their resolve have made a deep impression, partly, I suppose, because our own lives in the United States are easy and, in some ways, empty by comparison. They know who they are and what they are about.'

Dick left thinking highly of Savimbi. 'Every Western journalist who has encountered him comes away with the feeling that he is a remarkable man,' he wrote. 'He has the mark of Cain on him from the South African connection. He is nonetheless remarkable. What can be said is that he has that quality so valued in Hollywood and American politics: charisma.'[1]

I too admired the personal qualities of the young guerrillas who had been our companions – their remarkable hardiness, patience, dedication, discipline, self-reliance, humour and sheer joyous laughter.

Our reports eased Tito's diplomatic task. He told me that officials and journalists in Europe became more willing to give him a hearing. Most were impressed by his demeanour whatever their doubts about his cause. Tito was invariably polite and tried to give straight answers. I never saw him lose his temper or composure, even in the most trying circumstances. Because UNITA was irrevocably tarred by the South African connection, he had to muster his arguments with cool logic and courtesy. Typically his case, and the case he scripted for Savimbi, would be developed from a simple opening statement that did not begin with a reference to Angola.

'We believe that SWAPO's struggle, next door to us, against Namibia's colonisation by South Africa is legitimate, just as we believe SWAPO's demand for one man, one vote elections is legitimate. In the past, before Portugal began decolonising, UNITA and SWAPO fought alongside each other against both the Portuguese and the South Africans. We were brothers, but now we are caught in a big game and the people supporting us are mutual enemies. SWAPO has bases in Angola and help from the Soviet Union; we asked for help from the West who pointed us to South Africa.'

Tito said SWAPO's desire for liberation and elections had been enshrined in countless United Nations resolutions. 'So isn't it illogical and inconsistent to ignore UNITA's similar claims for Angola? SWAPO wants to liberate their country – we want to liberate ours. SWAPO believes it would win elections in Namibia – we believe we would win elections in Angola.'

He said the coincidence of UNITA's interests with those of South Africa was for him an ever-painful problem, 'but we cannot allow ourselves to be liquidated to satisfy the principles of people who do not have our particular history and who do not live where we live. God did not ask our permission when he located us with South Africa as our near neighbour.'

He said he regretted this necessity for realpolitik.

'We wanted a different way forward. But we are not the pioneers of this kind of marriage of convenience. Stalin's pact with Hitler did not mean he wanted to embrace Nazism and Churchill's subsequent alliance with Stalin did not mean the British hungered after communism. For both Stalin and Churchill, the issues were survival. And that's also our issue – it's the same. Some people seem to feel we should be willing to be crushed by the Cubans and the Soviets. We cannot accept being eradicated in our own country. We won't do that. We would rather die on our feet than on our knees.

'I do want people to understand our case, but, if necessary, I and others prefer unpopularity to suicide. No one can sincerely look me in the eyes and tell me it would be better for my people to be massacred by the Cubans rather than accept aid from wherever it is available.'

Tito told me that it would eventually and inevitably be necessary for elections to be held in Angola. 'I don't understand the logic of some African countries who are pressing for black majority rule and elections in Namibia, while few of them have the courage to demand majority rule and elections in Angola,' he said. 'But I believe the MPLA will eventually enter into negotiations with us. There will have to be dialogue and reconciliation. That's certain. It's the only long-term solution.

'In UNITA we often talk about how good it might have been to have the Soviet Union as our ally. Moscow gives staunch backing to its chosen friends. However, ninety per cent of our people are illiterate or barely literate peasant farmers, so I don't suppose many, if any, of them know what Karl Marx used to say about people like them. Marx used to say it was difficult to apply his theories to "savages". I suppose it was people like us he was referring to.

'So, why should we want to be an African Hungary or Czechoslovakia? The fact is that we've been invaded – why should we not defend ourselves by any means?

'We do not foresee military victory. Our aim is to force the MPLA, which holds power never legitimised by the people's choice, to negotiate about a Cuban-Soviet withdrawal and to hold the elections that we all agreed upon in 1975. We will all have to make concessions so that we can make independence possible and society viable, with jobs, education and sanitation for the people. This would be considered a reasonable demand almost anywhere else on earth.

'And the logic of a Cuban withdrawal from Angola would be that South Africa would have to withdraw from Namibia. So there is a sense in which the Cubans are holding up not only our freedom but Namibia's.'

15

UNITA and the South African thrust north (1981–1983)

By August 1981 UNITA – buoyed by a commitment from a new United States President, Ronald Reagan, to resume clandestine weapons and cash supplies to the movement – had thrust far to the north and was raiding settlements all along the Benguela Railway.

'We want to be very helpful to what Dr Savimbi and his people are trying to do,' said Reagan.[1]

The South Africans themselves had renewed a thrust into Angola. Its soldiers pushed some 150 kilometres into southwest Angola, reassured by Reagan that there would be no pressure on Pretoria from him to leave South West Africa before the Cubans left Angola. Reagan had been sworn in as president on 20 January 1981.

The SADF's Operation Protea was launched on 23 August 1981 into Angola's Cunene Province. Its air force attacked and destroyed Soviet SAM-3, SAM-4 and SAM-6 missile sites. Its fighter-bombers shot down an Angolan MiG-21, believed to have been piloted by a Cuban, some 80 kilometres inside Angola.

The attack on the missile sites was followed by the largest ground operation across the border since 1975. Three columns of armoured cars captured two small towns, N'Giva and Xangongo. The South Africans claimed to have killed about one thousand SWAPO and MPLA troops and seized thousands of tonnes of weapons and other military equipment, including 13 Soviet tanks, 160 other military vehicles and anti-aircraft missile systems.

A Soviet non-commissioned officer, Sergeant Major Nikolai Pestretsov, was taken prisoner. Next to Pestretsov in his truck when he surrendered, while trying to flee N'Giva, were the bodies of his wife, a Russian woman in uniform, and two Soviet lieutenant colonels. Three South African airmen and twelve soldiers, none more than 22 years old, were killed when the helicopter ferrying them to a battle zone was brought down by a SAM-7 missile. It was the highest casualty toll the South Africans had suffered in a single incident in more than 16 years of fighting inside Angola.[2]

UNITA's drive north attracted little attention, but South Africa's Operation Protea assault drew widespread international condemnation. A UN Security Council resolution condemning the incursion was vetoed by the United States, which viewed with alarm the proof produced by Pretoria of Soviet Army personnel in forward military areas of Angola. Reuters reported that the Cunene region had become 'a gigantic no-man's-land in which only a few inhabitants remained in ruined towns and where the civilian administration had completely broken down.'[3]

Reagan put a public stamp of approval on Savimbi when, advised and guided by Tito, he invited the UNITA leader to visit Washington in November 1981.[4] He was hosted at the White House where Reagan compared him to Abraham Lincoln. Savimbi was received at the State Department by General Alexander Haig, the Secretary of State and the President's chief foreign affairs adviser. Haig assured Savimbi that ways would continue to be found to bypass the Clark Amendment and help him by channelling funds through third countries.[5]

Savimbi also met Chester Crocker, the Assistant Secretary of State for Africa and the architect of a peace plan for Angola and South West Africa that would take more than seven years of intense diplomacy to be brought to fruition. It was known in Washington that Crocker enjoyed a far better relationship with Tito than with Savimbi.[6]

Savimbi was required, as a preliminary goodwill step in the Crocker/Reagan peace plan, to release the two Soviet airmen, Kolya and Chernietsky, in exchange for three Americans held by the MPLA, including two mercenaries sentenced to long jail terms in 1976 after being captured fighting with the FNLA. Savimbi was reluctant to release Kolya and Chernietsky. He had hoped to use them to bargain for the release of some of his own followers imprisoned by the MPLA. Tito counselled him that he had to give way as part of the price for Washington's efforts to secure a Cuban withdrawal from Angola.

The release of the Soviet airmen involved negotiations on three continents over 18 months between seven different parties. The complex swap also involved the return of Sergeant Major Pestretsov plus the bodies of four Russians and one Cuban killed by the South Africans in exchange for the return of three bodies of South African soldiers killed by the MPLA/Cubans.

Kolya and Chernietsky were treated as honoured guests by UNITA in Jamba at a farewell dinner of impala stew before they were flown by the SADF to South Africa, from where they returned home to the Soviet Union.

As the evidence mounted that UNITA's advance northwards had real momentum, Tito offered me the chance in early 1983 to be the first Western journalist to witness a major battle in Angola in years of fighting. I accepted with alacrity. It also gave me the chance to fulfil an ambition to reach the Benguela Railway with the guerrillas. I suggested that Tito invite another witness to the reality. Gwynne Roberts, a reporter/camera operator, had made remarkable films inside rebel territories in Kurdistan and Eritrea. BBC TV's *Panorama* current affairs programme commissioned him to film our Angola journey.

Tito by now was flying frequently from London to Washington to liaise with the Reagan administration, and he was later posted permanently to the US capital.

16

Cangonga and the Benguela Railway (1983)

The Portuguese-Angolan pilot[1] of yet another second-, third- or fourth-hand workhorse DC-4 searched the forests and savannahs below, trying to locate landmarks to guide him to Savimbi's Luengue airstrip. He had filed a false flight plan when we took off from Zaire earlier in the day in January 1983.

The needle-thin target appeared suddenly near a lush green river valley and soon we were landing. The DC-4 rolled to a stop on the sandy runway, and as its doors opened we were hit by an explosion of sound: three African choirs, a pop group and a dance team competed against each other. I had seen this kind of UNITA display before, but Gwynne, new to it, was stunned by the colour and exuberance. Big trucks loaded several tonnes of medicine and aviation fuel we had carried from Kinshasa.

I looked for the wreckage of the crashed Fokker Friendship from 1981. It lay rotting among the trees, almost invisible, covered by mounds of branches and foliage.

Savimbi stood at the end of the airstrip surrounded by a phalanx of UNITA brigadiers, colonels and majors. Our initial meeting with him was brief, but he was in especially ebullient form. He said his forces had advanced spectacularly since 1981. They had surged far beyond southern Angola. We would see the gains and witness an action on the Benguela Railway. The journey there and back would be completed in a month, he said. It took two months, by which time we had covered more than 3 000 kilometres, some 800 of them on foot.

An Antwerp diamond merchant who had flown in with us to buy UNITA diamonds, some panned from rivers and others smuggled from mines in the northeast, said he had come to tell Savimbi that he had commitments from a group of West European businessmen of investments worth hundreds of millions of dollars should UNITA ever come to power.

Brigadier Demóstenes Chilingutila briefed us the next morning on the coming mission. Chilingutila, a stocky and muscled man, a former artillery specialist in Portugal's colonial army in Angola, had at one time fought against UNITA, which he joined after the Portuguese revolution of 25 April 1974.

Chilingutila said UNITA had greatly extended the area under its control in many battles with the MPLA and Cubans that had gone almost entirely unreported. He claimed the UNITA-controlled area was now roughly the size of the United Kingdom, extending all the way north to eastern stretches of the Benguela Railway. We would travel through that area and witness an attack on a railway town.

UNITA's army, said Chilingutila, now had two wings: semi-regular battalions 500 to 1 000 strong, and guerrilla Special Forces operating in groups of 15 to 30, or sometimes in company strength of 120. One guerrilla unit would be the bodyguard for Gwynne and me – Special Force Gamboa, named after a UNITA hero who died fighting the Portuguese.

We set out from Luengue in two captured Soviet Ural trucks. Mightily sprung, they ploughed on relentlessly over the roughest terrain, crushing small trees and knotted root systems, up formidable slopes and across fords and crude bridges.

Within two days we were passing Mavinga, 250 kilometres inside Angola, where Dick Harwood and I had picked oranges in 1981. Then it had been the furthest point of our journey. Now it marked the virtual beginning.

After six days we reached a broad and beautiful waterway, the Cuando River, beaded on either side by magical lagoons full of hippos and wildfowl and surrounded by tall, swaying papyrus reeds. This was a crucial point on the logistics route. Unlike rivers to the south, the Cuando was too wide and deep to be forded or bridged. To get the trucks to the war zone north of the river, the Chief of Transport, a 34-year-old Portuguese Angolan, Matos Leilinho, had set up a base on the mosquito-infested south bank where trucks were completely dismantled. Parts and sections were then put aboard a small metal ferry, powered by an outboard motor, and taken to a base on the north bank several kilometres upstream for reassembly.

Leilinho said it took eight days to get all the parts of a Ural across the river from the time his men, who he had trained as mechanics, began to dismantle it to when it was finally reassembled on the other side. The big problem with the Urals was their complicated electrical system.

We crossed the Cuando in an inflatable rubber boat, passing the metal ferry coming the other way carrying the chassis and back axle and wheels of a five-tonne East German IFA truck captured in fighting to the north. Watching Leilinho's remarkable, diligent and skilful team at work, I began to think that Tito's assertion that UNITA could win this war might be true.

Ten hours and 120 kilometres later, aboard another truck, darkness had fallen when we saw in headlight beams a raised, tarred road. We were joining the main highway which runs for hundreds of kilometres along Angola's eastern border with Zambia. It was on this road in 1976 that our French journalist colleague had leapt from

To get their trucks across the mighty rivers of southeastern Angola, UNITA mechanics dismantled the vehicles on one river bank, ferried the parts across to the other side, and reassembled the trucks there. It took eight days to reassemble some vehicles. (Source: Fred Bridgland)

his vehicle thinking it was about to crash after remembering his recent helicopter crash in Zaire.

We plunged back into thick forest after a few kilometres and arrived at Chilingutila's forward base camp, called Kandende. Remarkably, there was electricity throughout, provided by captured Soviet generators. Our huts were newly built of fragrant fresh green grass and the beds were made up with laundered and beautifully embroidered sheets. Bushcraft was in the style of the Chokwe tribe, whose traditional territory we had now entered. There were artistic little twirls in the roof thatch, and behind my hut there was a shower area where neatly peeled logs had been laid densely across a small pit so that your feet stayed clean while the water drained after a dousing. Throughout the widely spread base ran arrow-straight paths lined by fences made from tree limbs stripped of their bark to expose the pink pith. The precision and neatness reminded me of the trim orderliness of army military cantonments I had visited while posted in India.

The evening before our departure from Kandende, we were guests of honour with Chilingutila at a stunning concert in a wood and thatch amphitheatre, floodlit by the Soviet generators, with tiered seats for the troops. There was a modern African ballet, followed by a wisp of a girl who wowed the soldiers with an amazingly sensuous traditional dance. They whistled and cheered as her navel vibrated and she glided towards Chilingutila, in the seat of honour, tipping her hat at him like some African Marlene Dietrich before contemptuously turning her quivering back on him and exiting the arena. Mariko, an Angolan Sinatra famous throughout UNITA's territory, clad in a green toga and known only by one unique name, crooned in English, 'The people of Angola have been sold as slaves to the Russians, Cubans and the East.'

And then the evening turned magical.

The resident troops of 333 Battalion sang war songs in rich harmonies and thrilling descants. As they sang there was a hilarious spoof in the arena on elders and their wives at a village dance, with soldiers cavorting in drag and others in greatcoats and boots several sizes too big for them. The dancers drifted from the arena, leaving only the now-drunken village chief singing and rolling around hilariously in the dust. But as the chief evoked laughter, the soldier choir switched from war songs into haunting traditional tribal hymns to the spirits.

Women began shimmying into the arena carrying red hot charcoal on shovels, and as they built the glowing pile the floodlights were dimmed. And then the chief, now more inebriated than ever, began picking up the red-hot charcoal pieces with his fingers and placing them on his tongue. The singing grew more and more unearthly, almost intoxicating, until the chief had a whole mouthful of charcoal burning

UNITA soldiers in a traditional spirit dance, commonplace in UNITA territory. (Source: David Kane)

bright and shining red through his black cheeks. It was the most mesmerising and inexplicable spectacle I have ever witnessed.

Later, I asked Tito how it had been done without damaging the tongue or the inside lining of the mouth. 'African magic,' Tito laughed.

From Kandende we walked for another nine days north to Sandona, Savimbi's base during the fight against the Portuguese. In awesome feats of endurance, the soldiers carried their own heavy weapons – cannons, mortars, rocket launchers – dismantled into manageable components. Village women, some with infants on their backs, carried mines, mortar bombs and anti-tank rockets on their backs and heads. UNITA was transforming into one of the most remarkable foot-slogging armies since the Romans.

Wooden cage traps set out next to paths to catch leopards told when we were approaching villages. On village outskirts women spread

Ammunition and weapons for UNITA combat troops were carried Vietcong-style on the heads and backs of columns of civilians. (Source: Fred Bridgland)

carpets of leaves for us to walk upon and brushed our shoulders with palm fronds in traditional Ovimbundu and Chokwe greetings.

Along the way we were joined by some guerrillas whose style differed dramatically from that of the smart semi-regulars. These men fascinated me. They were a different breed. Their clothes were ragged and seemed like an extension of their skins. They walked alone, not in the orderly files of the battalion. Tied to and in their knapsacks they carried all their worldly wealth, including blankets made from beaten tree bark, for the ethos of these guerrillas was that they had to live off the countryside and fruits of the forest and not rely upon conventional supplies. As well as their Kalashnikovs, they all sported big knives and village-made axes. When we passed the bole of a tree filled with evil-looking green rainwater, one guerrilla shocked the semi-regular soldiers when he withdrew a thin wooden tube from his hair, matted with dirt and leaves, and drank from the fetid-looking basin. He explained to me, through an interpreter, that the water at the bottom of those pools was sweet, and all his guerrilla comrades carried drinking tubes.

The guerrilla leader, Lieutenant Colonel Verissimo (first name unknown), was a huge man with a brilliant smile. He had been one of Savimbi's original guerrillas fighting the Portuguese in 1966 and had refused all offers to live a 'soft' life with the semi-regulars. He had been in the forests for nearly twenty years and had reached such a symbiotic relationship with the vegetation that, had he lain down, he would have been almost indistinguishable from a toppled tree trunk. He seemed to know everything about the forest. Which plants were edible, medicinal or poisonous. He interpreted animal sounds and birdsong and said he could tell from certain birdsongs whether the enemy was approaching. He and his men knew where to find wild bees' nests and harvest the honey.

It was sheer pleasure to be back in the heart of the wilderness. We passed under waterfalls tumbling hundreds of metres and along ravines clothed in curtains of delicate green ferns. It was pure Rider Haggard country.

At Sandona we were greeted by one of UNITA's brightest young officers, Colonel Ben-Ben Arlindo Pena. Ben-Ben had immaculate manners, was intelligent and decisive and, Tito had told me earlier, was brave in battle. Ben-Ben, who had trained with the French military in Morocco for several months, commanded the respect of his troops through the strength of his personality. He became a good friend.

115

Sandona was just 65 kilometres south of the Benguela Railway. Ben-Ben introduced us at a rally to another semi-regular force, Battalion 017, which we would follow in their attack on an MPLA garrison in a railway town. The rally propaganda was powerful. Tiny girls gently presented Ben-Ben, Gwynne and me with bunches of wildflowers as a choir of 50 women sang a soft lullaby. Then Battalion 017, their adrenaline pumping at the prospect of battle, launched into an electric song and dance routine. Ben-Ben translated. 'Cubans, if you hear a small noise, you know UNITA has arrived. If you hear a second, you're dead.'

On 9 February 1983 the attack force moved out: 520 semi-regular soldiers of Battalion 017 armed with 75mm cannons, 81mm mortars, RPG-7 anti-tank rockets and Kalashnikov rifles; the 45 guerrilla soldiers of Special Force Gamboa; a 50-strong logistics team who had travelled with us from Luengue; a special unit of locally based explosives experts; a long chain of youths and women, some with children on their backs, carrying weapons and ammunition on their heads; and several hundred other locally based guerrillas who joined us here and there intermittently.

We moved up to a small transit base within 40 kilometres of the railway. There Ben-Ben told us that the target was Cangonga, a small railway town with a garrison of MPLA soldiers. A reconnaissance specialist, Lieutenant Colonel Antonino Philipe, had prepared a model about the size of a badminton court on the forest floor. Philipe's men had collected information about Cangonga over several months. His model used different-coloured sands, ash, bark, moss and twigs to pick out the town's buildings, including the MPLA barracks, railway station and shops, approach roads and paths, surrounding streams and hills. To the south was a red gravel airstrip.

Ben-Ben's plan was this: at first light, as the sun rose towards the horizon in the east, 100 infantrymen would launch a feint attack from the south, drawing the 300-strong MPLA garrison in their direction.

The main attack by 300 UNITA troops would follow from the darkness in the west. The other 120 troops of Battalion 017 would be held in reserve. A company of more than 100 of Lieutenant Colonel Verissimo's guerrillas would take positions to the west of Cangonga and another 100 to the east to pick off enemy soldiers fleeing from the beleaguered garrison.

We asked what would happen to the town's civilians, and Ben-Ben replied, 'It will not be possible to avoid some deaths among them, but I have instructed my troops to do their best to keep civilian casualties low.'

On 10 February, at 5.30 am, we began the final yomp towards Cangonga. It was a dramatic spectacle as three lines of troops streamed across river valleys and up into forest in the hills beyond. We stopped after three hours for a breakfast of cold rice and chicken. Suddenly, a succession of shots cracked out nearby. Ben-Ben hardly looked up from the chicken leg he was gnawing as he said without a trace of alarm, 'It's probably an MPLA patrol doing some hunting.' But how near? 'A kilometre maybe.'

While Ben-Ben continued eating, Lieutenant Colonel Philipe rapidly organised 30 guerrillas to shadow the enemy patrol and, if necessary, kill them. Scouts moved to and fro and gave reports to Ben-Ben as he sat against a fallen tree finishing his breakfast. The MPLA patrol was moving down a valley away from our resting place.

We stayed still and silent for four hours as the guerrillas continued to watch the MPLA patrol, eventually established as being between five and ten men strong. They were continuing to walk slowly down the valley, unaware of the presence nearby of more than a thousand of their enemy. Ben-Ben instructed that they should be allowed to walk away from the danger. He did not want to attack them and risk that some might escape and raise the alarm before the coming battle. It began raining very heavily, and the enforced delay caused by the MPLA patrol meant we had to move to the final position before Cangonga in pitch darkness. Without a moon, neither Gwynne nor I could see anything. Torches and matches were banned. Soldiers held our hands and guided us as we groped blindly through undergrowth, skinned our shins on fallen trees, slithered down muddy slopes and waded waist-deep across rushing streams. We stopped before midnight and, sopping wet, climbed fully clothed into equally sodden sleeping bags. It was a miserable, sleepless night, but as we lay still the battalion companies were being led to their attack positions by reconnaissance guerrillas. How they found their way through the wet blackness I'll never understand.

At 3 am on 11 February, a single rifle shot signalled to Ben-Ben, who had been with Tito on the MI6 training course in Portsmouth, that all his forces were in position. We began our final short hike towards Cangonga. Just after 5 am Ben-Ben gave radio-telephone orders for the attack to begin. We were about three kilometres southwest of the town when mortar and cannon fire opened up. Huge flames shot up in the distance, outlining buildings. We heard the crackle of hundreds of Kalashnikovs from troops moving forward line abreast from the west.

Walking in strict single file on a course charted by reconnaissance guerrillas through fields of anti-personnel mines, clutching the hands of soldiers in front of us, we at last reached the Benguela Railway and began closing on the town. We entered Cangonga at the western end of its airstrip to the staccato sounds of Kalashnikov fire. To the right, huts surrounded by giant sunflowers were ablaze. To the left, a building that was clearly the garrison's arsenal was burning and exploding periodically with great violence, prompting us to hit the ground to avoid flying metal shards.

The centre of the town was under UNITA control, but firefights were happening in every direction amid the crumps and crashes of mortars and rockets. We halted at the eastern end of the runway while Ben-Ben spoke with his field officers by radio telephone.

All hell broke loose.

Concentrated fire came from huts about 30 metres to the right. Some MPLA soldiers had regrouped and launched a direct counter-attack. Gwynne stood filming in the direction of the firing before both he and I were smashed to the ground in a mass rugby tackle by UNITA soldiers. Gwynne cursed them as they pinned us down to protect us.

Ignoring the danger, Ben-Ben strode upright throughout the counterattack, shouting orders while a section of our Gamboa Special Force bodyguard peeled off to deal with the MPLA soldiers who were invisible to me. The firing intensified as Ben-Ben led me, crawling, towards trenches near a whitewashed Catholic church. I dropped gratefully into one of the slits and moved past crates of Soviet mortar shells newly wrenched open by the defenders. Then, rounding a bend, I saw a dead MPLA soldier. He was sprawled on his back in the red earth, looking almost peaceful with a neat bullet hole in his forehead. Just a short time ago this young man had probably been eating his breakfast unaware that death was imminent.

From the trenches we were hurried into the church, which had been stripped of pews and altar and was being used as a military barracks. Jorge Valentim, UNITA's manic publicity secretary who, much to my dismay, had been assigned to accompany us on this mission, ranted tedious propaganda about how we were the first Western journalists to see how the MPLA desecrated and violated the sanctity of churches. I had no first-hand knowledge of the MPLA's attitude towards religion, but in this case UNITA's information man was talking especial nonsense. Although the MPLA's constitution, faithful to the Soviet model, had anti-religion clauses, there were several Bibles in tribal languages among the abandoned possessions of the 'Marxist' soldiers. It was an apt reminder of the danger of buying Eurocentric 'package deals' about any group in Africa. Nothing on the continent is as straightforward at close range as it seems from afar.

Just past a modern school building, devoid of furniture or books, there was an event of horror. Three UNITA soldiers appeared, dragging a body with the kind of lack of respect normally accorded a stuck pig. The body, with trousers pulled down below its knees, suddenly moved and groaned in agony. The MPLA soldier, a boy who looked barely 18, had a gaping head wound that looked fatal. I shouted at the soldiers to put the boy down, he was dying. Though, of course, they understood no English, they responded by laying him face down in the dust. If it is true that any man's death diminishes one, then witnessing the callous treatment of this terribly wounded youth made me feel unclean. As journalists, we often claim that we are only there to observe. I don't buy that, and it cannot be an excuse for inaction, for opting out of humanity. When a moment arose, we asked Ben-Ben what his policy was towards enemy wounded. Those with slight wounds were treated and taken prisoner, he said. The badly wounded were left to die. What would happen to the wounded boy soldier? 'We'll leave him.'

Gwynne's personal diary caught the powerful emotions that overwhelmed him when he saw the boy being dragged by the scruff of his shirt and by his fallen trousers.

'When I saw his face and head matted with blood seeping from a white wound on to his brown skin, pity swept through me and I was almost in tears as I filmed. This poor creature was in abject despair and terror. He groaned and, when he saw me filming, dropped his head and arms in humiliation. What had such a young lad done to deserve this – forced possibly by poverty to join the army? I felt sick at heart – half disgusted with myself for being there to film this, but also hating everyone for reducing a human being to such misery.'

Gwynne pleaded with Ben-Ben that the boy be given treatment. Ben-Ben ordered three male nurses to work on the wounds. Ben-Ben promised Gwynne that the boy would be taken to a camp for prisoners but, despite several inquiries, we learned nothing more of his fate. I am certain he must have died.

We were unable to count the total MPLA dead. Two badly wounded UNITA soldiers lay on the dirty concrete floor of a desolate schoolhouse. One man's leg, shattered by mortar fragments, had been splinted. Another, immobile and covered by a rain cape, lay dying – a male nurse said a mortar fragment had penetrated his ribcage. Another UNITA soldier, we were told, had died after being shot in his stomach.

Meanwhile, the phone rang in the stationmaster's office. Ben-Ben answered, and he said it was a neighbouring stationmaster wanting to find out about some explosions he had just heard. 'Here, nothing is happening. Everything is calm,' Ben-Ben said and put the phone down.

Saboteur teams began demolishing the town. A massive steel water tank that had served the Benguela Railway's great steam engines was blown up. The stationmaster's wooden house disappeared in one mighty blast. A road petrol tanker exploded like a giant bomb, making us hit the deck again as big metal fragments hurtled overhead. Work began on the destruction of the rail line. The Benguela Railway was single track, but sidings at Cangonga permitted trains to pass in opposite directions. Plastic explosives twisted the rails into grotesque shapes, ensuring that trains would not run over them again.

The train engine graveyard at the edge of the town was as nothing compared with the fates of the dead and wounded men. But waves of sadness nevertheless overcame me as I gazed at eight crippled giant steam engines, some dating from the 1920s. They had been built in Glasgow and Manchester ('Beyer, Peacock and Co. Ltd, Manchester,' said the cast-iron logo on one of them) by the same kind of proud, grease-stained, overalled working men as my own northern England forefathers. I was never a train-spotter, but I knew that these machines, crammed together in maintenance sidings, were objects of a special kind of beauty, engineering marvels of great strength specially

Engine graveyard on the Benguela Railway of magnificent giant engines built in British industrial centres of Glasgow and Manchester. UNITA stopped the Benguela Railway from functioning by attacking these engines with rocket-propelled grenades. (Source: David Kane)

manufactured with tenders fore and aft to burn wood as they crossed Africa. UNITA had put RPG-7 shells through all of the engines to deny their use to the MPLA. It was a sad end to epic careers which began in the cold damp of Lancashire and Clydeside, were spent working in the warmth and colour of Africa, and were now terminated in a terrible war.

Six hours after the battle began we left Cangonga with Ben-Ben, a platoon of 017 Battalion, our logistics men and the guerrillas of Special Force Gamboa. We passed between burning huts as firefights between MPLA soldiers and their UNITA pursuers continued in the distance.

Booty had been gathered by UNITA soldiers: blankets, small Japanese petrol-driven generators, radios, rubber buckets, sewing machines, boots, cooking pots, corrugated iron roofing. One soldier, wearing a large red Cuban sun hat, was ordered by Ben-Ben to remove it and replace it with his guerrilla cap. Many soldiers were leading 'liberated' goats; others had live ducks and chickens tied to their packs.

It had been a day that was professionally exciting, and emotionally and philosophically profoundly sobering. Hundreds of civilians, about one-third of them children, were being led away for 'resettlement' in UNITA-held areas. Who knows how they felt? In civil war peasant people are as helpless as chaff in the wind. Liberation is rarely for them.

Ben-Ben halted the southwards march after three hours. I slumped immediately on to the forest floor and fell into a deep sleep.

17

Remarkable guerrillas (1983)

Heading back south, we crossed a wide grassy plain where there had been a recent skirmish that UNITA had won. Angolan kwanza banknotes were scattered all over the plain. Near a thick clump of trees stood a wrecked Soviet BRDM-2 armoured car which Ben-Ben said had been hit by UNITA RPG-7 rockets. From its innards still seeped the sweet and hideous smell of death, and through the shell holes I saw the gruesome remains of three soldiers who, according to Ben-Ben, had been identified by MPLA prisoners as those of Cubans known as Captain Aguiar Gonzales, 'Vladimir' and Idale. The dead men subsequently haunted me, and one night later I dreamed that one of the Cubans, his corpse almost beyond recognition as a human, showed signs of life. And there, despite the carnage, was Kathryn, a deeply compassionate being, taking the dead man's head gently in her hands, looking into his eyes and rubbing noses with him, willing him back to life.

Ben-Ben briefed us that 35 MPLA soldiers had been confirmed killed in the Cangonga battle. Seven had been taken as prisoners. Besides the two UNITA soldiers who died, six had been wounded. There had been no Cubans in the garrison. Ben-Ben said he had deliberately left several avenues of escape for the MPLA. 'It is always so in our attacks,' he said. 'If the enemy feel trapped, they resist heavily and our casualties increase. In our kind of war, we must keep our soldiers' morale high, so it is more important to keep our casualties light than to inflict very heavy losses on the enemy.'

Nearly 600 civilians, including 200 children, had been rounded up from the town and brought to the forest bases. They would be distributed, said Ben-Ben, two or three families to a village, in UNITA's area of control. Political commissars, he added, would keep an eye on them until they were fully integrated or 're-educated'. If any of the civilians were unhappy about being taken off to a new life in the forest, they were keeping quiet about it. And why not? In their situation, I'd wave the flag and sing the anthem of whichever movement was momentarily in charge.

The big failure of the attack, said Ben-Ben, had been the destruction of the MPLA arsenal. 'The MPLA staged a resistance from that warehouse and my troops said they had to hit it with a rocket-propelled grenade. I'm quite angry because we needed that material for our stockpiles.'

The big plus, he said, was that the fall of Cangonga would allow UNITA to punch a secure logistics route through to a semi-regular battalion and several companies of guerrillas who had already infiltrated into country more than 300 kilometres north of the Benguela Railway.

For me there were other more personal and esoteric lessons learned, and satisfactions gained, from the journey to and from Cangonga which had little to do with the big questions of military, political or economic strategy concerning men of power in the West and East. I had already formed a warm and lasting friendship with Tito, and I had come to like others in UNITA, with some exceptions. This had something to do with a quality of warmth and vivacity in Angolans in general, because people who have come to know Angola from a different perspective, that of the MPLA for example, reported similar personal reactions to the country and its people.

The best time of the day for me in the forest came just before sunset when a halt was called to the march, which on some days stretched for 40 kilometres. While I collapsed into a state of exhausted immobility, I watched Antonio, the guerrilla assigned to me as a batman, build my open-sided canvas-covered bivouac in an exhibition of bushcraft and speed that would have left Robert Baden-Powell gasping. First he prepared the bed – a low earth platform surrounded by a shallow channel to divert rainwater run-off. He swiftly harvested saplings to form a frame for the canvas roof. Antonio, who I guessed was perhaps 18 or 19, then tore strips of bark from a *chimwanji* tree to tie the canvas to the frame. The bed was completed with a 'mattress' consisting of a layer of fragrant leaves covered by a canvas sheet and blanket. All was ready to settle down for the evening in great comfort. It was there when, for the first time, I read Joseph Conrad's *Heart of Darkness* by the light of a fire Antonio built and tended alongside the bivouac: 'The silence of the land went home to one's very heart – its mystery, its greatness, the amazing reality of its concealed life.'

By 'silence' Conrad must have meant the absence of European city noise. During those Angolan forest nights, cicadas, nightjars and owls chittered and called from dusk until dawn, and near rivers and swamps frogs made music like thousands of Tibetan bells. Beyond my bed, the fires of the guerrillas glowed in every direction and there was laughter and talking. On clear nights the heavens were filled with racing meteors and millions of winking diamonds of other worlds – an awesome and humbling tapestry.

Although Antonio and I could only talk in pidgin Portuguese and three or four words of Mbundu, we communicated reasonably effectively with signs and gestures. Just as Stockholm Syndrome captors and hostages become bonded, so journalists and guerrillas living together in extremely tough conditions inevitably develop a close identity of interests. I was totally dependent on Antonio, and other members of the logistics team, for food, shelter and life itself. By the end, I regarded him as a young brother and gave him the only gift I could offer, my Swiss penknife with all its gadgets.

Antonio was amazing. Whenever I began to slow down, suffering from the pace of the march, he would be there waiting, straining under the 20-kilogram load on his back and head. While I sank down at the end of the day, drained of energy, Antonio would lower his load and his Kalashnikov and immediately start building the bivouac and lighting the fire. Soon hot water would appear to bathe sore feet. Scalding coffee would be served. Nothing was too much trouble, and his kindness and concern is etched indelibly in my memory and will always influence my thinking about Africa. As the war descended into greater violence and Savimbi succumbed to madness, I wonder to this day if he survived and whether we might ever meet again. I hope so. I would like him to know how highly I liked and respected him.

There are equally positive memories of Ben-Ben. The first is of him striding upright and purposefully to direct the counterattack when we were under MPLA fire on the airstrip at Cangonga. Another was one evening after the battle as we twiddled through various radio stations. The dial hit Radio South Africa, which reported Foreign Minister Pik Botha saying his country was willing to 'consider' giving aid to any anti-Soviet liberation movement in black Africa that asked. The statement was heavy with irony because the South African government, without informing its own parliament, was already aiding at least three liberation movements, including UNITA. Ben-Ben collapsed in laughter at Botha's absurd duplicity, and said, 'We're not even having to ask them!'

A personal nurse, a gentle man called Jacko, was attached to Gwynne and me. He tended my wounds with salves and bandages when a tree, felled by our advancing truck, hit me and gouged two deep channels of flesh from my right arm. Jacko also dug *bitacoia* maggots from my feet and ankles with a hypodermic needle. The *bitacoia* fly, common wherever there is uncleared refuse, leaps from the ground and burrows unnoticed into feet and ankles and lays its eggs. There the maggots hatch, grow large and are first noticed as painful sores, when you can see their waving black heads beneath your skin. Unless the maggots are removed your feet begin to rot. Ben-Ben reckoned I had picked up the *bitacoias* at Cangonga, where the pumped water system had broken down and pigs rooted among rotting garbage.

The *bitacoias* and occasional bouts of diarrhoea apart, personal hygiene was not a great problem. Hundreds of streams and rivers flow swiftly from the Angolan plateau into various great African waterways. Crystal-clear, cool, sandy-bottomed and free of the debilitating bilharzia parasite common elsewhere in Africa, they were good sources of drinking water and made excellent bathing pools. Among the best times on our trek were those spent swimming with the guerrilla leaders while clouds of yellow, blue, green and orange butterflies danced over the stream banks.

Our 'great march' enabled us to understand how Angola's vast forests and sparsely populated Land at the End of the World were vital allies of UNITA as it frustrated the Cubans and Soviets. I learned how easily the soldiers could fade into the bush when I went to a river to bathe. I thought I was alone, but as I began to walk back, after getting dressed, some dozen guerrillas rose from the long grass within metres carrying rifles and anti-tank weapons. Special Force Gamboa, assigned to protect me, had moved unseen and unheard by me into position with the stealth of leopards.

One evening, as we sat eating, Gamboa's commander, Lieutenant Bonaventura (first name unknown), demonstrated the gap that surfaces from time to time between European and African perceptions.

Bonaventura said something which made Ben-Ben, highly educated and well-travelled, collapse in laughter.

'The lieutenant wants to know how easily his platoon could infiltrate Britain,' said Ben-Ben. 'I tried to explain to him about customs, immigration officials, coastguard patrols, police and that there was very little thick forest.' Earlier, on the battlefield, Bonaventura's men had acted without regard for their own lives to protect ours. Now he had endeared himself further.

At one village, as we continued south, we watched as a UNITA economic agent and trading officer bartered clothing and salt in exchange for villagers' surplus food and for ivory and animal skins. Villagers had walked as far as 200 kilometres carrying crude axes and bags made of skins. Barefooted and dressed in ragged clothes, they had brought elephant and warthog tusks, balls of wild beeswax and python, leopard and crocodile skins, which they exchanged for trousers, shirts, blouses and brassieres, stuffing these into big black plastic bags to carry back to their villages. The rate of barter exchange was seven pieces of clothing for an elephant tusk and six for a leopard skin. The agent said he had full-time workers in the area sifting streams for diamonds: in a good month they sometimes found nearly 2 000 industrial-quality diamonds.

Once back in Jamba, we slept between crisply ironed sheets in large huts with electric light. We ate off English china in a mess where waiters served egg and chips. The tablecloths were sky blue, and the coffee came in silver pots. And there was welcome cold beer in cans imprinted with an exhortation to 'Keep South Africa Tidy.'

18

'I can only tell you the things that happened as I saw them, and what the rest was about only Africa knows' (1983)

Later in 1983, as we worked together towards completion of the Savimbi book, Tito urged me to return to Angola yet again. The war was becoming bigger, bloodier and more complex. This time, he said, I would be able to push north of the Benguela Railway with one of the movement's best guerrilla commanders and watch an attack on a town in the diamond-mining province of Lunda during a rainy-season offensive.

It was November 1983. I decided also to make a television film and took with me a young Scottish cameraman, David Kane.

With us on the flight from Paris to the forest airstrip at Luengue via Kinshasa was Rony Brauman, the president of Médecins Sans Frontières (MSF, Doctors Without Borders). Brauman, a physician who specialised in tropical diseases, set up a major operation by the Paris-based MSF to treat UNITA's sick and wounded.

Shortly before David and I arrived, there had been a massive battle for Cangamba, about 150 kilometres south of the Benguela Railway, the last major MPLA stronghold within UNITA 'liberated' territory. Savimbi committed some 6000 fighters against the 3000-strong MPLA garrison. South African Air Force Canberra bombers and Impala fighter-bombers pounded the town

Tito said that some one hundred UNITA fighters lost one or both legs in the Cangamba battle. Most had been wounded or killed in dense minefields that surrounded the town. The wounded were treated by Brauman's volunteer doctors and paramedics.

By the end of the 11-day August battle, Tito claimed that more than 800 of the soldiers, some of them Cubans, defending the Cangamba garrison lay dead, and more than 300 had been captured. The rest of the garrison fled northwards. He said 63 UNITA fighters had died. He also released photographs of a government Antonov transport plane sitting with its back broken by UNITA artillery fire on the Cangamba airstrip.

No foreign journalists witnessed the battle for Cangamba.

The MPLA's story differed from Tito's account. On the day he said that UNITA had overrun the town, the MPLA announced in Luanda that it had initially beaten back the assault, but that South Africa had then rushed to UNITA's aid, taking command of the offensive and bombing Cangamba until it had 'ceased to exist'. The MPLA said its forces had retreated in order to save civilian lives. Before the withdrawal, it said, 1100 UNITA fighters had been killed for the loss of only 53 MPLA lives.[1]

The starkly different versions of the Cangomba battle 'facts' were typical of so many unwitnessed accounts of the conflict. It reminded me so much of one of my favourite aphorisms of the South African author Herman Charles Bosman: 'I can only tell you the things that happened as I saw them, and what the rest was about only Africa knows.'[2]

Whatever the precise truths, there were no doubts about the consequences of the unwitnessed Cangamba battle. UNITA had cleared from its midst a dangerous threat: thousands of its forces had been freed from the Cangamba siege to join other strike forces heading north of the Benguela Railway. David and I would follow them, said

Tito. UNITA morale had soared while that of the MPLA had hit a low. As the battlefields spread and became more savage, American news media speculated excitedly about an impending UNITA drive towards Luanda that might bring down the MPLA.[3]

The annual rains had begun. They were breathtaking: purple and deep pink skies while clouds, incongruously, were shades of dark green before turning black.

UNITA's hospitality base near Luengue had changed. The huts were more spacious. There was a special mess for visitors. Dinner on the first evening was a rice and antelope stew, washed down with lager beer from South West Africa. But outside it was wild: a lioness had recently been shot after she killed a UNITA soldier. As we went to bathe the next morning in the exquisite clear water of a sandy-bottomed stream, a big herd of sable antelope burst out of the reeds.

We began pushing north aboard captured Ural trucks, passing a 200-hectare collective farm producing maize, sorghum, tobacco, beans and a variety of vegetables, one of several UNITA had created out of virgin bush. We crossed a remarkable 25-metre-wide road bridge that UNITA engineers – or maybe South Africans? – had constructed across the Cuanavale River. We were again escorted by a bodyguard of tough Special Forces, heavily armed and smartly dressed in navy-blue uniforms.

We reached the Benguela Railway on 12 November and from there began a 12-day march northwards, passing through entirely different terrain than anything I had previously experienced. High rolling hills were topped with forest and gouged by cliffs and ravines. Emerald grass was sprouting, brought on by the rains, which regularly drenched us.

We stopped in villages where the people again brushed our shoulders with palm branches and laid down carpets of green leaves for us to walk upon. We were met in one village by an old friend from eight years earlier, Colonel Smart Chata, UNITA's secretary for justice and a leader of the Chokwe, one of the largest tribes of southern and central Angola, second in size only to the Ovimbundu. The Chokwe are internationally renowned for their exceptional craft works, particularly their mask carvings. The artworks illustrate Chokwe spiritual beliefs, mythologies and oral history.

Smart spoke beautiful, precise English, delivered with all the restrained, polite mannerisms of a decent kind of English country gentleman. So it was a surprise and a delight to see him transformed – or as his real self – as he addressed a rally in his native Chokwe. It was a full-blooded performance of incredible vigour and sensual body movements, which British politicians would get arrested for. We watched initiation dances for boys and girls. And we watched women pounding millet to a traditional tune but with new, unsubtle words: 'Cubans, you have to get out. Savimbi says so.'

Smart said, 'We encourage people to maintain the traditional culture, because our culture is what makes us Africans. At the same time, we incorporate that culture into our politics.'

Travelling with us as interpreter was a new UNITA secretary of information, a delightful man called Dr Jaka Jamba. Jaka was an intellectual whose PhD from the University of Geneva was based on an aspect of the life of Blaise Pascal, the 17th-century French philosopher, theologian and mathematician, and author of the philosophical argument known as Pascal's Wager, a deep, probabilistic argument on whether or not God exists. There, in the middle of 'darkest' Africa, I learned from Jaka one of Pascal's greatest aphorisms: *'La cœur a ses raisons que la raison ne connaît pas.'* (The heart has its reasons which reason does not know.) Jaka said it was his greatest wish, when peace came, to be a teacher of Angolan history. He picked up little orange fruits from the forest undergrowth and squeezed them to show us the rubber sap on which a big Angolan wild rubber boom was based in the 19th century. The 20-year upsurge collapsed in 1902 when trees from the Amazon became the main international source of rubber.

We had marched 120 kilometres north of the railway when we entered the base camp of Brigadier Geraldo Sachipengo Nunda, the 31-year-old commander of UNITA's 'Northern Front'. Nunda's immaculate base was spread over many square kilometres. It had a hospital, communications centre, military parade ground, an open-air wood-and-thatch theatre, a football pitch and a command and communications centre. Straight paths marked neatly by bark-stripped stakes linked the different parts of the base. All the time, high overhead, droned Soviet-made Ilyushin and Antonov transport planes ferrying supplies from Luanda to the railway town of Luso, in the east, where MPLA and Cuban troops were cut off from road and rail communication by UNITA forces.

Three battalions of semi-regular troops were at Nunda's base. They had crossed the Benguela Railway and forged northwards following the battle I witnessed at Cangonga on 11 February.

A military rally was planned at the parade ground for 23 November. SAM-7 missile teams assembled, and there were Chinese 12.7mm anti-aircraft guns in place. The atmosphere at the base – far north into what outside analysts were interpreting as MPLA/Cuban territory – was electric. But just as the rally began, a spectacular rainstorm descended. Water plunged from the skies, heavy blankets of it, accompanied by thunder and lightning, which pounded the earth for three hours. The rally was modified: the smartly kitted battalions still went through their conventional drills, but then they crowded around the little grass pavilion in which we sat with Brigadier Nunda. Throughout the chilling, drenching downpour, they sang and danced non-stop, rolling joyously in the mud, as if to say they were unstoppable.

Brigadier Geraldo Nunda, commander of UNITA's Northern Front, briefs a guerrilla battalion before the battle for Alto Chicapa, 29 November 1983. (Source: David Kane)

UNITA battalion dance and sing before going into battle, 1983. (Source: David Kane)

We moved out on 24 November towards the target with 2 000 of Nunda's troops. The soldiers no longer wore their spick-and-span parade ground uniforms. They were dressed in ragged, dirty clothes, rather as Wat Tyler's English peasant army must have looked 600 years earlier. On their backs and heads were mortar tubes and plates, mortar shells, rocket launchers, rockets, machine-guns, sacks of maize flour, cooking pans and blankets. We passed an abandoned settlement where the houses were made of red laterite bricks. Nunda said it had been an MPLA outpost until it was cleared in a UNITA operation. Now the houses were roofless, and the rain was dissolving the walls. That night we camped on a great hilltop, and when we heard the cries of babies, we realised we had women porters with us carrying their children in back-slings and weapons and ammunition on their heads.

Eight daylight hours were spent on 25 November ferrying the troops, the porters and us across the headwaters of the Cuango River in two inflatable rubber dinghies and two bark pirogue canoes. We swam in the swift-flowing river and admired a pathetic little baby monkey the soldiers had picked up and were carrying as a mascot. A nurse dug a *bitacoia* maggot from my foot, and a barter deal was done with a herdsman for some of his cattle. They were slaughtered and transported across the river in big, bloody hunks for feasting on that night.

On 27 November Brigadier Nunda revealed the target – Alto Chicapa, a town of about 5 000 people some 150 kilometres north of the railway line. We met the intelligence team who had been monitoring the town for months beforehand. On the forest floor was a large-scale sand model of the town. The intelligence men pointed out an airstrip to the northwest, two water towers and the municipality's electric power generator. Defensive trenches were indicated on the model, along with a series of civilian houses for 4 000 people who, the intelligence team said, were UNITA supporters. The total enemy force was estimated at 700. The last convoy of supply trucks had visited the town seven weeks earlier. Villagers reported that MPLA morale was low because of poor food and clothing supplies. There were no Cubans.

Nunda, destined to play a major heroic role in Angola's future, briefed us on his plan of attack. At 10 pm, on the night before the assault, UNITA soldiers would erect a rough wooden bridge across a small river to the northwest of Alto Chicapa. Two battalions, each of 600 men, would cross the bridge and get into positions, one to attack from the west and the other from the north. Other troops would be held in reserve. A 200-man artillery unit would be placed to the west of the river. There was a possibility of intervention from MPLA air bases. For protection, UNITA units were carrying SAM-7 missiles and 12.7mm anti-aircraft guns. But Nunda thought the battle would be so short that there would be no time for the MPLA to deploy aerial support. 'Enemy morale is very low, and within one hour everything will be over,' he forecast.

In darkness on the morning of 29 November we went with Brigadier Nunda across the river to the west of Alto Chicapa as the assault began at 5 am. Heavy mortars and cannons put down artillery fire. Then we heard the rattle of massed infantry rifle fire. At about 5.30 am, a white Very flare was fired, a signal to the artillery to stop their bombardment, and by 5.40 am the infantry fire also had stopped. We approached the town with Nunda from the north where MPLA dead littered the scrub. Huts were burning, but there were no people around, only chickens and goats. Reaching the main street, bound and blindfolded MPLA soldiers were already being interrogated by UNITA intelligence officers. Most of the soldiers in the central garrison seemed to have fled before the attackers reached it, for no bodies were there.

While David filmed, soldiers were removing weapons and useful materials, and destroying the infrastructure. I wandered around Alto

Chicapa. It had obviously once been a pleasant town, with fine Portuguese colonial-style bungalows, a hospital and a big restaurant where travellers had perhaps washed down their meals with chilled *vinho verde.* But now there was little furniture in these buildings. There were no beds in the hospital wards. In the clinic, medicines were spread in jumbled piles all over the floor.

There had been no electricity recently in Alto Chicapa. The generator, which was dismantled and taken away by UNITA engineers, was in working order, but there was no fuel to drive it. Because there was no electricity, there was no water, which needed to be pumped. As a result, all the town's toilets were unflushed, filthy and stinking. An open-air swimming pool lay empty and littered with debris. In the houses, hospital and restaurant, wood fires had been lit on the floors. There were two East German trucks with no wheels. The primary school was well stocked with Japanese and Czechoslovak pencils and attractive but propagandistic arithmetic books. I picked up a maths book, in Portuguese but printed in East Germany, in which children were asked: 'If it takes three bullets to kill two counter-revolutionaries, how many does it take to kill four?'

I spoke to some prisoners. Their replies needed to be heard and interpreted with great caution. They were terrified. With good reason. All the evidence I had seen and heard showed that UNITA executed MPLA captives. Sergeant Andre, the 22-year-old leader of an MPLA logistics platoon, said, 'We don't know why we're fighting, and the Cubans don't accept to stay here (in Alto Chicapa) with us. They don't bring us food here because we have no Cubans or (East) Germans. This is why troops are deserting. There have been three desertions from my platoon. They are leaving because of hunger, and often we survive by stealing.'

Nunda said there had been less resistance than he had expected. Partly, this was because there had been only 500 enemy soldiers in the town against the 700 suggested by the intelligence units. Twenty-five

MPLA prisoners taken by UNITA after the 29 November 1983 battle for Alto Chicapa. More often than not, MPLA prisoners were subsequently executed. (Source: David Kane)

MPLA troops were killed and eleven taken prisoner. No UNITA soldiers were killed or even wounded.

Compared with the earlier battle I had witnessed at Cangonga, Alto Chicapa was a complete walkover – a sledgehammer to crack a nut. Only a few weapons were captured, but Nunda was happy for strategic reasons. He could now push his battalions yet further north into Lunda Province, where Angola's richest diamond fields were located.

We left the brigadier in Alto Chicapa, to begin the return trek south, as he discussed with his officers the site of a new forward base. 'My soldiers were disappointed with the battle,' he said. 'They feel they were not really tested, and they want a new and bigger target soon. I'll have to decide on one.'

I would meet Nunda again many times over many years in unexpected circumstances and places.

As we marched back, we met another battalion yomping northwards to reinforce Nunda on the Northern Front. I had lost an enormous amount of weight on a constant diet of soggy rice, tinned pilchards and poor-quality French corned beef, rejected in France but given by the Paris government to UNITA. So it was a relief when the guerrillas discovered a large wild bees' nest high in a tree. They smoked out the bees, retrieved the nest and carved it into big slices. We sat in the forest sucking honey, and the occasional dead bee, from the wax honeycombs. Pure luxury and indulgence.

It took ten days to cover the 150 kilometres back to the Benguela Railway at a captured town called Munhango, where we were guided through minefields and saw, with great sadness, that after a battle there on 20 April, UNITA had created another railway engine graveyard. Its fighters had fired anti-tank rockets into the lovely old British-manufactured double-tender steam engines. We comforted ourselves with deliciously ripe mangoes from the deserted orchards around Munhango.

From Munhango it took four days on the Ural trucks to get back to Luengue. We arrived at the same time as two Canadian and 34 Portuguese hostages taken on 13 November in a battle for Cazombo, a small town near the border with Zambia.

'I can only tell you the things that happened as I saw them'

The capture of Cazombo was of great importance for UNITA. It finalised control of the whole 1 100-kilometre Angola frontier with Zambia, and it meant that more border posts could be opened through which Zambians and Angolans could pass to trade with each other.

The Canadians were missionary nurses, Nora Draper and Marion Wilson. They had been led with the 34 Portuguese on a 650-kilometre march to UNITA's southeastern bases.

Draper told me they had been captured by UNITA guerrillas from a clinic outside Cazombo where she and Wilson were treating up to a thousand poverty-stricken villagers each day. The Canadians said they had not expected to be attacked, although they knew there were regular ambushes of MPLA convoys on roads approaching Cazombo, and that earlier in the year all their own personal goods being delivered from Canada had been lost in a UNITA ambush.

'I had just finished stitching a small head wound on a child when the soldiers arrived,' said Draper. 'I didn't know who the soldiers were until I noticed Savimbi's portrait on some of their rifle butts. Their captain assured us we would be safe, but we were very frightened for the first two days.' The Portuguese, however, said they had learned from the local people that a big UNITA force was in the area and that an attack was imminent. One had even dug a trench in his garden in anticipation of the attack.

The Portuguese were released unconditionally soon after the Canadians were freed on Christmas Eve 1983. But there was no such luck for Rodolfo Esteves Lantegua, a 34-year-old Cuban soldier captured in banal circumstances near Nova Lisboa. When two Africans he thought were MPLA soldiers asked him for a lift in the military truck he was driving, he agreed to help. But they were UNITA men.

Lantegua asked me to convey, somehow, a message to Fidel Castro about his plight. He said he wanted me to tell Castro that, despite his capture, 'I remain faithful to the ideals of the revolution and of

Che (Guevara). Only death will make me forget the revolution.'

Despite his brave show of defiance, Lantegua's spirits were low.

'My main problem is that there has been no word from my country. That makes me think. I don't understand why my state has not spoken out about my situation.' But, he added, he would rather stay a prisoner for 20 years than give up his revolutionary ideals. I knew Lantegua was still alive three years later, but I am sure he must eventually have been killed, in line with UNITA policy of executing all captured Cubans.

There were more hostages to interview – 66 Czechoslovak men captured earlier that year, on 12 March 1983, with 38 of their wives and children, including an 18-month-old toddler and a female medical doctor, Dr Rudeschkova. The Czechoslovaks were technicians and managers at a big Czechoslovak communist government aid project, a pulp mill at Alto-Catumbela on the Benguela Railway. The pulp mill had become derelict after Portugal's withdrawal, and the Czechoslovaks had been trying to resurrect it.

Some 1 500 UNITA fighters attacked the mill complex and led the Czechoslovaks and their families into nearby mountains and then on a two-month, 1 200-kilometre march through swamps and forests to Savimbi's Jamba headquarters. UNITA commanders said 30 government soldiers were killed in the attack, for the loss of one on the rebel side. Guerrilla sappers blew up the mill's power plant and heavy machinery, three bridges, a locomotive and dozens of trucks.

Food on the march was basic – maize porridge shared by hostages, soldiers and porters. After 24 days, salt ran out, as did sugar for the bitter coffee carried by the guerrillas. Then, 39 days into the march, death struck the Czechoslovaks.

'Jeroslav Navratil was a handsome sportsman,' said Dr Rudeschkova. 'Without any warning signs that he was ill, he just lay down and died.' Jeroslav Navratil's body was placed in the wet Angolan earth by the guerrilla rearguard. Dr Rudeschkova believed Navratil, aged 37, was a diabetic without knowing it, and that the disappearance of sugar from the diet had killed him. Several women became so weak that they were carried by guerrillas on rough stretchers.

All the women and children, and seven of the men, were immediately released to a senior representative of the International Committee of the Red Cross for return to Czechoslovakia via South Africa. Twenty men were kept as hostages. The farewells were so traumatic that, as the women, children and sick men were driven away to freedom, UNITA officers tried to stop TV cameramen from filming the departure.

I met and talked to the men hostages at the end of my trek back from Alto Chicapa. By then they had been held for almost ten months and they were getting desperate. One of the men, Lumú Novostny, slipped me a note with his wife's name and Prague address on it. He whispered to me that I should assure her he was okay. I wrote to her on return to Brussels, where I was then working. Savimbi demanded a payment of US$300 000 from the Prague government for the release of its citizens. Foreign Minister Stanislav Svoboda refused to make the payment, warning Savimbi that UNITA's image was in danger of changing from that of 'a national liberation movement into a pack of bandits who kidnapped our citizens for ransom'.[4]

The hostages were held two to a hut, but with no communication permitted between the huts. They had no radios, little writing material and few books – one had read VS Naipaul's *Among the Believers* several times. Their food was monotonous – soggy macaroni and tinned meat, with fresh antelope once a week, and no fruit or vegetables. Ten developed hepatitis and some suffered from malaria. One was operated on for a double hernia by a UNITA nurse. And another complained, Schweik-like, 'My big problem is whether I'll come out with my last three teeth intact.'

Savimbi eventually released the men unconditionally when, 16 months after the attack on the pulp mill, Stanislav Svoboda reluctantly visited Jamba. I subsequently received a letter from the man who had slipped me the address of his wife. He thanked me for having contacted her and invited me to stay with his family in Prague.

'Everything I have will be yours, except my wife of course!' he wrote.[5]

19

British captives (1983–1984)

The response of Cuba and the Soviet Union to UNITA's thrust north of the Benguela Railway was to send more troops and weapons to the MPLA. The Cold War in tropical Angola got yet hotter.

In the first three weeks of September 1983, at least ten Soviet cargo ships unloaded in Luanda harbour arms including Soviet-built T-62 tanks, 24 helicopters and four naval patrol boats. Another 40 Soviet military technicians arrived to strengthen air defences, and 5 000 Cubans reinforced Havana's army in Angola, bringing its strength to more than 25 000.[1]

As the UNITA drive north intensified, South Africa launched another major invasion of Angola. Operation Askari began on 6 December 1983: 10 000 soldiers crossed the border and attacked targets in south-west Angola, supported by waves of South African Air Force Mirage and Impala fighter-bombers. Pretoria claimed 324 SWAPO and nearly 100 MPLA troops were killed and a Cuban taken prisoner. Some 25 Soviet tanks were destroyed and a Soviet SAM-9 mobile missile system captured.

Brigadier Nunda meanwhile thrust deep into the Lunda diamond-mining region with a force of 2 500 men – the three battalions with whom I had been at Alto Chicapa, plus another that had yomped from the south. On 23 February 1984, Nunda's men overran the mining town of Cafunfo. Following the usual UNITA tactic, the fighting began at 5 am and lasted only 50 minutes. According to foreign eyewitnesses, the MPLA garrison offered little resistance and most of its defenders fled. Twenty MPLA soldiers and eight Filipino miners were killed. Nunda's men marched off with 106 hostages – 16 Britons, four of them former SAS special forces; 40 Portuguese, including five women and four children; and 50 Filipinos, one of whom was carried all the way on a stretcher because of a bullet wound in his foot.[2] For 32 days, the hostages trekked to the Benguela Railway. Another four days in trucks brought them to Jamba, where they were kept under armed guard.

The Portuguese and Filipinos were released immediately and unconditionally. But Savimbi was angry with the British government because he had warned London months beforehand that Britons on contracts with the MPLA were likely to be killed or taken prisoner as the war escalated. The Britons would not be released. Savimbi outlined his bargaining position with a British journalist soon after the hostages reached Jamba.

'They (the hostages) are in good hands, but if Britain does not talk (to us) we will keep them for a year or two, or however long is necessary.'

Less than three months later, under a hostage return agreement whose essential details were kept secret, the United Kingdom sent Sir John Leahy, head of the Africa Department at the Foreign Office, to Jamba to receive the British hostages at a midnight ceremony on 12 May 1984. Some Foreign Office officials regarded Sir John's excursion as humiliating and distasteful. '*Opéra bouffe* (French comic opera) in a jungle setting,' sniffed one.[3]

Sir John, who stayed for 48 hours in Jamba and held three hours of talks with Savimbi, said he was impressed by the UNITA leader. He was neither the first nor the last international civil servant or political leader to be charmed by Savimbi, whose underlying psychopathy had yet to be uncloaked. The southern Africa correspondent of *The Times* of London noted that the British official, tight-lipped and uneasy on his arrival in Savimbi's lair, warmed to his host. In his farewell speech he was fulsome in praise of Savimbi's 'great qualities of leadership and colourful style'. It had been suggested to him before he left London that it was degrading to have to go and beg for the release of British citizens.

'I have not had to beg for anything today, and if this is humiliation I can take a lot more of it,' Sir John told a farewell ceremony of cheering, singing and dancing Angolans.[4]

Battles were by now commonplace across wide swathes of Angola. South African weapons deliveries to UNITA tripled, and all lingering doubts about the existence of close relations between UNITA and South Africa were swept away on 14 September 1984 when Savimbi was the only black African leader to attend the inauguration in Cape Town of Prime Minister PW Botha as South Africa's new state president.

Among UNITA's most spectacular attacks was the planting of 800 pounds of explosives in a hostel occupied by Cubans and Soviets on the main street of Huambo. The hostel exploded on the evening of 19 April 1984, leaving, said Tito, more than 200 dead, including 37 Cuban officers and three Soviet lieutenant colonels. The Soviet news agency TASS reported that women and children had died in the 'monstrous crime'. It did not mention Soviet or Cuban victims. However, the official Havana daily, *Granma*, said 14 Cubans died and 66 were wounded. 'Once again a group of self-sacrificing Cuban building workers offered their generous lives for the duty of helping in the economic and social development of other peoples,' said the newspaper.[5]

The truths of the growing avalanche of UNITA and MPLA claims and counter-claims were almost impossible to weigh, except as a general indication of the widespread scale of the fighting in a war still almost entirely hidden from the eyes of the outside world. By the end of 1985, Western intelligence agencies estimated that the Cuban troop presence in Angola had risen to 31 000, and that they were supported by 3 500 Soviet and East German personnel.

20

'Only peace will allow us finally to realise who we are' (1983–1986)

Tito, following his organisation of my travels to Angolan battlefields, had meanwhile risen to giddy heights in the UNITA leadership pantheon. He was recalled from London to Jamba, after four years of diplomatic service abroad, at the end of 1983 and promoted to the post of deputy secretary for foreign affairs with the military rank of lieutenant colonel. By then UNITA had taken so much territory that it had become a state within a state, extending its military campaigns throughout the country.

Unknown to me at the time, Tito had quietly married a young Angolan woman, Raquel Matos, in London. The reason he never got married to his first love, Ana Isabel Paulino, who was part of the group of young UNITA women who had received secretarial and language training in Paris, would only become clear to me later. Tito's relationship with Raquel was destined to be tragic. But for the time being his star was rising inexorably.

He was sent by Savimbi for a month at the end of 1984 to Washington, DC, to join the campaign for repeal of the eight-year-old Clark Amendment, piloted by Democratic Senator Dick Clark of Iowa, which banned covert US military aid to UNITA. The amendment was repealed on 11 July 1985, paving the way for the free flow of direct assistance to UNITA by the government of President Ronald Reagan.

The book Tito and I had worked on together for six years was published in the United States and Europe in 1986 and two years later as a paperback. Titled *Jonas Savimbi: A Key to Africa*,[1] it was widely regarded as highly controversial. The reviews it received ranged from favourable to damning, to a large extent depending on reviewers' preconceptions and ideological sympathies. Both Tito and I were sanguine about the mixed reviews – it was what we'd expected. The South African issue was a constant hot potato, and most sympathisers with the MPLA were viscerally hostile to UNITA quite apart from the South African connection. But Colin Legum, a notable South African-born anti-apartheid activist who spent most of his career as Africa Editor of the London *Observer*, wrote, 'Bridgland has performed a dauntingly difficult task with skill and honesty.' The British centre-left weekly *New Society* commented, 'A thoroughly researched and finely written book.' Personally, I reckon overall that the book had conveyed some of the many complexities of the Angolan conflict.

What the book did undoubtedly do was to raise greatly Savimbi's international profile, and shortly afterwards there were rumours that Tito was to be made vice president of UNITA. Tito's friends within UNITA said he asked not to be promoted to that rank. Instead, he was appointed foreign secretary, making him effectively number three in the movement's hierarchy. He was posted permanently, in January 1987, to Washington to liaise with the Reagan administration, the CIA and the black American churches.

Raquel, with whom he now had an infant son, Kaley, did not accompany him to America. Instead, she returned with Kaley to Jamba, on Savimbi's orders.

Tito's task as UNITA's premier diplomat had become a little easier. By dint of his own efforts, UNITA's war gains and a changing international climate, his arguments on behalf of the movement were being given more credibility. Politicians and intelligence personnel were regularly visiting UNITA's bases. More journalists followed the guerrillas into combat.

Diplomats went to the main Jamba base to negotiate the release of Britons, Czechoslovaks, Canadians, West Germans, Brazilians, Portuguese, Bulgarians, Japanese, Filipinos, Spaniards and Italians captured from government centres. The United States, even before the repeal of the Clark Amendment, had already greatly increased its 'secret' aid to Savimbi.

Tito set himself several major objectives in Washington. His UNITA predecessors in the US capital had clung tightly to the life-raft of the American Right. Tito wanted to cast off. He knew that as long as UNITA was engaged in war with a Moscow-based movement, it would have automatic right-wing support. But the right had no intrinsic interest in the more profound and subtle concerns of Angolans and of Tito himself. The right's commitment was viscerally anti-communist, but Tito had no illusions that it was also often racist. 'Because UNITA has South African support, they assume we must be "good" black Africans,' he told me.

He had no wish to discourage the right – UNITA needed every friend and supporter it could get. But he believed it was futile to work only with ideological right-wingers whose embrace, and stereotyping of Angolans in banal clichés, he found stultifying. It amused him as much as it exasperated him. He began to lobby liberals, Democratic Congressmen and churchmen, rarely demonising the MPLA but always arguing that his movement had a case which at least deserved a hearing.

He began making inroads into America's black community.

Florence Tate was a militant follower of the American branch of Pan-Africanism, the idea that people of African descent in the world-wide diaspora share a common oppression and destiny. Tate had twice served as personal aide to Washington's black mayor, Marion Barry. Florence became close to Tito, discovering that many of his ideas about releasing the potential of Africans through education and economic development, as well as politics, mirrored her own.

'He was a sweet boy with moral and intellectual strength who gave the impression of performing effortlessly,' said Tate. 'But it cost him, and whenever it all threatened to become too much he would drop by my home, and we'd talk for hours.'

Tate, politically astute, suggested Tito woo black churches way beyond Washington and the capital's politically correct cults. So he began addressing black rural congregations, many of them with similarities to his father's village flocks. Among the converts was Charles Evers, brother of Medgar Evers, the civil rights leader assassinated by a white supremacist in 1963 in Jackson, Mississippi. Charles succeeded his murdered brother as Mississippi field director of the National Association for the Advancement of Coloured People.

Around September 1986, I met Charles in Fayette, Mississippi, where he was the first black American to have been elected mayor of the town. He told me that he immediately liked Tito and understood his arguments, suffering far less angst than many a white liberal. 'My own blood brother was murdered because he campaigned for voting rights and educational opportunities for blacks,' said Evers. 'My black Angolan brother is also fighting for voting rights. How can I, so close to a legend in our civil rights campaign, deny Tito the same right?'

Some Democratic Congressmen and Senators gave Tito a hearing and began arguing the need for multi-party elections in Angola. The sympathies of Gillian Gunn, a senior researcher on Africa and Cuba at Washington's Center for Strategic and International Studies, were with the MPLA, the subject of her London School of Economics PhD.

'I was deeply anti-apartheid and anti-South African and vowed I would have nothing to do with anyone connected with South Africa,' she told me. 'Tito took me by surprise. He argued with formidable logic, but he was also a good listener and always courteous. He had a grace and gentle humour about him which made UNITA palatable to many people who didn't like the movement. Many detractors came away from a meeting with Tito with a wider view. My own convictions did not change, but I recognised him as a fine person.'

Tito also shunned the right-wing public relations agency Black, Manafort, Stone and Kelly, hired on behalf of Savimbi by the Saudi Arabian government. Known for short as Black Manafort, the agency's first client was a 34-year-old New York property developer, Donald Trump, nearly forty years before he became the 45th President of the United States. Sundry right-wing Senators and international dictators, including Zaire's Mobutu Sese Seko and Ferdinand Marcos of the Philippines, were among Black Manafort's clients.

Tito pushed support for UNITA beyond the American arena. He won backing in Lisbon from João Soares, who was the socialist Mayor of Lisbon and later Portugal's culture minister. The son of socialist President Mario Soares, João so greatly admired Savimbi that he named one of his sons Jonas, after the UNITA leader.

With personal support that blew hot and sometimes cold from Savimbi, Tito began talking to the 'enemy'. He pursued a dual strategy: strengthening UNITA in every way possible while opening contacts with the MPLA. Tito told me believed fundamentally that MPLA and UNITA followers would ultimately have to accept each other as fellow patriots, negotiate an end to the war and find a way forward together. He had come to acknowledge that humankind could not eat slogans, nor could problems be solved with ideology alone. He knew how desperately the people were caught up in a maelstrom of Cold

War manoeuvring and desperate domestic politics in which they were pawns.

One of his closest MPLA contacts was Angola's ambassador to East Germany, Mendes de Carvalho, who had shared a prison cell with Jonatão Chingunji under the Portuguese. Tito and De Carvalho used to meet in East Berlin. Savimbi sometimes said he had instructed Tito to make contact with the MPLA, but on other occasions he accused Tito of taking initiatives without his permission. On another occasion a Cuban government contact of Tito's organised a meeting for him with a top MPLA official in the Ivory Coast. Many MPLA people Tito met shared his belief that it was time to strike a creative deal. Tito read the work of the Kimbundu poet Artur Pestana, pen name 'Pepetela', who, although an MPLA supporter, had begun questioning how Angola had descended into hell.

In an article, Pepetela wrote, 'We were plunged into the East-West conflict and now we don't even know who we are. Every aspect of our lives is imbued with alienation and contradiction. Black market vs. official planning, proletarian ideology in a rural society, pro-Soviet rhetoric while doing business with the West. Only peace will allow us finally to realise who we are.'

21

Cuba's top defector (1987)

It was in the US, and with State Department and intelligence cooperation, that Tito opened up the possibility of another fascinating new journalism venture for me in Angola.

Cuba's troop strength in Angola had grown to 37000 by 1988, by when there were also present an estimated 950 Soviet advisers. However, all was not well between Fidel Castro and his two top generals in Angola – Rafael del Pino and Arnaldo Ochoa Sánchez – and with the new Soviet head of state, Mikhail Gorbachev.

General Del Pino, aged 50 in 1988, was one of the most flamboyant products of the Cuban Revolution. As a teenager, he too had fought against Fulgencio Batista, the US-backed military dictator of Cuba from 1952 to 1959. In 1961, he was hailed as the hero of the resistance to US President John Kennedy's abortive CIA-led Bay of Pigs invasion of Cuba. As a young pilot, Del Pino had shot down two American B-26 warplanes as they approached Cuba. After the air campaign, Fidel Castro publicly proclaimed him Hero of 'Playa Girón' (the Bay of Pigs).

Del Pino rose to become commander of the Cuban Air Force in Angola in 1975, carrying out the initial clandestine surveys for the arrival of Cuban troops and subsequently spending years trying to locate and kill Jonas Savimbi.

Del Pino flew to Moscow on 20 April 1987 to liaise with the Soviet Air Force on the annual draft of Cuban fighter pilots for training in Russia. Perestroika (reconstruction) and glasnost (openness) were newly in fashion at that time, following the appointment in 1985 of a new Soviet leader, Mikhail Gorbachev.

'There was great confusion among young Cubans studying in Moscow,' Del Pino told me in a remarkable meeting I eventually had with him in July 1987. 'They saw the Soviet government under Gorbachev reversing itself after 70 years of socialism and adopting a variety of reforms. There were the beginnings of private medicine, private restaurants, small private businesses. It was in stark contrast to what was happening back home where if some unfortunate cripple, for example, made milk shakes in his house so that his schoolchildren could have a snack he would have his mixer confiscated.

'Even in the midst of their confusion they (Cubans in Moscow) did not lose their sense of humour. They told a joke about the Cuban Communist Party entering important talks with the Soviet Communist Party for the transfer of Lenin's tomb to Havana because Fidel Castro was the only man left who wanted to be the saviour of World Communism.

'I got back to Havana on 8 May and told Carlos Aldana, in charge of the Department of Revolutionary Orientation in the Central Committee, that I was surprised that none of what was changing in the Soviet Union was being published in Cuba. Aldana said it had to be censored or the Cuban people would turn anti-communist.'

Three weeks after his return, on 29 May 1987, Del Pino put his wife and three children aboard a Cessna light aircraft for an ostensible routine leisure flight. He took off and touched down 150 kilometres away at the US Naval Air Station on Key West, Florida, to become the most senior defector ever from Fidel Castro's Cuba. Castro played down the escape, alleging that Del Pino was emotionally unstable. But later he admitted that Cuba's security had been endangered. Del Pino had been so close to the leadership that he could brief interrogators in depth about the many things that were happening in Castro's inner circle.

Tito, through his high-level contacts, was introduced to Del Pino, who said he wanted to meet Savimbi. His minders agreed to permit him to travel through Zaire into rebel territory in Angola to meet the man he had been trying to kill. Tito suggested that a film be made of the meeting. He offered, through my then agent, Richard Gollner, the chance to film exclusively Del Pino's venture into UNITA territory and possibly to write a biography of the general. Britain's Channel 4 television channel commissioned the film enterprise.

Tito arranged for me to meet Del Pino in July 1987. I flew into Washington and, on Tito's instructions, met a man in the Hay-Adams Hotel, near the White House. I forget how we identified each other, but the man, who was obviously a CIA employee, drove me 22 kilometres westward into Virginia to the then small town of Tysons Corner. There, in a Marriott Hotel, I met Del Pino, stocky, grey-haired and bespectacled, in a large conference room with security agents dotted around the perimeter. I could not help thinking that it was like living a scene in a James Bond movie or a John le Carré novel.

Our conversation, hours-long and wide-ranging, was conducted through a silver-haired, immaculately besuited, very cool and smooth interpreter who I presumed was Del Pino's CIA minder.

If Tito were to bring this project to fruition, it would be an enormous coup and his reputation in the UNITA ranks would soar and be permanently ensured.

Del Pino told me that his unease with Cuba's 'internationalist mission' in Angola had grown steadily from its start.

157

'Castro was drunk on the 1975–1976 successes in Angola,' he said. 'There was great pride and excitement about the adventure among the Cuban people. They believed it was a just war because Castro is very intelligent, and he presented it very skilfully. He persuaded the people that we were going into Angola because of the South African invasion, that it was a war of national independence as opposed to a civil war, and that we were there to help the people liberate themselves from the South Africans.'

All Cubans at the beginning wanted to go to Angola, Del Pino asserted. Public morale was high, and it gelled with Castro's personal ambition for international renown. He told the people that the South Africans feared the Cubans.

'The *povo* (people) loved that rhetoric. He whipped up national patriotic sentiments and convinced people that we had an invincible army. Before units left for Angola he would tell them, "Don't worry, we've already won the war." Our people were happy and proud, but then they did not know we would lose young men for many years as the commitment in Angola came to preoccupy all of our military personnel.'

Castro, said the general, got most things right. But he'd made a crucial mistake: he never imagined that Savimbi would resist, and he believed that UNITA was dead and buried.

Del Pino shared Castro's belief in total victory for the first three or four years after the Cubans had helped put the MPLA in absolute power at the expense of the multi-party elections that had been promised under the Alvor Accords of 15 January 1975. Del Pino believed surviving UNITA groups to be isolated from others and acting on their own. It was just a matter of mopping up, with armoured cars and helicopters, a few badly trained, poorly armed black Africans.

Mightily as the Cubans tried, they were simply unable to get Savimbi, who was now being dubbed the Black Pimpernel by the international media. On two or three occasions Del Pino himself flew a MiG-21 and shot up ground troops with whom Savimbi was travelling. The UNITA leader kept escaping.

The failure to kill or capture Savimbi was a source of increasing frustration to the Cubans. 'It was not until 1979 that it dawned on us that we could be facing a long war,' said Del Pino. 'It was then that UNITA guerrillas shot down for the first time one of our helicopters. It happened at a village called Maria Delida, about 400 kilometres from Luanda. The Mi-8 helicopter was firing rockets at a small group of guerrillas who stood their ground and returned rifle fire. One bullet penetrated a fuel tank, and when another rocket was fired the flame ignited leaking fuel and the helicopter exploded. All ten Cubans aboard – the pilot, co-pilot and eight soldiers – were killed.

'My friend, Colonel (later General) Harry "Pombo" Villegas, said it meant we now faced a very difficult situation, and we would be bogged down in Angola for many, many years. Villegas said the UNITA action showed that some of its fighters had lost their fear of aircraft to the extent that they had become willing to stand their ground and return fire, rather than running or hiding. This is something that takes time and courage to master.

'It would get more difficult for us because they were learning not to be afraid. Pombo knew about these things because he was one of the *Olivos* (literally 'Olive Drabs') who had fought with Fidel right through the Sierra Maestra campaign against Batista, and he was one of only three guerrillas who survived the campaign under Che (Guevara) in Bolivia.'

The legendary Guevara served as a minister in Cuba's first communist government until 1965, but then resigned to apply his theories of guerrilla revolutionary warfare first in the jungles of the Congo and then US-aligned Bolivia. Guevara's quixotic attempt to inspire an uprising in the Congo failed ignominiously. But he believed he could rouse Bolivia's tin miners, who lived in appalling poverty, to insurrection. This was also a disaster – fatally so. Few Bolivians rose in support and on 7 October 1967 Bolivian government Special Forces, armed and trained by the CIA for the military dictator General René Barrientos, trapped Guevara and his men in a ravine. There Che was riddled with bullets and died soon afterwards either from his wounds or summary execution.

Ironically, one of the last people with whom Guevara held talks in Africa about his theories of revolution was an aspiring young African who wanted to launch guerrilla warfare against the Portuguese in his own country, Angola. Jonas Savimbi told me that he and Guevara had two long meetings in 1965 in Tanzania and Algeria, in the course of which Che encouraged the then 33-year-old Angolan Maoist to go back into his own country, set up guerrilla bases among the peasantry and survive initially without help from outside.

Guevara entered Bolivia through the back door in 1966, the same year that Savimbi and his first small band of guerrillas entered Angola, also through the back door. Guevara died. Savimbi survived and, in a great irony, his guerrilla techniques and willpower were put to their greatest tests against Che's close comrade, Fidel Castro.

Del Pino said the 'old guard' *Olivos* were not a success in Angola. Castro clung to them out of loyalty and his sense of romanticism about the Sierra Maestra years. 'But they weren't young any more and their thinking did not change. They made a lot of mistakes, and when the MPLA realised the *Olivos* were no good, it hired former Portuguese counterinsurgency commandos who began replacing the *Olivos* and training 500-strong MPLA commando Special Brigades.'

Cuban counterintelligence reported increasing support for Savimbi from 1979 onwards as his guerrilla army grew and UNITA's operations spread. For Castro, said Del Pino, there could be no turning back. 'He needed success for the MPLA both for his own personal pride and as part of his quest to be an international figure. And, increasingly, he needed the internationalist mission in Angola to distract attention from all the internal economic problems and crises he continued to have in Cuba.'

Incidents piled up that gradually undermined Del Pino's faith in the Cuban Revolution he had fought to achieve and defend. In 1983, some one hundred Cuban troops were unable to prevent a devastating defeat for MPLA forces besieged by UNITA in the 1–14 August battle for the southeastern garrison of Cangamba. (See Chapter 18 for conflicting versions of the battle.) After what Del Pino described as an Alamo-style resistance by the Cubans and the MPLA, UNITA fell back with heavy casualties, but many Cuban and MPLA soldiers also lay dead.

Cuban survivors, said Del Pino, were helicoptered to safety after a massive row broke out between Cuban and Soviet planners. The latter wanted to pursue the retreating UNITA forces through the south-eastern forests. Castro cabled from Havana that all surviving Cuban forces were to withdraw from Cangamba. The Cuban leader described the Soviets' wish to pursue the retreating guerrillas as 'absurd'. Castro's brother Raúl, head of the armed forces, followed up Fidel's cable with a 'categorical, irrevocable' command to withdraw from Cangamba. 'Do not waste one more minute,' ordered Raúl.

Del Pino alleged that Angola became more and more a punishment posting for those whom Castro perceived to have failed him elsewhere. He gave as an example Colonel Pedro Tortolo, who was in charge of Cuban troops on Grenada when the Caribbean island was overrun by American forces in 1983. Tortolo was stripped of officer rank and sent to serve as an army private in Angola with 30 other demoted officers.

Standards of command, discipline and technical maintenance in Angola also began to decline. In 1984, Del Pino, by then back in Havana as deputy chief of the Cuban Air Force, visited Angola to investigate a series of losses in crashes of fighter-bombers, transport planes and helicopters. Many had crashed through sheer carelessness, but the loss of one young flyer in particular angered Del Pino. Lieutenant Raul Quiala Castenada was a promising pilot who had been sent to Angola for combat duty even though he had never done any night flying. One day, Castenada's commander in eastern Angola ordered him to fly a night mission in a MiG-21 and bombard any area where he saw fires burning.

'It was irrational to suppose that any bombs tossed out at night at unspecified targets were anything other than wasted,' said Del Pino. 'But it was criminal to send out a kid on that mission who had never flown at night. He crashed and died. His family was told, according to the routine, that he had died heroically in combat.'

Del Pino fretted that the Cuban dead were not sent back for burial at home and that the island's young men, far from home in Africa's HIV/AIDS belt, were beginning to succumb to the killer virus. The first HIV/AIDS case was diagnosed in Cuba in 1985, and informed wisdom is that the virus arrived on the island as Cuban soldiers returned home from tours of duty in Angola and other parts of Africa in the 1980s.

The last straw for Del Pino came when one of his own sons, serving in the air force in Angola, disappeared on a mission in 1985. He was co-piloting an Antonov An-26 light transport aircraft carrying soldiers from Luso, in the east, to Luanda, a flight of some 800 kilometres. When no one was able to trace wreckage, Del Pino flew to Angola to coordinate the search. He had found nothing after a week and reported that his son and all the missing men must be dead. 'That same night we heard, over the BBC from London, that they were all alive and well in Zaire,' said Del Pino. 'Talks started with the government of Zaire, which was very hostile towards us, to secure their return. I launched an inquiry into what had happened and opened a can of worms.

'As soon as the plane had taken off it flew into heavy cumulus storm clouds. They found they were unable to make contact with the ground by radio and, unknown to them at first, the plane's navigational system was malfunctioning. Although the instruments indicated they were heading at 310 degrees for Luanda, they were in fact flying almost due northwards on a heading of 350 degrees. By the time they realised their navigational system had gone wrong they had only five minutes' worth of fuel left, and they were flying over mountains. They spotted a stretch of road on a small plateau and made an emergency landing. They believed they were on Angolan territory, but since UNITA controlled nearly all the countryside, they burned the aircraft and all their documents before beginning their march to safety. In fact, they were in Zaire, and they were picked up by Zairean soldiers who didn't believe their story. They were eventually released after difficult negotiations and flown home to Cuba.'

Among the first things Del Pino discovered in his inquiries was that the then commander of the Cuban forces, in Angola, Colonel Tomas Benitez, had changed all radio frequencies for security reasons and failed to inform air force personnel in Luso. 'And then I discovered that the navigation systems of many aircraft had not been inspected or serviced for five years or more and that most of the entries in service logs were fraudulent. I sent the most damning report back to Havana. What was the outcome? Colonel Benitez was decorated shortly afterwards and returned to Cuba to command the Revolutionary Armed Forces in Oriente Province. The men on the plane were investigated for two months, reprimanded for surrendering four rifles to the Zaireans and reduced to the ranks.'

Del Pino said he had also become weary with government corruption in Cuba, particularly the practice in which Air Force pilots were deployed to flush out wildfowl from mangrove swamps when Castro went shooting at one of his weekend-retreat homes. On one occasion, Del Pino alleged, a helicopter crashed, and the pilot and co-pilot died when a flock of ducks flew into the rotor of the low-flying craft.

Del Pino admitted that he had benefited from a corrupt system in which politicians accumulated great riches 'while our young men died in Angola'. He said he was able to buy Western goods of every kind at very low prices in special shops for military officers. Castro, he said, used to give his generals luxury houses. Castro offered him another one just before he defected.

'I wanted to leave for many reasons,' said the general. 'But Angola was one of the main ones. It had become a dead-end street – Cuba's Vietnam. Only Fidel and Raúl had any faith in victory.'

Del Pino's final visit to Angola was in February 1987 when he helped plan, with the Soviet high command, an offensive that later that year would erupt into warfare on an unprecedented scale. Back in Havana, he continued to contribute to the planning of the Soviet-inspired campaign.

On 29 May 1987 Del Pino made his flight into a new life.

The fate of General Arnaldo Ochoa Sánchez, Castro's other top man in Angola, and for many years Cuba's top military icon, was drastic. Ochoa's career had been so dazzling that he was widely seen as a contender to succeed Fidel Castro as Cuba's leader. By Cuban standards, he was an independent thinker, with a tendency to bypass set rules and regulations. With Del Pino, he had also fought in the Sierra Maestra under Castro and Che Guevara in the late 1950s.

By 1987, he was deputy defence minister, second in military power only to Castro and the Cuban leader's brother, Defence Minister Raúl. But before he could take up his post Fidel Castro accused Ochoa of corruption, which included, but was not limited to, the sale of diamonds and ivory from Angola. As the investigation continued, Ochoa was accused of taking pay-offs from South American drug traffickers in exchange for letting them use Cuban territorial waters for drug drops and pick-ups. Raúl Castro, who was personally close to Ochoa, pleaded with his friend to reveal 'everything' so that matters could move forward.

Ochoa was stripped of his 'Hero of the Republic' title and went on trial in a military 'Court of Honour' on 13 July 1989, charged with treason. He was found guilty and sentenced to death. Ochoa, who was widely popular with his troops and the general public, is alleged to have testified, 'I was sent to a lost war (in Angola) so I could be blamed for the defeat.'

In one account of his execution by firing squad it is alleged that Ochoa asked not to be blindfolded. His trial and death remain matters of intense controversy and lack of detail. One unproven allegation is that Castro and Raúl used him as a scapegoat to cover up their own enrichment from the burgeoning drug trade. Arnaldo Ochoa Sánchez was aged 59 when he died.

A short time after I interviewed Rafael Del Pino, my then agent, Richard Gollner, visited him, at Tito's invitation, at the Marriott Hotel venue at Tysons Corner to finalise arrangements for the film with the general. It was agreed that Del Pino, with extremely tight security, would be flown to Zaire and from there fly through the back door into UNITA's territory in Angola.

I resigned my job, as *The Scotsman's* London-based diplomatic correspondent, to concentrate on preparation for the filming. Del Pino sent me a letter in which he said, 'I am really enthusiastic about your project, and I believe it will be the most interesting documentary yet made on the tragic suffering of Angola.'

But, as I was advising my successor on some of the ins and outs of the diplomatic reporting task, I received a bombshell telephone call from Tito in Washington. He said General Del Pino had suffered a 'nervous breakdown' and would not be able to take part in the project. Devastated, I asked Tito whether this hitch was short-term or permanent.

'Terminal,' he said, without any immediate explanation.

22

Peace agreements (1988)

There were dramatic developments in Angola in 1988. The Cuban-MPLA and the South African-UNITA military alliances fought themselves to physical and financial exhaustion in great battles on the Lomba River, near Mavinga, and at the small town of Cuito Cuanavale, some 100 kilometres to the northwest of the Lomba. The clashes, spread across eleven months, amounted to the biggest land battle in Africa since the battle for El Alamein in North Africa between British and German forces in 1942.[1]

The Lomba River/Cuito Cuanavale showdown was a major turning point in southern African history. But no reporters witnessed the carnage in which thousands of men were killed or wounded – mainly MPLA and UNITA soldiers, but also Cuban, South African, Soviet and East German military men. Secrecy, propaganda, obstruction and outright lies from all sides made press coverage of the conflict a journalistic nightmare.

Having fought themselves to a standstill, the main foreign players – South Africans, Soviets and Cubans – all realised that the best they could achieve was a lean peace rather than a fat victory. Soviet leader Mikhail Gorbachev, who had committed an estimated £1 billion to the Cuban-MPLA Lomba River offensive, said there would be no more money to purchase weapons for the MPLA: Angola's 18-year war was unwinnable. The South Africans too wanted out. The war was eating up Pretoria's financial reserves, already hard hit by international economic sanctions. There was also anger among many sections of the white electorate as teenage soldiers returned from the secret, unreported war in Angola in body bags or maimed for life. And although South African troops and artillery maintained ground superiority, its ageing air force was no longer a match for Cuba's and the MPLA's modern Soviet warplanes.

The Cubans too had had enough. Angola was consuming 11 per cent of the Caribbean island's annual budget and, despite a decade-and-a-half of support by Havana for the MPLA, the Angolan economy was in ruins. Some 400 000 Cuban fighters had been rotated through Angola, so that nearly every Cuban family in a population of ten million had been affected by the war. HIV/AIDS had been introduced into Cuba by men returning home from Africa. The veterans of Angolan service were being referred to as the 'generation of disenchantment', with comparisons being made with US Vietnam veterans.

Tito and I were in less regular contact after the publication of the Savimbi biography in 1986. I was intensely busy in a new posting to Brussels as *The Scotsman's* Europe correspondent. He had left London and spent a long period from 1984 onwards in Jamba, where Savimbi tried to persuade him to become vice president of UNITA. He declined and returned to Washington in 1987. An extraordinary cat's cradle of peace negotiations, conducted by Chester Crocker, the US Assistant Secretary of State for Africa, was happening in locations across the globe. Tito was UNITA's representative at many of the peace talks, which culminated in the New York Accords, signed at UN headquarters on 22 December 1988 by the foreign ministers of Cuba, South Africa and Angola.

'Something beautiful is happening,' Tito told me by telephone each time he returned from a negotiating session, without ever revealing the magnitude of Crocker's enterprise. He was invigorated by the talks – all his diplomatic efforts had been directed towards the ultimate goal of achieving peace and reconciliation. He said he was convinced that the winds of change were blowing both UNITA's and Angola's way. He believed an end to war was within grasping distance.

Tito during his Washington years.

'We need to prepare the ground to bridge the confidence gap between the MPLA and UNITA,' he told me. 'Both sides are trying to talk more candidly about our mistakes and successes. Many people have friends and relatives across the conflict lines, and young people in particular are willing now to talk about reconciliation. What can bring us together? We have to become very flexible, not rigid or intransigent.'

However, Tito was not present when the New York Accords – Chester Crocker's ultimate achievement, but in which Tito had played a crucial role – were signed. In December 1988, he was back in Jamba and barred from witnessing the fruits of his labours.

The New York Accords decreed several trade-offs. Both Cuba and South Africa withdrew their armed forces from Angola. The Cubans were able to withdraw from their Angolan quagmire without loss of face. South Africa also withdrew from South West Africa, paving the way for the territory to become independent Namibia and for SWAPO to come to power in the country's first all-race general election.[2] Having surrendered Namibia, South Africa got a bonus, under the Accords, in the shape of the expulsion of the African National Congress army, Umkhonto we Sizwe (Spear of the Nation), from its military bases in Angola and Zambia.

With the Cubans gone and the ANC neutralised militarily, Nelson Mandela was released from 27 years of imprisonment. Negotiations began on South Africa's political transition, leading to the country's first all-race general election between 26 and 29 April 1994.

Mikhail Gorbachev was free to concentrate on the Soviet military's continued withdrawal from Afghanistan and on serious domestic political and economic problems. The Berlin Wall came down ten months after the signing of the New York Accords.

For the MPLA and UNITA the New York Accords offered an opportunity to settle at last their 18-year civil war at the negotiating table free from external interference. In an agreement brokered by Portugal, the United States and Russia, the MPLA and UNITA signed a peace accord at Bicesse, a western suburb of Lisbon, on 31 May 1991. The Bicesse Accords officially ended the civil war and provided for Angola's first all-party parliamentary and presidential elections to be held on 29 and 30 September 1992. The accords were hailed from Washington to Moscow as a model for post-Cold War peacemaking.

For Tito, the Accords should have been the high point of everything he had worked and fought for. He had persuaded the Reagan administration and Congress to send to UNITA the kind of weaponry, including Stinger missiles, that led to a military stalemate and forced the MPLA to agree to a ceasefire and the holding of elections. The government had realised it was not strong enough to crush Savimbi, while Savimbi himself realised he was not yet strong enough to overthrow the government militarily.

In reality, the signing of the Bicesse Accords marked the beginning of tragedy for Tito and his close and extended family.

23

A shock game-changing revelation (1988)

I had not recovered from my deep disappointment about the cancellation of the Del Pino film project when Tito phoned once again, in September 1988, and asked me to fly to Washington: he needed to talk to me urgently. I asked what this was about. He said he could not explain by phone. I said impatiently that I was not in the habit of just jumping on planes to make 12 000-kilometre transatlantic return journeys for casual chats with pals.

He said I must come. There was an unusual edge of anxiety in the voice of a man who nearly always exuded calm and whose courage, intelligence and kindness I had come to value greatly. 'Let me ask you this,' I said. 'Is this a matter of life or death?'

'Yes.'

'You're serious?

'Yes.'

Mystified but deeply concerned about my friend, I flew to Washington.

Nothing before in the thirteen years I had known Tito prepared me for the horror of what he related to me that late summer in my room in the downtown Vista Hotel. Everything was surreal, beginning with big placards in the hotel foyer publicly advertising the US Secret Service annual convention.

My relationship with Tito had already tugged my life, and the lives of my wife and three daughters, in completely unforeseen and hugely challenging directions. Now, in the US capital, Tito added a terrifying twist to the story.

'There are things I need to tell you I have never told you before,' he began. 'You need to know them because there are things that might now happen that you would otherwise not understand. And I need to tell you because your family has loved me and because you are a man who understands Africa.'

I smiled wryly. Truth be told, the more I learned about and lost my heart to that extraordinary continent, the less I felt I really understood it. Africa is unfathomable to outsiders much of the time.

I was totally unprepared for what came next. It was the most disturbing conversation I have ever had. Tito said the situation within Savimbi's movement was more complex and traumatic than anything he had previously shared with me. Each time he returned to Savimbi's forest headquarters, he now told me, he did not know whether or not he would come out again or whether he would be killed.

My eyebrows must have lifted incredulously.

He reminded me that when I was researching and writing *Jonas Savimbi: A Key to Africa* he had told me that his parents, Jonatão and Violeta, disappeared during an MPLA military offensive and were presumed dead. It was what he had been told and what he believed when he first talked to me about his parents.

'But when I was based in London (from 1980 onwards) I began to hear stories that they had not been killed by the MPLA but had been beaten to death on Savimbi's orders,' he said. 'I have confirmed with certainty, following a long and detailed investigation, that that is the truth. Without any doubt. Also, my sisters and remaining brother and their husbands, wife and children are under arrest and have been severely beaten. They are under constant threat of imprisonment or death.'

He apologised for not telling me this earlier, but said, 'I've been carrying all this heavy extra baggage. But I want to try to complete this peace mission, secure my family's safety and try to prevent UNITA from going to hell.'

He went on to drop a series of further bombshells.

Tito said he had put together the details of this different narrative only slowly but steadily, on evidence supplied by family and friends from Jamba, some of them now in exile. In 1980, he had travelled ahead of Savimbi to Morocco to prepare a diplomatic offensive in the West. As part of that initiative, he had contacted me and reminded me of my book 'promise'. While in Morocco, Savimbi told him about his parents' deaths, and he had believed his leader's account of how they had been killed by the enemy. He had no reason to believe otherwise. His father was joint creator of the movement: he and his wife had been the pillars of the clandestine movement in the Portuguese-occupied towns. Tito had been born and grown up at the heart of this founding family. 'My father was a deeply devout Christian of strong character and discipline. His example has affected me very much, even at times when my own religious faith was weak.'

Jonatão was widely and deeply respected and regarded Savimbi almost as a son. Tito's two oldest brothers, both dead, had been elevated to martyrdom in UNITA: both Samuel Kafundanga Chingunji and David Samwimbila Chingunji were commemorated in the movement's bases in song, dance, poetry and giant revolutionary painted banners alongside standards of Che, Mao and Savimbi. A school for political thought had been built in Jamba and named after Samuel. Tito said Jonatão at first refused to believe the evidence amassed by family and friends that Samuel and David, and their younger brothers Estevão and Paulo, had actually been killed on Savimbi's orders.[1] Jonatão felt personally insulted that people should associate Savimbi with such evil. The rumours were being spread by those who wanted to destroy UNITA, he felt. Savimbi used to address Jonatão as 'my dear uncle', and many people thought, incorrectly, that the Chingunji and Savimbi families were related by blood.

Jonatão and Violeta arrived, in March 1979, at UNITA's temporary Delta[2] base, just across the border in South West Africa, after a months-long trek through central and southern Angola. Jonatão became troubled after he began discovering the extent of Savimbi's prodigious sexual promiscuity and callous treatment of women. The leader had a growing harem of 'official' wives and concubines, some as young as fourteen.

'He was taking wives from everywhere and everyone, and his children from these relationships were scattered through southern Angola,' said Tito. Savimbi's sexual proclivities had extended beyond most 'normal' concepts of lust. He chose wives for many of his senior officers and slept with them in bizarre *droit de seigneur* rites of passage before they married.

Jonatão was confronted with a mammoth existential and ethical crisis when Savimbi began making sexual advances to his youngest daughter, Lulu, when she was just 17, and also Helena, Tito's married twin sister.

Eduardo Chingunji told me several times, and in many conversations, 'This was dynamite for my grandad. He didn't believe in polygamy. He wrote to Tito, who had arrived in Morocco to begin preparing UNITA's international diplomatic offensive, saying, "I cannot allow this man, who is our president, to continue harassing my daughters."'

At the time, Eduardo, who has been an important source for this book, was a civil engineering student in London. He is the son of Samuel Kafundanga Chingunji, Tito's oldest brother. I hadn't been introduced to Eduardo by 1979–1980, but sad circumstances brought us close together in London from 1986 onwards.

Jonatão realised he had to act to protect Lulu. It led him to a wider critique of Savimbi's iron grip on the movement, which had developed into a cult of personality that Jonatão considered to be at odds with UNITA's founding egalitarian and collective leadership ideals. He began listening seriously to conflicting evidence about the deaths of his sons and reluctantly accepted that Savimbi had ordered the murders of Samuel, younger sons David and Estevão, and probably also another son, Paulo.

'David Samwimbila died in 1970 while commanding an attack on a Portuguese train on the Benguela Railway,' said Tito. 'I've now heard more detailed accounts of what happened in that battle, and I now believe that Samwimbila was shot from behind on Savimbi's orders. Kafundanga was poisoned to death. The "official" accounts that he died from cerebral malaria are not true. Eduardo – Kafundanga's son, my nephew – can describe to you what happened and how his mother, Kafundanga's wife, Grace, and her children were subsequently ignored by Savimbi.

'Estevão, I have been told, was shot on Savimbi's orders, by one of Savimbi's personal bodyguards, in May 1976 as he was leading an attack against MPLA forces. Paulo died shortly afterwards in a "motor accident" somewhere in Cunene Province. In view of all the accumulating evidence, concrete and circumstantial, I obviously have grave doubts about this account.'

Jonatão demanded a meeting with Savimbi. He believed that with his reputation and counselling skills he could secure the safety of his surviving family members. So, although he demanded that Savimbi stop sexually harassing Lulu, he did not immediately raise the issue of his dead sons. But he did request that Tito be recalled from abroad to collect his remaining family and that they all be allowed to leave Angola and rebuild their lives elsewhere.

Savimbi, Tito learned, was enraged by Jonatão's demands. A few days later, Savimbi's bodyguards arrested and tortured his parents and also Lulu and Helena.

'I did not at first believe the stories, or maybe I preferred not to believe them,' Tito told me. 'But as I got more and more accounts of their deaths, I had to face the truth.' He said that at a public rally Savimbi had accused his parents of witchcraft and plotting to kill him. Savimbi alleged that Violeta had powers of witchcraft so great that she could fly. She also ate people, Savimbi told the rally, and said she had killed Jonatão's oldest sons Eduardo and David by his deceased first wife, Isabel.[3]

Jonatão and Violeta were subsequently killed on Savimbi's orders in late 1979, said Tito. According to one version, related to both Tito and Eduardo Chingunji, the couple were beaten and then tied by ropes to the back of a truck and dragged through the bush. Violeta died behind the truck and Jonatão succumbed soon afterwards to his injuries. They were buried together in the same grave by a distant Chingunji relative, Isaias Kawema, who later confirmed their murders to Tito and Eduardo. Savimbi falsely told rallies that Tito had condemned his parents' witchcraft practices.

'For years Tito hoped that his parents would turn up,' Eduardo Chingunji, who was very close to Tito, told me in 1986. 'He only seems to have realised the truth towards the end of 1983 when he met some young relatives who had been beaten and imprisoned at the time his parents died.'[4]

Tito made further highly disturbing revelations. He said his oldest sister, Xica, 'the most innocent and least political member of my family', had been executed in October 1983 on Savimbi's orders. Her only offence, he asserted, was to have the Chingunji surname.

Francisca Chingunji Domingos, known affectionately as Xica, had become an instant celebrity when she arrived at Jamba towards the end of the 1970s. Savimbi paraded her at rallies as the sister of the movement's great revolutionary hero, Samuel Kafundanga Chingunji. Xica was subsequently denounced as a witch, said Tito, by one of Savimbi's 'witch-finders', a chief named Xavier. She was also denounced by one of Savimbi's chief bodyguards and executioners, General Samuel Epalanga, by one of Savimbi's brothers, Abel Savimbi, and by an evangelical pastor.

Xica's alleged crime was that she had caused miscarriages of three women by witchcraft. The execution by firing squad of Xica, seven months pregnant at the time, was supervised by a Savimbi aide named Melgasso. Xica was blindfolded and made to stand next to the grave that had been dug for her. She was riddled with bullets, and as her body fell into the prepared ditch her unborn baby was said to have been falling from her womb.[5] Her execution took place some time in October 1983.

Lulu, Tito's youngest sister, was an exceptionally strong, intelligent and independent-minded character. She had long believed her brothers Samuel, David and Estevão had been murdered on Savimbi's orders. She considered the UNITA chief repulsive physically, spiritually and in every way possible. Lulu, Tito reported, born in November 1960, was beautiful, and she also had enormous courage and self-belief. Not only had she constantly refused Savimbi sex; she openly berated him. Portugal's mournful, nostalgic *fado* folk songs – popular among Angolans – were banned in Jamba by Savimbi because he said they indicated a Portuguese mentality. So Lulu began roaming at night among the huts singing *fado* in what everyone knew was deliberate defiance of Savimbi.

So feisty and contemptuous was his sister's conduct, said Tito, that she was more often in than out of the movement's fetid underground prisons. All her teeth were broken in frequent punishment beatings and Tito had pleaded unsuccessfully with Savimbi to allow her to receive dental treatment abroad.

Even during Lulu's spells out of prison, Savimbi subjected her to terrible pressure. He sent her to teach, with Helena and Raquel, at UNITA's model secondary school, the *Polivalente*, which was always on the itinerary of important foreign visitors to Jamba. When the women arrived to begin teaching they were confronted by pupils carrying banners emblazoned with 'We refuse to be taught by traitors.' The three were beaten up by pupils while Savimbi's bodyguards looked on.

During one of her stretches in prison Lulu attempted to commit suicide, according to evidence gathered later by Eduardo Chingunji. Although she became increasingly rebellious, she grew less able to cope with regular sessions of torture and with conditions in the pit prisons, where there were no toilet facilities. She was found in a critical state one morning after a suicide attempt some time in 1989. Pinto Chikoti, a fellow prisoner who later escaped to Luanda, said he was told by guards that Savimbi then issued an order for her to be killed and that she disappeared.

According to Chikoti, Kamy Esteves Pena, another Savimbi aide who ran a death squad, removed Lulu from prison. In front of Savimbi, she was kicked and beaten. 'That was the last time she was ever seen alive,' Eduardo told me years later. 'There was no way out for Lulu, who was one of the most graceful, courteous, strong and unwavering women I have ever known.' Lulu was aged only 28 when she died.

Tito's lone surviving brother, the youngest, Dinho, was a soldier serving at the front when news reached him of his parents' deaths in 1979. He later vowed revenge. Savimbi at another rally denounced him as a counter-revolutionary. Eduardo said Dinho subsequently disappeared and has not been seen again since. He is presumed to have been executed.

Alarm bells were by now sounding loudly and wildly in my head. If all this was true, this was savagery, pure evil and sheer madness beyond anything else I had knowledge and experience of in my foreign reporting career. My book on Savimbi had stirred huge controversy and I had staked my reputation heavily on its reasonable accuracy. Facts were tumbling out from Tito about his leader in total contrast to previous narratives. I took careful notes. I faced a moral and professional responsibility to tell a different story and explain why. Although Africa thrilled and intrigued me, I now really questioned my powers to understand its politics and cultures.

Tito said Savimbi had refused permission for Raquel and their son Kaley to leave Jamba to join him in Washington. Indeed, Raquel had told him, Savimbi was now talking about the entire Chingunji family as a plague that had to be totally eliminated. Tito said she told him that the hatred he had of the Chingunji family was beyond imagination or rational thought. Savimbi had warned her that her siding with the Chingunjis made her a traitor to the UNITA cause.

Tito said he challenged Savimbi on a working visit to Jamba in 1984 about the deaths of his parents. He said he knew most of the facts and believed Savimbi had ordered the killings. Savimbi's response was that on the day in question, at an unknown date in 1979, he had been ill and the executions of Jonatão and Violeta were the fault of his bodyguards who had taken precipitate action on learning of the witchcraft allegations against the couple. Tito said the reply was so lame that it was obvious to him that Savimbi was lying. No action was taken against the bodyguards, but he said Savimbi promised to protect the rest of his family from persecution. For the moment, that was an apparent promise that had to be grasped.

It was abundantly clear to me, after hours of talking on that September day in Washington, that Tito faced possible murder by a man I had liked, a man I could not have conceived of previously as my friend's potential assassin.

How, I asked Tito, did he expect me to deal with this devastating new information, which ran totally counter to the narrative of *Jonas Savimbi: A Key to Africa*? At some stage, it was obligatory that I would have to publish the truth. I had a clear duty to do that. He asked out of fear for his relatives in Jamba that the information remain confidential for the time being.

'Either I will give you a signal that the time has come to act, or you yourself will know, without me, that the time is right to go public,' he said. He said he knew that the only way surviving members of his family could be saved would be if he redoubled his efforts and worked his guts out diplomatically to bring Angola to permanent peace.

'It is the only way that I will be able to ensure that the family comes out of this quagmire alive. I have to search deep within myself to find the best way of dealing with this. If I am seen to overreact, all my family might die,' he said.

We embraced. I flew back to London in a state of profound shock, a deeply troubled man. This was all beyond a nightmare. My friend, whom I had come to love, was ensnared in a moral and practical dilemma of Kafkaesque proportions. I felt grateful and, I hope, humbled that he had trusted me enough to share his dreadful burden. But I was also deeply disturbed. I was unable to see how my life and that of my friend were now likely to develop. I would have to reappraise huge and important issues in which I had been immersed for more than a decade. Rough times beckoned. In due course I would be accused of planning to assassinate Savimbi with an African poison. I would receive death threats. A person I loved would be threatened with mutilation. And worse. Much, much worse.

24

The murder of Jorge Sangumba (1980)

The Chingunji family were not the only prominent members of the movement to suffer the consequences of Savimbi's megalomania. Jorge Sangumba, whom I got to know and to respect, was a brilliant graduate of Lincoln University, near Philadelphia. He was Savimbi's first foreign secretary and had established close links with a wide range of governments, journalists and intelligence agencies. For a long period in the 1970s he was UNITA's chief spokesperson.

Sangumba, sophisticated and widely read, began criticising openly Savimbi's erosion of collective leadership. He told Savimbi that he was no longer thinking straight and that he needed help from the entire top leadership to move the party forward. A political settlement of the Angolan conflict was a necessity. It was essential to enter dialogue with the MPLA, otherwise the war might continue for generations. Sangumba, Tito told me in Washington, tried also to begin a debate on how the movement could lessen its dependence on South Africa.

Savimbi regarded Sangumba's challenge as intolerable. He was put on trial in 1980, charged with plotting to kill Savimbi. The UNITA leader was unhappy about Sangumba lending young guerrillas his copy of Niccòlo Machiavelli's *The Prince*, a textbook for absolute rulers on how best to preserve power by the judicious use of violence and deception.

The last offence was possibly the most damning. Sangumba was accusing Savimbi of attempting to return his people's resistance to a kind of Khmer Rouge-style Year Zero. Tito told me that gradually all writing, poetry and political philosophy other than Savimbi's own had been banned in Jamba. People were ordered to call Savimbi *O Mais Velho* (The Elder), as though he were God-like. He had come to share with his old mentor Mao all the veteran Chinese leader's paranoia, duplicity, rages and cruelty.

Angolan writer Sousa Jamba, in his novel *Patriots*, published in 1992, accused Savimbi of organising Sangumba's murder.

'He was beaten to death by Savimbi's secret police,' said Jamba, a former UNITA political commissar and senior interpreter. 'Savimbi has been able to convince journalists and others that Sangumba is still alive.' Following Sangumba's execution, Sousa Jamba said he was thrown into an unmarked grave and all copies of a small book he had written, *Know Your Party*, were confiscated and burned.

Jamba added that Savimbi also ordered the killing, in 1980, of the then UNITA chief of staff, Brigadier Pires Chindondo, a close friend of Sangumba. Chindondo had confronted Savimbi for forcibly incorporating his wife, Aninhas, into his entourage of concubines and mistresses while Chindondo was away for months at the war front. Chindondo's younger brother, Captain Piedoso Chindondo, was also executed after he supported Pires' complaint.

For years journalists and others who asked Savimbi about Sangumba's welfare and whereabouts were told he was on an education mission 'in the north'.[1] Those who inquired about Chindondo were told he had fallen under the wheels of his jeep and died from his injuries.

According to some accounts, Sangumba had been sentenced to die and was hacked to death with machetes. Others said he'd been beaten to death. Either way, it was an act of incredible savagery and betrayal of a man who had served the UNITA cause well. I cannot begin to imagine what he must have been feeling in the final moments of his life as Savimbi released his attack dogs on his former foreign secretary.

Tony Fernandes, who wrote UNITA's founding constitution with Savimbi in 1964, told me in an interview[2] that there had been show trials of Sangumba and Chindondo in Jamba in 1980. No evidence was led other than a statement by Savimbi accusing them of plotting a coup. 'I had just arrived in Jamba, in February 1980, from representing UNITA overseas,' said Fernandes. 'I was naïve. Others told me Savimbi's so-called evidence was a death sentence.'

Fernandes, soon afterwards, was in a meeting with Savimbi and mentioned Sangumba. Savimbi replied that he had already been executed. 'I was taken aback. I talked to a few other people who said Jorge had been beaten to death by Kamy Pena's execution squad on Savimbi's orders.

'I was subsequently arrested and imprisoned myself on a trumped-up charge. My offence was being a sympathiser of Ronald Reagan. And then, when Reagan was shot, I was accused of saying it was a good thing because Savimbi would no longer get American help. I was completely baffled.' Fernandes was also accused of criticising UNITA's links to South Africa. 'I was beaten with fists and clubs. By now, I realised there was a lot of killing going on.

'There was a full "embassy" of three Americans in Jamba at that time (around Sangumba's death). There were also white South Africans mingling with us, eating at the same tables and dancing with Angolan girls. I can't believe that none of them knew what was going on.'

Leon Dash wrote, in a 30 September 1990 *Washington Post* article, that Savimbi saw Sangumba's criticisms as a threat to his control of UNITA. He ordered the imprisonment and beating of Sangumba in 1979. 'Imprisoned in one of UNITA's damp prison pits dug deep into the soil, the jovial Sangumba is alleged to have dwindled to a thin, haggard and sickly reflection of himself before he died.'

I asked Fernandes why no one, other than Sangumba and a few others, seemed to question Savimbi's increasingly deranged behaviour.

'It's difficult to explain,' Fernandes said. 'But under the way Savimbi ruled, you became less than a nobody if you were charged with an offence. There is no other way I can describe it. Being confined to the pits was sometimes worse than being killed. As well as being a Maoist, Savimbi was also a Machiavellian. I was publicly beaten. I was put in a pit prison for 36 days and then spent eight months under house arrest with no job and no privileges.'

After studying at Lincoln University in the early 1960s, Jorge Sangumba had married an American academic and journalist, Connie Hilliard, currently Professor of African History at the University of North Texas and a board member of the *Dallas Morning News*. The couple met in 1973 at a conference in London on southern Africa when Sangumba was UNITA's foreign secretary and Connie was a Harvard University postgraduate student. They married in 1975, just a few weeks before Angola's civil war erupted.

Subsequently, they spent barely a month together as Jorge shuttled between Angola and world capitals. Connie annulled the marriage when it became clear that she would not be allowed to join Jorge in the Angolan bush. Nevertheless, she continued to regard him as a man of courage and integrity who would never back down on his political principles. When Savimbi visited the United States in October 1989, some seven years after Jorge had been executed, he invited Connie to fly to Washington to talk with him.

'He tried to convince me that he (Savimbi) had enemies who were lying about Jorge being dead, and that Jorge was actually in a remote area of Angola where he had settled down with some peasant woman,' Connie told me.[3] 'I returned to Dallas heartsick and confused ... For many years after that conversation with Savimbi I was haunted by dreams in which Jorge would show up on my doorstep and insist that he really was alive. I'm not sure I've ever fully recovered from his death.'

25

Witch burnings and other atrocities
(1983 onwards)

It was Savimbi's cold-blooded way with women that enmeshed Tito ever more tightly into the web of *O Mais Velho*. The story is so preposterous, so devilish, that I feel almost too uncomfortable telling it for fear of being disbelieved. Tito told me the basic story, and I have fleshed it out from numerous other sources.

Tito and a slim, beautiful girl called Ana Isabel Paulino fell in love with each other in 1974 in Silva Porto when Tito, aged just 19, was released from São Nicolau penal colony and appointed chief of Savimbi's bodyguard. Ana was a teenage secondary schoolgirl in Silva Porto, who later I often saw in the small city. She was beautiful and vibrant, she dressed colourfully, and she always seemed to be surrounded by laughing friends. Tito and Ana agreed to marry and raise a family when there was peace.

Ana Isabel was sent by Savimbi on an advanced secretarial and language course in Paris, from 1977 to 1979, arranged with the French DGSE secret service. When she returned to Jamba, she was appointed head of UNITA's secretarial school, training 20 young women at a time in touch-typing, shorthand, Portuguese, French and English.

When Tito was posted to Morocco in 1980, Savimbi claimed Ana for his own. She was forced to become his 'number one' official wife in his harem of mistresses and concubines. She accompanied him abroad to America and Europe, dressed elegantly in the latest fashions, her presence promoting Savimbi as a modern and sophisticated man.

Before sending Ana to Paris, Savimbi is alleged to have raped Raquel, his own niece, and had also made her one of his concubines. When Raquel's parents protested, they were executed.

Raquel turned up in London in 1982 to begin a college course and assist in the UNITA office. She had, in fact, been sent on a mission by Savimbi to seduce and spy on Tito. How willingly he succumbed I do not know, but he and Raquel were both at that time intensely lonely people bearing almost impossible burdens about terrible events inside the UNITA movement. Nevertheless, succumb he did. Raquel, however, broke down and confessed to Tito the nature of her assignment and how Savimbi had ravaged her and murdered her parents. She begged him to take her or she would, at best, be returned to concubinage with Savimbi, or, more likely, killed like her parents.

'Raquel was an emotional wreck,' said Eduardo Chingunji. 'Having heard her story, Tito told me her situation was so dire that he could not reject her.'

Eduardo believes Raquel fell truly in love with Tito. It was hardly surprising. He had apparently effortless charm. He was young, handsome and highly intelligent, the hero of a whole younger generation back in the Angolan grasslands and forests. He was also her only chance of survival.

Tito was not in love with Raquel, at least not initially, according to Eduardo. 'But I know he felt huge compassion for her,' he said. 'He was also in a classic Catch-22 situation. It spelled danger for him if he spurned her, and he realised that for her it was a clear matter of life or death.'

They married in London, unbeknown to me. There was no public ceremony. In 1983, Raquel became pregnant and at the end of the year visited Jamba. She and her son by Tito, Kaley, born in 1984, were not allowed out again by Savimbi. Raquel subsequently bore twin boys by Tito.

With both Ana and Raquel back in Jamba, living in Savimbi's compound, Savimbi effectively had 24-hour control over Tito, although most of the people continued to think Tito was Savimbi's favourite son.

It was soon after Raquel's return to Jamba that things took a very dark turn. Tito described this to me when we met in Washington in September 1988.

On 7 September 1983, Savimbi summoned everybody to a 'very important rally' on the central parade ground at Jamba. Savimbi's bodyguards and commandos were ordered to ensure that no one missed the event.

As people flowed towards the arena – where international television crews had filmed senior American, British, Portuguese, French and Czechoslovak politicians and officials reviewing Savimbi's troops – they saw a giant stack of wood at its centre and blindfolded men tied to trees at the edge of the parade ground. Savimbi arrived with his senior officers. All were wearing scarlet bandanas and neckerchiefs.

Soldiers were drawn up in battalions and companies to pay military honours to Savimbi on his arrival. Bela Malaquias, who was among the gathered crowds and who later penned an autobiography based on her experiences as a member of UNITA,[1] wrote: 'The atmosphere was one of terror.' Revolutionary songs were chanted by the soldiers. One line, Malaquias recalled, went: 'Friends, just listen to the teachings of our great King, Jonas Savimbi. Only him do we follow!'

Malaquias said there were jugglers, traditional dancers and a karate demonstration before Savimbi rose to speak on a day that would be remembered as *Setembro vermelho* (Red September). According to accounts gathered by Tito, Eduardo Chingunji, Bela Malaquias and

The parade ground at UNITA's Jamba base.
This photo was taken around 1982.

others, Savimbi said witches had been plaguing the movement, causing soldiers to lose their lives on battlefield front lines. Some witches
would this day breathe their last and would no longer be able to
sabotage the war effort, UNITA's leader told the gathering.

An armed detachment walked towards the blindfolded men. The
soldiers lined up, fired and the men slumped dead, still held by their
ropes to the trees.

Savimbi had only just begun.

He ordered every person in the crowd, children also, to pick up a
twig each and cast it on the woodpile. The giant bonfire was lit. *O Mais
Velho* called names of women and asked them to step forward. They,
he said, were witches who had been condemned to death. Some had
children – they too would die with their mothers because 'a snake's offspring is also a snake'.[2] Savimbi's all-women propaganda music troupe,
the so-called *Departamento de Agitacão e Politica* (Department of

Political Promotion), or DAP, applauded and danced to the news. Most DAP members were Savimbi concubines.

Savimbi said what was about to happen would be an example to everyone: people practising witchcraft would be burned. Anyone who defended the condemned women would be in big trouble. 'These witches did not spare the soldiers wounded at the front in defence of the homeland who are now in hospital,' Malaquias recalled Savimbi telling the death rally.

Malaquias went on: 'The military had been convinced by Savimbi that front-line deaths were the result of interventions by women witches. Once they had been manipulated, they worked hard to prepare for the burning alive of the women. They shouted in unison, "Death to the witches!" … All this was being done by a man who hyped himself as the people's saviour.'

The women whose names Savimbi had read out were ordered to stand before the presidential platform. A woman called Judith Bonga was called first. Judith was so shocked that she was unable to move. Commandos grabbed her and threw her into the flames. Eyewitnesses said she jumped from the fire and begged for mercy. Savimbi always wore, at his waist, an ivory-handled pistol that fascinated reporters so much that they made it almost as famous as the man himself. Now he drew the gun and, together with one of his senior generals, forced Judith back into the fire where she perished.

Victoria Chitata begged Savimbi to save her small son, who was dragged with her to the bonfire. No one moved and she and her son died together in the flames. Victoria cried out for someone to save her son, who she said was innocent. No one moved.

Aurora Katalayo, Violeta Chingunji's younger sister and Tito's aunt, was a paediatrician and haematologist who had trained as a doctor in Switzerland. She was also the widow of a popular and outspoken guerrilla commander, Major Mateus Katalayo, who she told relatives and friends had been killed on Savimbi's orders three years earlier. Major Katalayo had publicly castigated Savimbi for trying to break up his marriage. Leon Dash got to know Mateus Katalayo in the course of the first of his two long treks across Angola with UNITA's guerrilla fighters. Katalayo acted as interpreter for Dash. 'I suspected then that the smart, arrogant, blunt-spoken major would eventually clash with Savimbi,' said Dash. 'Mateus was much too cynical to deify any man.'[3]

Aurora Katalayo had resolutely refused Savimbi's invitations to sleep with him either before or after Mateus's death. Aurora, by several accounts, vehemently protested her innocence as she was frog-marched from the crowd with her four-year-old son Michel.

'I've done you no harm. I do not deserve this. After this day, it's the beginning of your end,' Aurora is alleged to have said. She cursed Savimbi's soul aloud, calling him a criminal and warning that he had condemned himself and would never be victorious as she and Michel were pitched into the flames. The proof Savimbi gave of Aurora's witchcraft was the 'Swissification' of Michel and his 12-year-old sister M'Bimbi, but, said Tito and others, she died only because of her resistance to Savimbi's sexual advances.

When Clara Miguel was called to be burned, she had her infant daughter in her arms. According to reports, she did not say anything but tossed her child into the arms of the closest pair of hands before she walked forwards to her death. 'In an act of great betrayal, Clara's husband ran towards her and kicked her (as she advanced towards the fire). I suppose he wanted to demonstrate, such was his panic and fear, that he had nothing to do with the witchcraft of his wife and child and that he unconditionally supported President Savimbi's action to rid the party of all dangerous women,' wrote Malaquias.

One lone man, João Kalitangue, died on the pyre. Kalitangue, a qualified nurse, had for many years cared for Savimbi's mother, Helena Savimbi. Kalitangue's wife, Isabel, a kindergarten teacher, and their four children aged 7 to 15, including a mentally handicapped daughter, and a 12-year-old nephew were also burned to death.

I discovered years later that another woman murdered by Savimbi in the flames was Arleta Navimbi Matos, sister of Tito's wife, Raquel, and yet another of Savimbi's many concubines. Navimbi was pregnant by Savimbi at the time of her death, having already given birth to a daughter by him, Celita Navimbi Sakaita. Her crime, according to Savimbi's witch-finders, was having flown over the UNITA leader's main residence several times to prevent him winning the war.

Tony Fernandes, at the time a senior Politburo member before his defection nine years later, witnessed the burnings. He described them to me as the most horrific events he has ever experienced.[4] Fernandes defected in 1992 and later became Angola's ambassador to Britain from 2005 to 2006.

Ermelindo Kanjungu, who quit the movement to study in Portugal, told *The New York Times*[5] that as a child he had watched the Red September burnings from the crowd. He said the executions by fire were supervised by Savimbi. He described watching some victims trying to flee the flames only to be thrown back on to the fire. Kanjungu, aged 22 at the time of the interview, said that when the children of Aurora Katalayo and João Kalitangue were cast into the flames Savimbi bellowed: 'The party is not going to support the children of witches.'

Kanjungu said he and his fellow students compiled a dossier of atrocities committed under Savimbi. They sent their document to the UNITA leadership with a demand for change. When they were denounced by Savimbi as traitors they decided to go public.

'Savimbi,' said Kanjungu, 'is a leader caught between modern political ideas and African traditional practices. And, of course, to eliminate the opposition is a Stalinist practice.'

Savimbi called a halt after 13 victims had been consumed by the fire.

A remaining group of condemned women, who were to have been

burned, had their heads shaved with broken bottles by traditional healers before they were led away to underground cells where the witch-doctors searched their vaginas for magic charms. The group included 12-year-old M'Bimbi Katalayo, who had just watched her mother and brother die; Eunice Sapassa, one of Savimbi's former lovers; Tita Malaquias, Bela's sister, from one of UNITA's leading families; and Francisca Chingunji Domingos (see Chapter 23).

The reprieved women were led barefoot and made to kneel, in some awful rite, while an old chief smeared their heads, arms and legs with ashes from the pyre on which the others had died. They were pronounced guilty of plotting to overthrow Savimbi and of casting spells that caused setbacks at the front and made soldiers' wounds unhealable.

Several of those detained were subsequently executed over a period of months. Francisca 'Xica' Chingunji was among them. Eunice Sapassa was hacked to death with machetes. M'Bimbi Katalayo was shot dead with three other young girls.

Tita Malaquias, who Savimbi accused of using trigonometry in witchcraft practices, was pardoned and later escaped from prison to tell the tale. Tita's sister Bela, who later wrote the book,[6] was also imprisoned. Bela said many women continued to arrive in the underground pit prisons. Some committed suicide.

Bela, attempting to explain Savimbi's obsession with witchcraft and his relentless drive to dominate women, wrote, 'If they were beautiful, if they had long hair, if they were educated, if they were *petit bourgeois*, if they were unyielding, if they were intelligent, if they were outspoken, if they good relationships with their husbands, they risked being labelled a witch.' Bela said Savimbi socialised his followers into 'evil and anti-social psychopathic behaviour by creating an atmosphere of fear and paranoia'.

Bela was taken to a prison camp deep in the forest.

'There were more than a hundred naked women lined up undergoing a series of rituals,' she wrote. 'I was terrified and tried to understand what I was seeing. A "magic" doll named Yeta, decorated with beads and studded with pins in its head, was placed on the ground. The chief healer approached me and said, "You're staring at me as though you are a white. Get undressed and go to the end of the line." Reluctantly I obeyed. A ventriloquist projected speech onto the Yeta doll, which was asked if one particular woman was a witch. In a squeaky voice, Yeta asserted that she was a witch and should be sentenced to death.'

Malaquias said some of the women were housed in huts while others were confined to pit prisons, from where they were taken at intervals and shot.

In just a few hours, on that day, in Washington in September 1988, Tito had changed so much of my own personal and professional life and future. I had to reappraise fundamentally important and, I believe, historic events in which I had been immersed for more than a decade. Savimbi was not only tyrannising, bestialising and murdering his own people, but he was surely condemning the whole movement to defeat in the long run.

Although Tito knew he had to work insanely hard to protect his family and placate Savimbi's demons, there was more to it than that. The movement his father had believed in, helped found and lead, had come a long way in its quarter century of existence. With a peace breakthrough imminent that could end the civil war, the movement – rather than Savimbi – was so near its founding goal that Tito told me he felt he would be letting down his father, his dead brothers and millions of ordinary UNITA followers if he gave up now. He felt he could not sacrifice the overall cause – that is, UNITA's early ideals – for an immediate settlement of his own family's personal grievances. He said he felt inviolate and indispensable in his diplomatic role: the contacts he had made and the relationships he had forged were essential for Savimbi. 'It is important for me to survive and for multi-party elections to be achieved. There will be a reckoning one day with Savimbi. But not yet. Now it is impossible. Only after the elections.'

Tito believed he was protected by his strong Christian faith. 'I feel that God requires me to pursue the greater cause,' he said.

Tito said there were two people I could trust in the wake of what he had told me: Olga Mundombe, one of his close assistants in Washington, and his nephew Eduardo in London.

Olga, whom I met many times in Washington, and continue to meet, was a member of a leading UNITA family of educationists from Tito's home town of Silva Porto who had fled into exile in Zaire to escape Portuguese rule. Olga had completed degrees in biology and international public health at American universities on missionary scholarships. Eduardo was in London beginning studies for a degree in civil engineering. Eduardo and I became close from the late 1980s onwards, and remain so today.

26

Rumble in the *django* (1988)

Barely three months after the public burning of women and children, in mid-December 1988, Olga phoned me from Washington in a distressed state. She said Tito had been recalled to Jamba on 9 November for a conference with other UNITA overseas representatives to discuss the imminent signing of the New York Accords. He had been due back by 25 November for a scheduled important meeting with black church leaders in Birmingham, Alabama. He also hoped to meet civil rights leader Jesse Jackson. He was further scheduled to be interviewed on three BBC Radio programmes.

Instead, another UNITA leader, Jeremias Chitunda, had arrived in Washington, announcing that Tito had been given new responsibilities in Jamba and would not be returning. Chitunda gave Olga an order from Savimbi to return to Jamba. She refused but pleaded with me to travel there to check that Tito was safe. Rightly or wrongly, she believed that I, as the author of *Jonas Savimbi: A Key to Africa*, was the only person Savimbi might listen to seriously.

Both Olga and Eduardo Chingunji had implored Tito not to return. 'Savimbi will get you, just like the rest of the family,' Eduardo said he had told his uncle. 'He knows he will have to kill every last Chingunji

196

to stop the truth from being known.' Eduardo said he reminded Tito that his trapped sisters had warned him never to return – they might die, but at least someone would survive to tell the story.

But Tito believed he had done such a fine job in Washington that Savimbi could not move against him. He thought he was inviolate because of his major diplomatic achievements, working closely with National Security Adviser Colin Powell, Assistant Secretary of State for Africa Chester Crocker, Herman Cohen, the then presidential adviser on Africa, and with senior CIA officials.

To me, Tito had somehow seemed composed despite his terrible troubles. Olga, one of Tito's closest friends, saw things differently. She told me that Tito felt deeply disturbed and mentally tortured by Savimbi and that he had been on the verge of a nervous breakdown for months. He was drained emotionally and physically and had frequent blackouts and fainting fits.

'The more success Tito achieved (diplomatically), the more Savimbi sent demeaning messages and the more he humiliated the Chingunji family in Jamba, either imprisoning them or punishing them in some other way,' said Olga.

Eduardo said, 'It was driving him crazy. All he knew was that the slightest mistake could cost him his life and that of his entire family.'

Tito's diplomatic successes had gained him international recognition. The achievements were way beyond anything Savimbi could once have dreamed of: funding amounting to hundreds of millions of dollars; supplies of sophisticated weaponry; invitations to meet US Presidents in the White House Oval Office. But Savimbi now argued that Tito had done all this for his own self-renown, not for the honour of the party.

Eduardo said Tito had further discovered that one of his subordinates in the Washington office, Marcos Samundo, was sending secret belittling reports about him back to Savimbi through the UNITA leader's right-wing lobbyists. Sousa Jamba said Savimbi had developed an intricate network of informers, not only Samundo, who reported back to UNITA's leader.

Eduardo, who also asked me to go to Jamba, said he told Tito that all his efforts at compromise had failed. Savimbi had constantly refused to send Raquel and their child to join Tito in Washington. The entire extended Chingunji family in Jamba was being held hostage against his continued loyalty. In early 1988, during one of Tito's visits to Jamba, his wife and surviving sisters and brother urged him never to return. Go out and never come back, they urged. That way, at least, the story of Savimbi's murders would be known to the outside world. 'We'll look after ourselves.'

Tito did briefly consider refusing to go back but quickly rejected the possibility. He had promised the family that the more things he achieved for UNITA diplomatically, he was sure the more things would improve for them.

He had by now again embraced fully the Christian faith of his childhood and believed that God might protect him. But he also knew there was a chance that it could be the end. 'Either all the family live, or we all die together,' he told Olga. 'I would rather die on my feet than live on my knees.'

A few days before he left for Angola, Tito visited Connie Hilliard, Jorge Sangumba's widow, and her second husband, Terrill, in Dallas. 'He said he wanted some respite from politics,' Connie recalled. 'So we spent time showing him some of the sights in Dallas, went out for dinner and relaxed in each other's company, generally avoiding any discussion of Angola. Except when, as Terrill reminded me, Tito said something briefly to the effect that his work in Washington was being undermined and that Savimbi had become critical of what he was doing.'

I agreed to travel to Jamba. I had no choice other than to take the risk. Tito was my friend. He had confided in me. He trusted me implicitly, and I him. I could not have failed him and been able to live with myself.

And so I stepped into one of the most bizarre and dark encounters of my life. I flew to Johannesburg before being picked up by a light plane at Pretoria's small Wonderboom Airport which flew me to Jamba.

Just before midnight on 21 December 1988, I was ushered past guards toting AK-47 rifles into a circular open-sided conference hut, known as a *django,* deep in the forest near Jamba. Savimbi was sitting in a big red chair facing 13 pistol-packing uniformed members of his Politburo. Tito, his face drawn and haunted, sat in the middle of the Politburo men. We hardly dared look at each other.

I cast my eye around the rest of the semi-circle of guerrilla commanders opposite their leader, their faces lit by the glowing red embers of a fire in the centre of the *django*. Some, I knew, were men of extraordinary physical valour. Others, I equally knew, were moral cowards.

Savimbi welcomed me warmly, saying it was always a pleasure to greet me on my ventures into UNITA territory. What had brought me there on this occasion?

I began with what I thought was the blandest possible statement. I had come, I told Savimbi, on behalf of people who were puzzled about why Tito had failed to return from Angola to his high-profile post in Washington. I felt obliged to act on their behalf because, while working closely down the years with Tito on the book, I had come to regard him as my brother.

It was a bad start.

Savimbi exploded. His face contorted. His prominent eyes blazed. The voice that had thrilled countless rallies and bewitched and enchanted foreigners boomed as he berated me. I could almost feel physical shock waves.

'We have always welcomed you, but now you come here in a very arrogant manner puffing yourself up and saying Tito is your brother and getting him into a lot of trouble.'

He fixed his prominent flashing eyes on me, swept his arm towards the Politburo and shouted: 'These are Tito's brothers, the ones sitting around him who have been fighting imperialism in our country, not agents of imperialism like you and others who come to divide us.'

Savimbi raged on.

'You come here with a sense of white superiority thinking you can teach me lessons. I am older than you and all my life I have had to fight white racism, starting with the Portuguese. I never accepted that, and now *you* have come here to insult me; and I have never accepted to be insulted by anyone, not anyone.'

Turning towards his guerrilla chiefs, he roared, 'Haven't I always said that imperialism will try to divide us?' The commanders loyally rejoined, 'Yes, that's right President.' 'Correct, President.' 'Absolutely, President.' Tito, I noticed, also nodded agreement weakly. But I was sure I could see tears welling in his eyes.

Savimbi swung back towards me and continued his tirade, which I estimated lasted more than an hour. I was so close that I could feel the physical force of his anger, like a succession of blast waves. 'I am so insulted by what you have said here that I think maybe you should just go, get out of here.'

Except that there was nowhere I could *just go*. I was as deep in the African bush as it was possible to be – a region with no roads, no towns, no development of any description, other than UNITA bases, for many hundreds of square kilometres, saturated with wildlife and by heavily armed guerrilla fighters fiercely loyal to their Big Man. The only way out was aboard the tiny plane that had flown me in from Pretoria and which was scheduled to return the next morning.

Savimbi went on. 'Our struggle is a big one, bigger than your book. Your book (published the previous year) may be thick (it was 670 pages!), but it is a very thin thing in the history of our struggle. We have survived without it and, if necessary, we can die without it.'

I felt curiously relaxed, but not for long. I did not know it at the time, but Savimbi had just returned from meeting South African President PW Botha in Pretoria. Botha had told him that the next day, 22 December 1988, South Africa would sign the New York Accords with the Cuban government and the MPLA government. The Accords would oblige South Africa to withdraw from Angola and South West Africa/Namibia. Botha had told Savimbi that South Africa intended carrying out the agreement to the spirit and the letter of the law. That meant that all South African assistance to UNITA was stopping with immediate effect. It ensured that Savimbi was already in an ugly mood by the time he saw me.

At one bizarre moment in the *django* – bizarre, because I had neither voiced nor written by this stage a single public allegation against Savimbi – he raised his left palm towards his comrades-in-arms and said to me, 'I don't know what Tito has been telling you, but I can tell you there is not a spot of blood on my hand! Yes, it is true that Tito's parents were killed, but not by me. And these stories that Tito's brothers were also killed by me are lies … You people are making it impossible for Tito to begin his new job. He is in a state of nervousness each day wondering what new story will be coming to divide him from his brothers.'

This made me abruptly aware that Tito was in mortal danger, and perhaps me also. Although I had made no public allegations, I did know by then that Savimbi's hands were soaked in the blood of his own people. But I had no way of knowing whether Tito had confessed that he had revealed to me, just two months earlier, the truth about Savimbi. If he had, it's possible I would not have left Jamba alive.

Savimbi invited opinions of me from his commanders. One of his most sycophantic loyalists sprang to the challenge. Savimbi's nephew General Elias Salupeto Pena attacked my opening remark about completing my book with the help of Tito.

'Do you think,' he sneered, 'that Tito is UNITA? Tito is not UNITA. He is not bigger than UNITA. But the people of UNITA are Tito's true brothers. It is in Angola with his own people that he will be loved and cared for, not by you. The way you come here and insult our president in front of the entire Politburo shows you are very racist.' I had interrupted several times, but here I objected angrily to this latest Pena remark. It had no truth, I said.

Savimbi cut in with a cruel taunt.

'There is you friend Tito. So what do you want to do with him now? Take him to a room where you can discuss alone? Or take him out (of Angola) altogether so that you can be the guarantor of his safety?'

If only it had been possible.

At one point Jorge Valentim, the movement's toadying information secretary, who reminded me of a marabou stork and with whom I had clashed frequently, leaned across to Tito, tapped his knee and hissed, 'These imperialists not only spread all these lies about your family, but they are writing untrue things like "Tito is the most intelligent man of the movement, he is the cleverest one," trying to divide us.' It was a craven and sickening act by Valentim, ingratiating himself with Savimbi by mocking Tito's intellect.

Tito nodded, near to tears in helpless agreement and then, to my relief, joined in the attack. He mumbled disjointedly that I was wrong to speculate that there was any unusual reason for his failure to return to Washington. 'You know yourself, Fred Bridgland, in conversations with me, that you have always asserted the brilliance, like a shining star, of Mr President, who has taught me everything I know.'

It was clear to me that his attack on me was a coded message that, whatever may have happened to him since his return to Jamba, he had not revealed to Savimbi that he had told me earlier the true inside Savimbi story – completely different from the thrust of my book. He had preserved my life by attacking me as he struggled for his own survival.

How totally helpless I felt, although I was aware of the need to stay totally calm and cool. Make a foolish slip and, in the bat of an eye, Tito could be doomed. In that atmosphere I came to realise fully that Savimbi was capable of extreme violence, moved by forces I scarcely understood. And yet he remained brilliant and dynamic, having created resistance to another form of tyranny. But I found myself pondering whether this man seated next to me was now a mad messianic genius, potentially out of control. Would a new kind of monster be unleashed if he came to power?

A profound moral challenge now faced me following this macabre encounter with Savimbi in the African forest. How was this former English council-house boy going to save his friend from this guerrilla chieftain who had learned the arts of war from Mao, Che, Clausewitz, the CIA and the South African Defence Force?

During his prolonged diatribe, Savimbi also made an extraordinary attack on the CIA, whose covert weapons supplies had kept UNITA alive. He said there was a young CIA agent posted in Jamba who had demanded to know where Tito was and to be able to meet him alone. This again was 'imperialism' at work, as far as Savimbi was concerned. The Americans, he said, were stunningly arrogant – for years they had deserted UNITA, and it was only in the last two years they had come back again to help.

'Even I can tell you that much of what they give us is completely useless,' Savimbi said. 'Yes, the Stingers (portable surface-to-air missiles) are very good, and the surgery and video equipment. But the rest is useless. Would you believe it, they send us water here and medicines which are past their date mark.'

As the hideous session wound down, Savimbi, in mercurial fashion, changed mood. He said he was sorry if he had insulted me and suggested I embrace all his comrades. I did so, like an actor in a surreal drama. When I embraced Tito, we got it all wrong, hardly daring to look in each other's eyes, but when I did look briefly those eyes were full of tears. We fluffed the movement's silly handshake, which involved bumping fists like that of some schoolboy gang.

The armed guards escorted me out. As I walked to my hut under the huge African night sky and billions of stars, I heard the sound of laughter from the *django* mocking the white fool in Africa. I scribbled notes on the encounter all night, not daring to fall asleep, as I awaited the arrival of the small plane at daybreak that took me to safety.

There was nothing more I could do in Jamba. I had all the information and clues I needed for the time being. First, it was necessary to get out alive and begin the struggle – I had no idea how – to try to save my friend's life. I was sure that Savimbi must have guessed that Tito had told me everything and that within weeks he would extract a confession from him to that effect.

I learned years later that, just a fortnight before I arrived for the rumble in the *django,* Tito's wife, Raquel, his twin sister, Helena, his younger sister Lulu, his younger brother Dinho and Dinho's wife, Aida, had been subjected to a three-day anti-Chingunji demonstration in Jamba, during which they were beaten and kicked. The demonstration began on 5 December 1988 in front of a big jeering crowd. For part of the time, Angélica Nduva Sebastião, an orphaned distant relative of the Chingunjis, was also subjected to the assault. Angélica, who was later freed and today lives in Huambo, said Dinho tried to shield the women, and especially Helena, who was eight months pregnant, from the worst of the assaults.

'It was a terrible thing,' Angélica said. Dinho was heavily wounded and bruised and his clothes were torn as he tried to resist the mob, who kept yelling that the Chingunjis were traitors. The women, except Angélica, were removed to various pit prisons. Angélica was eventually freed after being subjected to heavy interrogation by Savimbi's security police for about a month. 'I was only a child, but I was interrogated at one of the kangaroo courts, mainly about the Chingunji brothers' and sisters' plans for war against Savimbi. I kept telling them (the interrogators) that they had never spoken to me or others about such a thing. I said that all I knew was that they worked very hard for UNITA's cause, and especially Uncle Tito. I had heard exactly that from the President's own mouth at numerous rallies where he praised his (Tito's) incredible achievements for the Party. So I asked them what exactly did Uncle Tito and his siblings do, other than sacrificing themselves since the 1960s for UNITA and Angola? I was threatened several times with death if I did not cooperate, but I simply did not have anything to say.'

Of course, if I had known of this event at the time I travelled to Jamba I would have known just how extreme the danger was that Tito faced.

27
Death threats (1988–1989)

On my return to London, I immediately contacted Eduardo Chingunji, the son of Samuel Kafundanga Chingunji, the man considered Savimbi's natural heir until his mysterious death in Zambia in 1974.[1]

Eduardo was studying civil engineering at London University in 1988. He was then the only Chingunji at liberty in the outside world. We discussed how we could act on Tito's behalf in ways that would not expose him to Savimbi's wrath or immediate execution.

'I knew intimately the quandary Tito faced, how entangled his life had become,' Eduardo told me. 'He had joined UNITA to honour his father and elder brothers and to complete their unfinished work. He was facing excruciating dilemmas of how to do this work and at the same time hit on a viable solution that would save the remaining members of his family.

'I was full of trepidation about Savimbi's dark Machiavellian side. I was not at peace. I had warned Tito about Savimbi's deviousness.'

Tito and Eduardo were extremely close. Tito shared information and his anxieties on a regular basis with his nephew. It was Eduardo who urged Tito to reveal to me the real inside story of UNITA.

Eduardo and I decided to work through Amnesty International

and other human rights organisations in an attempt to put pressure on Savimbi to release Tito. We faced the severe handicap that we dared not reveal publicly that Tito had briefed us on the real facts: to do so would be to sign his death warrant. When we contacted Western diplomats and Savimbi's right-wing backers to say we believed Tito was in danger of death, they either did not want to believe Savimbi could act in such a way, or they believed Tito must have done something to deserve his leader's wrath.

And then Eduardo and I were confronted with the mysterious disappearance in Washington of Olga. Unknown to us, she had been kidnapped by a UNITA hit squad in scarcely believable circumstances and locked up in a mental hospital.

Within hours of Tito's departure for Jamba, Olga was visited in her Washington house in the middle of the night by three UNITA hitmen. She was told to write a public denunciation of Tito, saying he was plotting to assassinate Savimbi. Knowing it was cruel nonsense, she angrily refused, even when her brother, Emmanuel, a guerrilla major, arrived from Angola and told her she must cooperate and also return to Jamba.

Olga continued to refuse to collaborate. Then, at the beginning of December 1988, she was told that Tito had returned from Jamba to Washington and wanted her to meet him at Dulles International Airport. It was a ruse. Three men, including her brother, arrived in a car, but instead of going to the airport they took her to a private clinic, from where they managed to get Olga, now in an extremely fragile state, committed to Fairfax Hospital in Virginia as a mental patient. Olga assumes they knew the law and that was why her brother was involved because a close relative was needed for her to be committed. 'I still find it incredible that such a thing happened, much more so that it happened to me,' Olga told me.

'I was so shocked, and my story was considered so fantastic and unbelievable that they put me in solitary confinement with a surveillance camera for my own protection. They also gave me drugs to sedate me before they took me in handcuffs to the nearby Woodburn Medical Center for analysis by psychiatrists and other experts who concluded that my story was too fantastic to be credible. But, as you know, it's a true story.

'I decided right from the beginning that I should use some of the time to reach inside myself for some strength, to meditate and find a way of understanding all this evil. So I stayed silent and read and read.

'Ironically, when they eventually let me out of solitary it was the really crazy people who first realised I was not crazy! They kept calling me "nurse". Then one real nurse noticed I was reading newspapers. She began asking questions and she believed my story when I was able to show her newspaper stories about Angola featuring people who had appeared in my account to the doctors.' Olga was discharged and immediately phoned me in London.

Although Eduardo, then aged 23, and I realised we could not tell publicly what we knew about Tito, we decided we had to take some calculated risks because his life was clearly in danger.

We briefed, in confidence, Amnesty International's Angola specialist, Gill Nevins, who had her own sources about troubles within Savimbi's movement. Gill, with whom we liaised closely, issued a series of carefully worded statements that were the first that alerted the world publicly about human rights abuses by Savimbi against his own followers. Gill issued an official Amnesty statement saying: 'We have reports of well-known UNITA officials being extra-judicially executed.'[2]

I also approached a retired MI6 officer who, while still in the service, had been close to Tito but who was now brokering the sale of second-hand Chinese tanks to various Third World countries. While he was clearly deeply disturbed by what I told him, he said he found it impossible to believe that Savimbi could do such things.

In that, he was not unusual. The West's covert Angola actions in the African Great Game were working exceptionally well. With an Angolan peace agreement imminent, admirers of Savimbi believed he would come to power through the ballot box. His powerful backers in high places in the West either did not want to know that Savimbi could behave so evilly or else they chose to believe that Tito had done something so wrong as to deserve his leader's wrath.

We also went to the United States Embassy in Grosvenor Square, ostensibly to help secure a visa for Eduardo to pursue his civil engineering studies in the US, but actually to find someone in the US administration to whom we could tell the story of how Tito's life was threatened by Savimbi, Washington's man. We were ushered into a small backroom and questioned at length by two youngish men who I quickly realised must be CIA. The pair became very flustered, moving in and out of the room – perhaps seeking guidance from CIA head-quarters at Langley, Virginia? – as the questioning went on. We never heard from them again and Eduardo was refused his visa request.

We turned to television. A friendly producer at Channel 4 news service, Julian Norridge, understanding the story and the constraints Eduardo and I were under, made a half-hour programme on the history of the Chingunji family. Both Eduardo and I appeared, saying we believed Tito to be in potential danger while avoiding specific alle-gations against Savimbi that would make it clear Tito had briefed us. Our hope was that the publicity would make it clear to Savimbi that he could not harm Tito without negative consequences for himself.

Eduardo told Channel 4 that he believed Tito's life was in grave danger because he had evidence from his own sources that seven Chingunji family members had already been killed on Savimbi's orders. He said his grandparents – Tito's parents – had been beaten to death. Amnesty International said it had evidence from three reliable sources that Jonatão, 69, and Violeta, 60, were clubbed with rifle butts, kicked and then run over by a truck.

Sousa Jamba, who had won the Shiva Naipaul Memorial Prize following the publication of his novel about Savimbi, *Patriots*,[3] said: 'I am one of many UNITA members who have kept quiet until now about killings inside our movement in the interests of the wider struggle against Cuban and Soviet domination of our country.

'There are others who would like us to say nothing until the MPLA and UNITA are around the table in Luanda with Cubans sailing in shiploads to Havana each day. But the arrest and torture of Tito Chingunji has stretched our loyalty beyond breaking point. If we wait others may die.'

Sousa, in an article for *The Spectator*, headlined 'A Butcher with a Ph.D', said he had broken with UNITA because Savimbi was 'not only authoritarian, but had also presided over atrocities that all but beggar belief ... The way he and his fellow African dictators have treated their fellow blacks make the worst racist seem like a mere schoolboy bully.'[4]

Sousa characterised Savimbi as a highly complex man with many contradictions: 'He loved books and education but shot many intellectuals who fell out with him. He claimed to be fighting for democracy and a *laissez-faire* economy, but set up schools for cadres, of which I am a graduate, teaching Maoism. He claimed to be a democrat, but brooked no criticism ... He allowed a personality cult to evolve around himself. Musicians could only sing songs in his praise; others could write poems as long as they had the obligatory stanza honouring the leader. This cult was fanned by eager sycophants who wanted to be in the good books of the leader.'

Savimbi, said Sousa, had undergone an astonishing transformation from Chinese-supported revolutionary to conservative-backed 'freedom fighter'.[5]

Sousa, a highly educated and sophisticated man, surprised me one day in London when he came to my home in a highly nervous state. He said he believed that he had been bewitched by Savimbi as he slept.

From that moment Sousa's trenchant public criticisms of UNITA's leader dried up.

All hell broke loose after the Channel 4 documentary was screened on 12 March 1989.

UNITA representatives around the world gave press interviews saying Eduardo and I had been paid by the Angolan government to fabricate lies.

We received death threats by telephone night after night from Paris, Lisbon, Dakar and Abidjan, all capital cities where UNITA had overseas representatives. When a UNITA hit squad was rumoured to have arrived in London, Kathryn, from whom I was now separated, invited Eduardo to stay with her in Edinburgh and use her and my daughters' home as a safe house. Eduardo stayed with Kathryn for more than a month. Meanwhile, I received protection in London from Scotland Yard's Special Branch.

A big UNITA delegation featuring some of the movement's heaviest hitters, including Jardo Muekalia and Tony Fernandes, who was yet to defect, turned up in London and asked to meet Dinho and me in a hired room in a London hotel. It was March 1989 and the start of a series of events. They told us we should abandon our campaign because Tito was safe and well in Jamba: he was deeply disturbed by the stories beginning to appear about him in the outside world. Letters from Tito were given to both of us. Mine, dated 24 January 1989, in Tito's neat, clear handwriting, read:

To Fred Bridgland

I'm writing this letter to you wishing you well. I'm doing well and fine. I hope your family is well. Please give to each one of them my best regards.

Here I'm once more talking to you through this letter about matters that matter to me deeply and profoundly.

Through the many years I've worked with you we have shared different experiences as we went along. All was based and still is about the struggle of the Angolan people with UNITA.

Since 1987 we, that is me and you, started in Washington talking about my life and family in UNITA. We then broke the agreement which we respected in mutual acceptance while working for the book: to respect your free opinion without imposing our views and you would also not ask me about internal matters.

Everything that I told you, I want you to know from this moment that history will prove that Dr Savimbi is the only one that protected and still protects our family. Without him my family would not have survived at all.

I asked you to help me in every capacity possible. You said you could, indirectly through others, put articles in the papers as a means of exposing human rights violations in UNITA.

I want to ask you very honestly and sincerely: Please drop everything. When you came over last time Dr Savimbi asked you if you wanted to speak to me privately, you said no. I also said it was not necessary.

I committed personal insults to Dr Savimbi. Despite it all, he protects me every day. I hear you want to organise pressure groups in my support. I'm not in jail and never have been. Everything you, or anybody else, can do is create problems for me, stopping my brothers in the struggle to trust me.

I told you, Fred, that I will never quit Angola to stay abroad. I will never live in exile, whatever the reason. I still maintain this conviction. I joined UNITA because UNITA is the true liberation movement of the Angolan people. The MPLA or any other movement in Angola have no experience or capacity to truly help and meet the needs of the Angolan people.

I ask you to drop everything. I will fight against you if you insist. I'm an Angolan and I will remain so, come what may. The millions of Angolan families have given more than my family alone. I can't be selfish nor betray them. I'm with them for ever.

My best wishes to you and your family.

From

Tito Chingunji

I was outraged. So was Eduardo. We knew that Savimbi's team was lying and they knew that we knew they were lying. They all looked rather crestfallen. I remonstrated particularly angrily with Jardo Muekalia, whom Tito had mentored and worked with closely in London and Washington. I didn't give anything away that I already knew, but I told Jardo that this meeting was a cynical farce. I said angrily that I did not believe a word of Tito's letter. I told Muekalia that Tito had always supported and trusted him, but now he was betraying his own friend.

It was obvious to both me and to Eduardo that the letters from Tito had been written under immense duress. Tito used certain phrases that he and Eduardo had agreed beforehand would be code phrases indicating that he was in trouble – for example, 'The president always protects me,' and 'Eduardo, concentrate on your studies.'

The letters signalled that Savimbi was highly alarmed by the doubts being cast on his democratic credentials. I had no way of knowing whether our gamble had increased or decreased Tito's chances of survival. But Eduardo was in no doubt: 'After finishing reading the letters, I realised that the end of Tito had finally come. Our worst fears had been confirmed and I sat there in disgust. Tito had not even been allowed to return to Washington to collect his personal belongings.

'I felt sick as it all sank in. I told Muekalia I did not buy the story and that I was not going to allow Savimbi to get away with this one. Jardo was so nervous that he was not prepared to talk.'

Eduardo subsequently received information that a UNITA student conference in Jamba had denounced him as a traitor and that there were chants calling for his death. And eight years later, in 1997, some of the men who had participated in assaults on Tito, ordered by Savimbi, confirmed to Eduardo that Tito had written the letter to me while he was being beaten up.

'After he had finished,' said Eduardo, 'they told me Savimbi was impressed by the way Tito put the plea to Fred and gave him a rest from the beatings. They continued the following day.'

After Fernandes defected from UNITA in 1992, he too described to me how Tito was ordered by Savimbi to write the letters after first being beaten and tortured by security men.[6]

I showed my letter to the former MI6 agent who had been close to Tito. As he read between the lines he was visibly deeply shocked. He had little, if any, time to take action. He died a short time afterwards. I have no idea whether or not he passed on the information to active agents.

28
Show trial (1988)

What Eduardo and I did not, and could not, know at that time was that Tito had been arrested, tortured and put on trial before a kangaroo court from the moment he arrived in UNITA territory on 10 November 1988 from Washington, via London.

As Tito stepped from the small plane at Likua, north of Jamba, he was surrounded by hundreds of presidential commandos and security guards. Tito's own personal security detachment was immediately arrested, and he was taken to Bembua, Savimbi's luxurious lakeside[1] residence beyond Jamba, where his show trial began immediately. Tito's most loyal bodyguard, known as 'Little Tito', was beaten up so badly by Savimbi's commandos that his jaw was broken. He managed to flee and tried to reach Zambia to tell the story of what was happening to an international audience. He was caught and shot as he tried to cross the border river swamps into Zambia.

Tito's trial was presided over by one of Savimbi's ultra-loyal nephews, Elias Salupeto Pena, a man who proved as ruthless as his uncle. Tito was charged, along with Wilson dos Santos (his twin sister Helen's husband who worked at UNITA's Vorgan radio station), Savimbi's 'wife' Ana Isabel, and another senior official, Jeremias

Chitunda, of conspiring to overthrow and kill Savimbi.

During the initial hearing, orchestrated by Savimbi, the UNITA leader's bodyguards stormed into the giant meeting hut and dragged Tito outside, according to eyewitness João Vahekeny.[2] Vahekeny, UNITA's representative in Switzerland, had been summoned, with all the movement's other overseas officials, to attend the trial.

According to Vahekeny, and others who gave detailed information to Eduardo Chingunji, Tito was heavily beaten by Savimbi's guards. Those in the meeting hall heard Tito's screams and pleas to Savimbi to spare his life. When Tito returned inside, his immaculate clothes were in tatters and he was in tears, apparently already a broken man, according to Vahekeny.

Eyewitnesses said they saw Tito crawling and rolling around in mud as Savimbi's men kicked him and hit him with rifle butts. The guards could be heard shouting at Tito to confess to treason. He was charged in the meeting by Salupeto Pena of being a CIA agent and plotting to topple Savimbi. Savimbi cited black American churches as mentors and sponsors of the version of witchcraft in which Tito was allegedly involved. The 'evidence' of Tito's 'witchcraft' was a white surplice he sometimes wore when praying and which was found in his luggage.

Throughout the trial, Tito was taken from the meeting at intervals for renewed beatings. He survived all these beatings.

'None of us could protest at what was happening to Tito,' Tony Fernandes, who also witnessed Tito's crushing, told me: 'I looked at him and knew he was no longer himself. If I had been in his situation, I think I would have killed myself.'[3]

For the other overseas representatives, the brutality showed they could not dare to step out of line without dire consequences. Vahekeny told me and Eduardo confidentially, in February 1989, that he and other UNITA diplomats had been ordered by Savimbi to return to the outside world and argue convincingly that Tito had had to assume, at short notice, the newly created post of deputy secretary general. The post required him to be based in Jamba and therefore he would not be seen abroad for a considerable time. Vahekeny said another part of the cynical lie required him and others to say Tito, the UNITA architect of the peace process, was now working on a new UNITA strategy for eventual elections. Vahekeny said all the representatives knew full well that the story they were obliged to tell was a reprehensible lie. He told us Tito could be killed at any moment: he urged me and Eduardo to 'do something' to save Tito's life before it was too late. Vahekeny had previously also nervously urged me by telephone, in November 1988, to travel to Jamba to demonstrate concern for Tito's situation.

Vahekeny was a member of the Kuanyama tribe in southern Angola whose territory stretches across the border into Namibia. Vahekeny was worried at the time about the silence of his leader, the Kuanyama chieftain Antonio Vakulukuta, one of the founding members of UNITA. It was later established that Vakulukuta was already one of Savimbi's many victims. After a serious argument with Savimbi, the UNITA leader ordered the killing of his comrade, who was beaten to death by Savimbi's bodyguard. Vakulukuta died a lingering death in a bush hospital. UNITA eyewitnesses said he had been beaten so badly that his face was unrecognisable.[4]

Tito was moved among UNITA's chain of prisons, some in underground pits, others in shipping containers. His locations were kept secret except to Savimbi's closest confidants and guards. Savimbi delegated another nephew, Esteves Kamy Pena, an exceptionally cruel man who headed a death squad, to supervise Tito's imprisonment. Pena was told by Savimbi that Tito could be allowed to appear in public only selectively, for example when top American personalities known to be staunch UNITA supporters visited Jamba, to show that Tito was on active duty. Such visitors were never allowed to meet

Tito in private, only in the company of Savimbi's security men.

Following prolonged periods of torture, Tito was found guilty in a succession of show trials – presided over by Savimbi – with treason, working with the CIA to topple Savimbi, witchcraft and adultery with Ana Isabel Paulino. Tito admitted he and Ana had had an affair on the occasions when she had to visit Paris on UNITA business, but he denied the other allegations.

Three weeks after Tito's return from Washington, Savimbi ordered a large demonstration in Jamba against most of Tito's surviving close relatives: his wife Raquel, his twin sister Helena, his young sister Lulu, and his younger brother Jonatăo 'Dinho' and his wife, Aida.

First, on 5 December 1988, a new Savimbi brownshirt mob, The Revolutionary Organisation of the Students of Free Angola (Organisačo Revolucionário dos Estudantes de Angola Livre), destroyed the timber-and-thatch house in which the Chingunji relatives were living. They were then taken to a parade ground where they were accused of treachery and subjected to beatings in front of a large crowd. Jonatăo 'Dinho' was particularly heavily beaten when he tried to protect his wife, sisters and sister-in-law. 'Dinho was seen desperately shielding the women and children from the violent blows of the mob,' said Eduardo Chingunji.

Savimbi's commandos had encircled the area to prevent anyone from escaping. For most people who witnessed the horror, that was the last they saw of Dinho and the rest of the Chingunjis, although Helena did manage to say to Tita Malaquias, after the beatings, 'My cousin, I truly believe that Savimbi won't rest until he has killed each one of us, the Chingunjis, and I believe beyond doubt that sooner or later he is going to have his way.'

Helena, eight months pregnant at the time, was taken away to a distant detention camp. Shortly after she had given birth to a daughter she named Maezinha, both Helena and her infant child were executed.

Their final resting place is unknown.

Lulu disappeared forever and is presumed by Eduardo to have been killed in May 1989, on Savimbi's orders, by Kamy Esteves Pena's death squad. She was aged 28.

Jonatão 'Dinho' tried to escape to Zambia but was caught and beaten before being taken to one of Savimbi's secret prisons from where he disappeared forever, allegedly at the hands of Kamy Pena's squad. Eduardo Chingunji remembers Dinho's wife Aida as 'beautiful, phlegmatic and soft-spoken ... a docile and harmless person who never engaged in any politics.' She and her three children were taken away by a group of men commanded by one of Savimbi's secret police chiefs. They were never seen again. 'No one has ever come forward with any credible fresh information about how and when they were murdered,' said Eduardo.

Raquel and her three children by Tito were removed to a secret prison camp.

Meanwhile, Helena's husband, Wilson dos Santos, who was working in UNITA's Vorgan radio station, was arrested, charged with treason, severely beaten and jailed in one of Savimbi's pit prisons. Wilson had been looking after his three oldest children, Koly, Rady and Paizinho, by Helena; the children were sent to stay with a cousin and were later murdered.

A distant Chingunji cousin, Ulla Stella Chingunji, said she last saw her relatives at the 5 December 1988 rally where they were denounced and beaten. 'When they were being led by some soldiers, I called to them and asked where they were going. They only gave me a shy wave and shrugged. When I told my mother what I had seen, she begged me not to talk about it or mention the names of my Chingunji family again. It was confusing for me as a child. The image of them being led away without being able to talk to me remains stuck in my mind and eats away at me every time I think about them.'

Our quandary remained that we still could not reveal publicly what we knew about Savimbi's atrocities and threats. The only hopeful outcome of Eduardo's and my efforts – working with Amnesty International and Channel 4, talking to diplomatic and intelligence contacts – was that Savimbi now felt the need to parade Tito during nearly every visit to Jamba by foreign dignitaries: most of them saw Tito in military uniform with a pistol by his side (but without bullets), and most dismissed as nonsense our suggestions that he was in any kind of danger.

Typical was a visit by British Liberal Democrat MP Sir Russell Johnston, who had become an advocate of UNITA's cause, having been briefed and charmed by Tito. Sir Russell, who led the Scottish branch of his party for fourteen years, visited Savimbi in March 1989, after the show aired, and said on his return to London that he had spent an hour alone with Tito.

'He was certainly fit and well and denied having been tortured,' Sir Russell told reporters. 'Chingunji did not seem constrained. I watched him carefully while Savimbi gave a press conference and he laughed at the jokes as heartily as anyone.'

Sir Russell, one of the many Western liberal friends Tito had persuaded of UNITA's democratic credentials, said Tito explicitly told him he could not understand why Eduardo and I had suggested his life might be in danger. 'He (Tito) is very embarrassed by it all.'

The credulity of Sir Russell and others was a bitter blow. The British politician's remarks were widely reported.

At least we knew Tito was still alive.

29

Dark times (1989)

I was recruited in April 1989 by a Sunday newspaper to report, from Johannesburg, on South Africa's epic transition from apartheid to democracy.[1] Given my youthful ideals about the abhorrence of apartheid, it was a huge privilege to be posted to South Africa at such a historic time. But truth be told, Tito was weighing more heavily on my mind than Nelson Mandela on 11 February 1990 when, in the Cape, I watched the great South African make his sweet walk to freedom after 27 years of imprisonment.

From Johannesburg I continued to coordinate with Eduardo, Olga and Amnesty International's Angola specialist, Gill Nevins. Opportunities kept arising to pressurise Savimbi over Tito. Researchers and journalists passing through Johannesburg on their way to Jamba used to drop in to my office and ask to be briefed about Savimbi and Angola. I hoped Tito might be safe as long as questions were constantly asked about his wellbeing.

What I did not know for certain at the time I moved home to Johannesburg was whether or not Tito was being physically tortured. I now know that he was and that he must have been in uttermost despair when Savimbi executed his beloved youngest sister, Lulu, and other relatives. All his diplomatic efforts and personal sacrifices had failed to save them.

Tito particularly interested Shawn McCormick, a young analyst from Washington's Center for Strategic and International Studies. Tito's respect had grown for the skill with which Shawn helped him to establish Angola Task Forces in both houses of Congress, which kept more than US$80 million a year rolling to Savimbi from US government coffers.

'I soon heard about Tito when I first arrived in Washington,' Shawn told me. 'He was absolutely critical to UNITA's success. He was comfortable with Congressmen, heads of think-tanks and national security advisors, which helped UNITA transcend from the stupid right to moderate Democrats and Republicans.'

The bipartisanship of the Task Forces was Tito's remarkable achievement, said Shawn: 'When the Angolan government itself couldn't be seen anywhere on the Hill, in walks this young Angolan guy and gets a powerful caucus set up. He had a grace, a charm and a gentle humour about him. He dressed well, but not flashily. He spoke flawless English. He was highly diplomatic and never aggressive. Dennis DeConcini, chairman of the Senate Intelligence Committee, and Dave McCurdy, chairman of the House of Representative's Select Intelligence Committee, became close to Tito and played crucial roles in channelling covert aid to UNITA.

'His presentations were high quality – well prepared, delivered well and well received. For those who didn't like the movement, he made UNITA palatable. Detractors came away respecting him and with a different view of UNITA.'

Shawn called on me in Johannesburg on his way to Jamba in August 1990. By then, the so-called Border War had come to an end and the South African military had withdrawn from South West Africa, which gained independence as the Republic of Namibia in March that year. While the civil war continued in Angola, great progress was being made with peace negotiations. In May 1991, the MPLA and UNITA would sign a peace accord at Bicesse, 23 kilometres outside Lisbon.

I decided to tell Shawn everything I knew about what was truly happening and he became an invaluable ally in the attempt to keep Tito alive.

Tito was produced, on Savimbi's orders, in Jamba for a meeting with Shawn in the full uniform of a brigadier, with a holstered pistol at his waist. It was one of the last occasions on which Tito was produced in public. Despite a promise by Savimbi that he would be allowed a private conversation with Tito, Shawn was not allowed to speak with him alone. But as everyone walked from one meeting to the next, Shawn managed to sidle up alongside Tito and to tell him that Eduardo, Olga and I sent our love and had not forgotten him. Shawn reported back to me.

'I told him I had met with you and that you had told me the truth about his situation and the kangaroo court. He did not at first look at me directly. But he briefly turned towards me, and his eyes were filled with tears as though about to burst. He walked away. This was not the same Tito I had got to know in Washington. This chill ran down my spine because I felt that I was looking at a dead man. I just knew it would be the last time I would see him alive.'

Later, at a briefing by UNITA officers for Shawn and other visitors, Shawn tried to make eye contact with Tito, who sat at a table opposite him. 'No one talked to him or looked at him. Tito just stared the whole time at an overhead projector screen, even after the projector was switched off. I'll just never forget that.'

Shawn also managed to speak briefly with Wilson dos Santos, Tito's brother-in-law who had been charged with him in the mock trial in 1988, who said he had not been allowed to meet Tito for nearly two years. Shawn said he believed Wilson must have been released temporarily from house arrest to show that everything was normal.

On his return to Washington, Shawn tried to persuade government and intelligence officials that Tito and Wilson were in extreme danger. Few wanted to know.

'It was too heretical to speak out against Savimbi in Washington at that time,' said Shawn. 'You just got drowned out. There was near agreement on holding elections, with Savimbi, Washington's man, as the likely winner. They knew what had happened to Sangumba, but it had been widely forgotten. They clearly thought the same thing would happen with Tito.'[2]

Shawn said that if UNITA wanted to refute the claims about Tito and Wilson, all Savimbi needed to do was produce them in a neutral setting. 'If Savimbi lets them come to Washington with their families and speak freely then I will believe (that they are not prisoners),' he told me. Shawn added that he even knew someone who was willing to pay their plane fares.

Radek Sikorski, then a young UK-based journalist and later Poland's foreign minister, between 2007 and 2014, spent three months with Savimbi's guerrillas in 1989 after visiting me at my home in London. He tried to meet Tito, but wrote in an article that senior UNITA officials repeatedly evaded his requests to talk to him.

'The CIA officer on the spot thought that the allegations (of killings and human rights abuses) were sufficiently grave to confront Savimbi, after which the officer was withdrawn from Jamba, with the United States apparently bowing to Savimbi's ultimatum,' said Sikorski. 'The two defectors (Puna and Fernandes[3]) and a journalist (Bridgland) who revealed the allegations in the Western press have received repeated death threats … Savimbi has ended up believing his own propaganda. He cannot bear men of independent thought around him, and, instead of sharing our wariness of autocratic power, his officers accord him the reverence due to a traditional despotic African chief.

'In the beginning there was Savimbi's word, and the word became UNITA … UNITA has only one noted poet and lyricist – Jonas Savimbi himself. All institutions are mere appendages to his personal rule.

'Any person travelling with UNITA who has learned about the Soviet Union would feel as though they were touring a showpiece Soviet farm. Everything seems perfect on the surface, if the guides are to be believed, but once one tried to find out for oneself going beyond the established programme, armed guards would physically stop you "for protection" even though the enemy was a thousand miles away.

'He (Savimbi) remains an unrepentant Maoist … We can certainly admire his energy, charisma and craftiness. But let us have no illusions.'[4]

Sikorski was not the lone person having misgivings about Savimbi. Shana Wills, a senior researcher at Washington's Institute for Policy Studies, was a frequent visitor to Jamba. In her reports, she depicted Savimbi as charming, intelligent, articulate, dangerous and evil. She described how one US State Department official who had met Savimbi more than twenty-five times told her that each time he met the rebel leader he felt he was in the presence of 'pure evil'. She said the official frequently had to spend return flights from Savimbi's territory 'deprogramming African-American delegations who were charmed into thinking that Savimbi's vision for Angola was the right one.'

I was desperate to persuade UNITA's mentors in the US government that Tito was in extreme danger. I wrote to Hank Cohen, then the US Assistant Secretary of State for African Affairs, on 17 November 1991 pleading with him to use his influence with Savimbi to ensure Tito's survival. I wrote: 'I would be grateful for your advice on whether or not Tito Chingunji is still alive, and for assurances that Washington is exerting pressure for his freedom.' Cohen never replied.

One of Tito's American contacts, the activist Florence Tate, met

Cohen to make the same plea. He said he would see what he could do but again never replied. Senior researcher at Washington's Center for Strategic and International Studies Gillian Gunn also met him. Cohen told Gillian there was nothing he could do.

Later, on one of my visits to Washington to see Olga, we phoned a contact in the office of Cohen who by then had left government and become a highly paid political consultant. The contact said he would try to put us in touch with CIA people who had liaised closely with Tito. He eventually faxed a reply to Olga: 'Sorry, they don't want to talk about it: they don't even want to think about it.'

No one wanted to know at the highest level, apparently because a ballot-box victory was envisaged for Savimbi in a multi-party general election scheduled for 29 and 30 September 1992 – the first election since independence, after seventeen years of war and an estimated one million deaths.

Shawn McCormick said officials like Cohen were scared that the whole Angola peace process was in danger of being derailed, so he began his own disinformation campaign to prop up Savimbi. 'All he and other officials see is the elections,' said Shawn. 'And after that it's down to the Angolans.'

My advanced lesson in ruthless realpolitik progressed further when Democratic Senator Edward Kennedy's top researcher, Nancy Soderberg, called at my office on her way to Jamba in June 1991. Nancy, who later became US Ambassador to the United Nations, believed Tito was in trouble. I briefed her on how much trouble he faced and suggested she use her influence by writing to General Colin Powell to secure his help.

I knew General Powell had had dealings with Tito. During a visit I made to Washington in early 1988, Tito's phone rang and he apologised that he would have to break off our meeting. General Powell, then President Ronald Reagan's National Security Advisor, wanted him to go to the White House immediately to discuss business.

Nancy persuaded Senator Kennedy to write to Powell, who by now had moved from the White House to become Chairman of the Joint Chiefs of Staff in the Department of Defense. Kennedy told Powell: 'There are credible reports that he (Tito) had been tortured by UNITA and that his life is in danger.'

In his reply to Kennedy, Powell wrote, 'I don't believe I know Mr Chingunji and to the best of my knowledge I did not meet him during the long time I was National Security Advisor.'[5]

30

Tito is alive, says Savimbi (1992)

In early February 1992, Savimbi paid an official visit to Cape Town for pre-election talks with FW de Klerk, South Africa's last white state president. Savimbi called a press conference at the five-star Mount Nelson Hotel on the flanks of Table Mountain to proclaim his commitment to peace, justice and democracy.

A journalist friend, Chris McGreal of the London *Guardian*, and I plotted an ambush.

Savimbi paid tribute to South Africa's moves towards democracy and compared it to the Angolan peace process. Nelson Mandela by now had been free from imprisonment for two years. Answering questions, Savimbi confidently predicted that he would be elected president when Angolans went to the polls in September that year.

Savimbi did not know I was among the assembled journalists. I sat hidden by a pillar from his view at the back of the packed conference, but after a few questions I rose and asked my own.

'Can you tell the international community whether Tito Chingunji is still alive?'

If Savimbi was shaken by seeing me for the first time since the rumble in the *django* more than three years earlier, he did not show it.

'Yes, of course, Tito is alive and well, doing his job as deputy secretary-general and looking forward to the election campaign,' Savimbi told me and the other reporters.

Up rose Chris McGreal, as planned, from the other side of the room to ask why Savimbi did not simply put the whole Tito Chingunji controversy to rest by letting foreign correspondents talk to him.

Savimbi nodded like a sage and replied, 'No problem, you will meet him in Luanda soon and you'll be able to put your questions.'

Chris asked whether that was a promise. 'For certain,' said Savimbi. 'We don't want to display him as an instrument of propaganda. He is fed up with these demands. He just wants to get on with his job.'

As long practised, Savimbi turned on his formidable charm. Tony Fernandes, Savimbi's veteran comrade (yet to defect), cornered me and said 'The President' would like to talk to me. My heart sank, but following his promise that we would soon meet the living Tito it would have looked petulant to refuse. So dreamlike was my state during our conversation that I scarcely remember what was said, except for an assurance by Savimbi that Tito and I would soon meet.

That was good news. All our efforts seemed to have kept Tito alive and now, when he appeared in public in Luanda, it would thereafter be difficult for Savimbi to kill him.

Except that Tito was already dead.

31
Tito is dead (1991)

Seven months before his press conference in Cape Town in February 1992, Savimbi had summoned his executioners and ordered them to kill Tito, aged 36, and every remaining living member of the central Chingunji family and some of its more remote relatives.

On 5 July 1991, Kamy Pena, the commander of the execution squad, took Tito and Wilson dos Santos to a forest grove, where my friend and his brother-in-law were bludgeoned to death with rifle butts. I can't begin to imagine the terror and despair of it all for Tito and Wilson, both fine men.

Tito and Raquel by now had three children, including new-born twins, Katimba and Jonatão, born in a pit prison and not yet a year old. Raquel was beaten to death by a separate execution squad. The twins and first-born Kaley also were killed.

Tito's twin sister Helena, Wilson's wife, and their three children were shot dead. Tito's one surviving brother, Dinho, had by now 'disappeared' and has never since been seen again. He is presumed to have been executed. Dinho's wife, Aida, and the couple's three children were shot dead.

By the time the slaughter finished, there was not a single Chingunji left alive in Savimbi's territory, except for a few remote cousins.

I should perhaps have guessed the enormity of Savimbi's Cape Town lie, the obscenity of his guarantee.

I flew home to Johannesburg immediately after the press conference. In the early hours of the following morning, at about 3 am, the phone rang. This time Savimbi's attack dogs did not threaten my life. Instead they described to me how they intended ravishing and mutilating my partner, Sue. (My wife of many years, Kathryn, and I had by then separated and divorced.) I disconnected the telephone and we retreated for a few days into the Magaliesberg Mountains to the north of Johannesburg where there was no phone connection.

It was only in March 1992 – eight months after Tito's execution and one month after the Cape Town press conference where Savimbi had lied so grossly – that it was confirmed Tito had been murdered. Miguel N'Zau Puna, who for decades was Savimbi's loyal second-in-command, and Tony Fernandes, who co-wrote the UNITA constitution, defected while they were together in Lisbon. They called a press conference, and both said Tito had been executed on 5 July 1991 by Esteves Kamy Pena's death squad on Savimbi's orders. Puna had seen Tito's body.

Fernandes, in a subsequent meeting with me,[1] said the final time he had seen Tito was in early May 1991, two months before his death. Fernandes had been ordered by Savimbi to arrange a reception for a visit by Bill Richardson, a senior Democratic Party US Congressman who had been won over by Tito. Richardson later became Secretary of Energy and then Ambassador to the United Nations under the Bill Clinton presidency.

Fernandes had not seen Tito for several months. But youth rallies had been held at which young guerrillas, Tito's natural constituency, were told he had been plotting to kill Savimbi with help from a CIA faction.

'Savimbi built up the hatred against Tito for the day when he would kill him,' said Fernandes. 'He had to prepare young soldiers' minds because Tito was bright, youthful himself and loved by the youth.'

Savimbi needed to take his time because for years he had bragged that Tito was more to him than a son, that he was the best of his generation. 'That's what we all saw,' said Fernandes. 'We thought that Tito, of all the Chingunjis, would be spared. But Savimbi's love was calculated to within an inch to prepare Tito's smooth disappearance in a way that could not be questioned.'

Tito had been put on trial a long time before he was killed. The prosecutors, said Fernandes, charged that he had worked with the CIA to topple Savimbi; that he had joined a black American church to acquire witchcraft powers to reinforce his plot against the president; and that he had had an affair with Ana Isabel Paulino, the president's number-one wife. They said it was unforgivable that someone who had climbed so high had behaved so treacherously.

'It was a show trial,' said Fernandes. 'The people were moulded to believe there was a traitor among us. Only those designated by Savimbi could speak. No one could express dissent: it was forbidden to criticise *O Mais Velho*.

'Tito never did anything to undermine Savimbi. What offended Savimbi most was the fact that Ana Isabel never stopped loving Tito or appealing to him to save her (from Savimbi). I believe Tito never stopped loving her. There was nothing else against Tito – it all rested on Ana Isabel.'

Ahead of Congressman Richardson's visit, Fernandes was allowed to see Tito in prison but was not allowed to speak with him.

'I was deeply shocked when I saw how thin he had become: his clothes hung loosely on him. I was in charge of organising Savimbi's receptions for foreign visitors and persuaded him to begin feeding Tito properly. By the time Richardson arrived, Tito had put on weight. He told Richardson he was well and there were no problems.

He wore a pistol with no bullets. He went straight back to prison when Richardson left.'

Just before Richardson's visit, Raquel had given birth in her own pit prison to the twins, Katimba and Jonatão.

In December 1991, with Angola's first general election just nine months away and the administration of the then US President George HW Bush confident that Savimbi would win, Fernandes began preparing for another high-powered congressional visit. It was led by one of Tito's closest Democratic Party friends, Dave McCurdy, chairman of the House of Representatives' powerful Permanent Select Intelligence Committee. Tito had worked closely with McCurdy in setting up the Congressional Angola Task Forces. Another Tito admirer, Senator Dennis DeConcini, a Democrat from Arizona, chairman of the Senate's Intelligence Committee, was a member of the McCurdy delegation.

Tito's huge success diplomatically had been to make UNITA, once despised as a tool of apartheid, a credible force whose arguments were difficult to dismiss, in diplomatic circles, in foreign ministries and even among some journalists whose basic sympathies were with the MPLA.

By the time McCurdy and DeConcini were due to visit, Savimbi had moved out of his secure Jamba base deep in the forest to Luanda to prepare for the election. He bought a luxurious house, ironically named Casa Branca (the White House), in the posh diplomatic suburb of Miramar, as his campaign headquarters. In Luanda he demonstrated why he was widely considered to be one of Africa's most electrifying demagogues. 'Crowing like a cock and flailing his arms wildly, with his flashing eyes and nationalistic rhetoric, he whipped a crowd of 10 000 at one final campaign rally into a near-hysterical frenzy,' wrote the *Chicago Tribune*'s Africa correspondent Liz Sly. 'His supporters are confident that Savimbi, with his populist appeal and stirring oratory, will soon be sworn in as Angola's first democratically elected president.' Sly added that all this was 'in no small part due to the influence of Tito

Chingunji, UNITA's hugely popular Washington representative', who had unaccountably 'disappeared'.[2]

McCurdy did not merely request to see Tito. He demanded it. Fernandes told me he climbed fast the sweeping Casa Branca stairs to Savimbi's private quarters to brief his leader and suggest that Tito be fattened again and smartened up once more before meeting McCurdy and DeConcini.

'Savimbi,' said Fernandes, 'looked at me and said, "But Tony, don't you know? I had Tito killed a long time ago. Go away. Don't bother me." It was only then that I realised Tito was no longer alive. I was shocked and frightened. If he could kill Tito he could kill any of us. The first person I saw in the Meridien Hotel, where I was staying, was Puna. I told him what I had just heard from Savimbi and that for me it was the end. Savimbi is finished and I have to abandon UNITA.'[3]

Miguel N'Zau Puna told Fernandes he was already planning to defect. Puna, said Fernandes, had known for months that Tito had been murdered. Hours after both Tito and his brother-in-law Wilson were killed at dawn, on 5 July 1991, Puna was ordered by Savimbi to verify that the execution squad led by Esteves Kamy Pena had carried out his orders.[4]

Puna, in an autobiography,[5] said Savimbi told him: 'Little Brother, Security has eliminated Tito and Wilson and I'm not able to sleep because I'm not sure if they have really been eliminated or whether they managed to escape to Zambia. If they have gone to Zambia that will be very serious for the party. I have sent for you, my long-time companion, to go with Kamy to identify the bodies.'

Puna said he was consumed by fear when his own personal bodyguard was dismissed by Kamy Pena before he was taken to the execution site, beyond Jamba. 'I found the situation very strange and disturbing,' he said. 'I immediately began to think my time had come.'

At the edge of a clearing there was already a group of commandos wearing masks digging up two bodies from a shallow grave. 'Not having prayed for many years, I thought it was the perfect time to begin again. I recalled my childhood schooldays, and I am sure I asked God to forgive me for wrongs I had done.'

Puna advanced towards the two-hours-old bodies, blindfolded and lying side by side as they were exhumed. Their heads were terribly fractured and swollen, as though smashed with clubs, but they were still perfectly recognisable as Tito and Wilson. Puna concluded that Kamy Pena and his men had also killed Tito's three infant sons and Wilson's children. 'When I asked Kamy where he had taken the kids,' said Puna, 'his answer chilled me, "Sons of snakes are also snakes." That explained everything.'[6]

Puna confirmed to Savimbi that he had seen and identified the bodies. 'His reply was swift and cold. I can still hear it: "*Maninho* (Little Brother), I'm now much more relaxed because the dead don't speak."' Savimbi told Puna that it was important for him that he knew beyond any doubt that Tito and Wilson were dead. Savimbi, Puna said, was entirely responsible for the murders: 'Nobody could kill like that without Savimbi's permission.'

Puna felt traumatised and depressed by what he had witnessed, and four months later he was taken further aback when Savimbi gave him another extraordinary order. He said, at a meeting with Puna and five other top UNITA officials, that Puna must prepare a press statement to be issued internationally saying that he, Puna, had ordered the execution of Tito and his brother-in-law for the 'crime' of plotting to kill Savimbi.

Savimbi told Puna that UNITA would soon be visited by US Congressmen McCurdy and DeConcini and their delegation. Savimbi told Puna: 'They want to see Tito and Wilson in Luanda. I told them they were in the interior collecting data from the population.' UNITA would need to explain what was now their clear 'disappearance'. Savimbi went on to say it was logical that a 'traitor' like Tito should be executed by UNITA's interior minister, Puna himself.

And, indeed, there was a certain vile rationale to it. Puna, at Savimbi's side since they had trained together in China in 1965, was a very tough man in both physique and style. People who had met Puna might find it entirely possible that he had done the dirty work.

Puna said Savimbi told him UNITA was certain to win the coming election and then the whole matter would be forgotten. Puna, Savimbi said, would become part of the new Angolan government, his protection would be well assured, and the stories about Tito and his family would be buried forever. But Savimbi was stretching Puna's loyalty too far. It was not an order he was willing to accept. 'However, I knew the days were numbered for anyone who disobeyed him. I quickly realised that my time with UNITA was coming to an end. The deaths of Tito and Wilson were too much for me to swallow.'

Puna began planning his defection, coordinated eventually with that of Tony Fernandes, who had already managed to travel to London for treatment for a severe ulcer illness.

Puna left Jamba for Luanda, ostensibly to fly onwards to Cabinda, in Angola's far north, to campaign electorally for UNITA. While in Luanda, he received a telegram from Savimbi ordering him to return to Jamba the next day for an important meeting. A light aircraft was being sent to take him back. 'Bring all your family,' said the telegram, signed *O Mais Velho.* The young UNITA soldier who delivered the telegram said only two words to Puna: 'Don't go.'

'That boy saved Puna's life,' said Fernandes. 'I believe Savimbi would have killed Puna.'

Puna quietly moved his wife and children out of his hotel without his security detachment knowing. Leaving his computer and whisky supplies in his room to avoid suspicion, he moved into a friend's house and from there contacted José Ndele, a former senior UNITA leader

This photo was taken at the memorial service for Tito in Washington.

who had quit the movement decades earlier and become a successful businessman in Portugal and Switzerland. Ndele chartered a private jet, which flew to Luanda and parked in a secure and distant area of 4 February International Airport. Puna and his family were smuggled into the airport and on to the plane, which flew them to Portugal.

'We knew we had to leave the party together,' Fernandes told me. 'Puna, who was then in Luanda, was scheduled to address a UNITA rally in Cabinda, in the far north of Angola. Savimbi telephoned me at 4 am one morning and again at 6 am, and then every two hours, to order me to return from London to Luanda.' Fernandes instead travelled by train to Brussels, from where he flew to join Puna in Lisbon.

There, on 27 February 1992, they announced their defections from UNITA at a press conference. Sensationally, they said Tito and his entire family had been executed on Savimbi's orders, and they confirmed a large number of other killings and human rights abuses ordered by

From left to right: Florence Tate, a journalist, Olga Mundombe and Willietta Schley at the memorial service for Tito in Washington, DC.

the UNITA leader.[7] Fernandes subsequently went to Paris and gave another press conference in which he again confirmed the deaths of Tito and Wilson and said Tito's children had been killed by having their heads smashed against tree trunks. Fernandes and Puna flew to Washington and gave similar press briefings in April, and also to Congressmen on Capitol Hill and to officials at the State Department.[8]

These revelations were the first that the wider world and I myself knew of Tito's and Wilson's deaths.

It came as an immense and appalling shock to me, the sheer mad, cruel, destructive wastefulness of it. I had found it difficult to believe Savimbi would dare to go that far. Eduardo and Olga were always less sanguine.

Quickly, I knew the meaning of bereavement, a measureless despondency, a wrenching, dreadful deprivation of a friendship that had endured challenges and difficulties and had, I hoped, many good years to run. All our efforts and subterfuges to preserve Tito's life had failed. His death, I assumed, had been even more lonely than that of Steve Biko. His life had been snuffed out with perhaps even greater callousness, if that was possible. I found myself lying awake at nights wanting to reach out to him in his unmarked grave and hug him and tell him he was loved and that, in some scheme of things, his efforts and suffering and bravery had real meaning. I miss him immensely and for years afterwards I used to talk to him in my reveries.

It was a tragic and disgusting waste of one of Africa's finest young men – victim of a man of immense potential who was overcome by megalomania of a particularly evil strain. A former Savimbi admirer in Washington later told a BBC correspondent: 'Savimbi is probably the most brilliant man I have ever met, but he's also dangerous, even psychotic.'[9]

With Angola's presidential and parliamentary elections only six months away, the Puna and Fernandes defections caused a sensation. UNITA countered with a damage-limitation communiqué. Reversing all its previous public statements, UNITA said the pair had been detained for several years because they had tried to topple Savimbi 'by defaming him abroad and attempting to oust him in Jamba'. The communiqué added that the two men had now 'unaccountably disappeared'.

32

Death by chameleon (1992)

Now that the truth was out, I was free to publish my own understanding of the inside story of the savagery Savimbi had unleashed on his own people. The *Washington Post*, *The Scotsman*, *The Sunday Telegraph*, the Johannesburg *Star* and many others published my in-depth account of the events that led to the executions of Tito, his family members and others. The *Washington Post* ran my story on 29 March 1992 across three pages in its Sunday edition under the headline 'Angola's Secret Bloodbath: Jonas Savimbi and His Hidden War Against UNITA's leaders'.[1]

I wrote that Tito was the best-known of scores of UNITA members killed in bloody purges stretching over more than 15 years. 'The murders have long been hidden from the West, but the truth about what well-paid publicists continue to portray as a humanitarian movement is emerging. The story of Chingunji and other victims is important because, with Angola's first-ever democratic elections due in six months – after nearly 30 years of civil war – Savimbi hopes to gain ultimate power in the country and be embraced by Western democracies as an African saviour.'

Following publication of the *Washington Post* article, David Boren,

Democratic Senator for Oklahoma and Chairman of the Senate Intelligence Committee, said my report was 'a chilling one, if true … Mr Savimbi must accept responsibility for the fact that their deaths (those of Tito, Wilson and their families) occurred in a jurisdiction controlled by his political and military organisation. We cannot ignore their deaths. Mr President (George HW Bush), I ask unanimous consent that Fred Bridgland's piece which appeared in the *Washington Post* on March 29, 1992 appear in the record at the conclusion of my remarks.'[2]

The US government at last became alarmed about its chosen Angolan. The new Secretary of State, James Baker, acted. He wrote a personal letter to Savimbi in March 1992 demanding to know exactly what had happened to Tito. Some reports, said Baker, alleged that Tito had been executed several months earlier.

Someone, who I presume to have been a State Department insider, leaked to me Savimbi's classified 6 000-word reply.

It was true, Savimbi told Baker, that he had lied to the US government, members of Congress and journalists about Tito being a free man. Tito, he admitted, had indeed been imprisoned for a long time after he confessed to plotting to take over the UNITA leadership by killing him (Savimbi), in cooperation with Olga Mundombe, Fred Bridgland and junior CIA operatives, using 'a type of poisonous chameleon known in Angola'.

Chameleons, although completely harmless, are a source of mystery and fear in Africa where many people consider the small lizards dangerous. Fears about chameleons are related to witchcraft in many cultures around the continent. There are innumerable myths and beliefs about chameleons' legendary ability to change colour.

Savimbi went on.

'They (Mundombe, Bridgland and the CIA) had developed a plan to destroy my reputation, alleging, *inter alia*, human rights violations and drug use, in an attempt to create a climate enabling Tito to take over the Presidency … I concluded that the plan could not have enjoyed the support of President Reagan, senior members of his administration or the CIA Director, with all of whom I had good relations.'

Baker, perhaps the world's third most powerful man at that time, was further told that a UNITA Commission of Inquiry had established that Tito, Wilson and their families were killed, against Savimbi's will, on the instructions of Miguel N'Zau Puna.

Savimbi said Puna had concocted a false cover story saying Tito and Wilson had fled from captivity and been recaptured. 'Puna was a strong, even a harsh, disciplinarian,' Savimbi told Baker. 'He planned the operation (to kill Tito and Wilson) carefully and covered himself well … In the early days of the struggle, I often remonstrated when his excesses occurred.'[3]

About Tito's and Wilson's deaths, Savimbi told James Baker: 'I was determined that no harm should come to these two young men, not because I did not believe that Tito's intention to kill me should go unpunished, but because I was convinced that they could be rehabilitated … Everyone in the leadership was aware of my determination to have them released. We had, in fact, intended to have the two young men meet Congressman McCurdy and his delegation in January 1992. It may be that this prompted Puna to kill them so it could not happen.'

To which Puna commented later, 'If you come to Jamba for a short time, you will see Savimbi as a very good person. But if you stay for a long time, you will see very, very horrifying things.'

Savimbi said that in retrospect he regretted not having informed the Secretary of State earlier about the Tito-Bridgland-Mundombe-CIA assassination plot. 'We were fearful of damaging the relationship with the USA,' he wrote. 'But that, unfortunately, is water under the bridge.' Savimbi further told Baker that Tito's mother and his sisters Lulu and Xica had been convicted of practising witchcraft. But he said nothing about them being executed on his orders. Nor did he mention the Jamba 'Red September' witch burnings in 1983.

The State Department described Savimbi's defence as 'very unsat-isfactory'. Top officials said that by accusing Tito of being a CIA agent, Savimbi further gravely muddied his case, given that the US intelligence community had been helping Savimbi directly for more than a decade and that Tito was Savimbi's chosen point man with the CIA.[4]

I presume that Savimbi's bizarre letter merely confirmed to the State Department what it must surely already have known – that its man in Angola had lied to them all along about Tito. With the election looming, Savimbi nevertheless remained America's favourite Angolan son-of-a-bitch, especially because intelligence reports were saying he would be elected president. The US government was still expecting a Savimbi victory right up until the eve of the voting.

And Savimbi himself thought that he had victory in the bag: his top officials were euphoric. But Tito's ghost haunted them. Savimbi continued to be asked when Tito and Wilson would show up as part of his election campaign team. 'They will come,' he told the government-owned national newspaper *Jornal de Angola* on 29 December 1991. 'This is again propaganda (that they have been detained). Why should they not come? Everyone wants to come.' He said the problem was finding enough accommodation for everyone.

By this stage, Savimbi had become a kind of African Macbeth, believing in the spirit world with the ghosts of his brightest and best, whose lives he had ordered terminated, looking over his shoulder. He had sacrificed a whole generation and layer in his movement who had any intellectual competence, and he was now relying upon craven sycophants, many of them his own young relatives who, as campaigners, alienated more people than they won. Healing and recovery were looking impossible, with Savimbi increasingly unable to tell one lie from another, capable only of expedience at the expense of any morality, able to justify any murder.

George Chikoti, a senior UNITA defector, said Savimbi's targets were precisely those UNITA men and women who seemed most capable of challenging his dominance, immediately or in the future.[5]

Chikoti had been close to Tito. Back in 1974, he had been recruited by Tito to Savimbi's elite bodyguard unit. He quit UNITA in 1988, revolted by the string of human rights abuses springing directly from Savimbi's orders. In an interview with the *Washington Post*'s Leon Dash, Chikoti said Savimbi had routinely ordered the beating to death of suspected opponents and the burning to death of women and children on charges of witchcraft. The killings in UNITA, Chikoti insisted to Dash, began in the early 1970s during the clandestine movement's nine-year anti-colonial war against the Portuguese and escalated under the more strenuous demands of the war against the MPLA and the Cubans. 'Savimbi has killed, beaten or tortured any capable leader who could replace him,' said Chikoti, who after his defection rose to become secretary-general of the Brussels-based Organisation of African, Caribbean and Pacific States.

When I later met and interviewed Chikoti in Luanda, he asserted that, 'Morally, Savimbi has no basis to become Angola's president, but he doesn't want anything less. Savimbi grabbed Tito early to make him his right-hand man and so that he could be controlled. He tried to hide his killing of Tito's parents from him, and then when Tito discovered the truth, he tried to persuade him they were witches.'

33

The peace collapses and war resumes (1992–1993)

In the event, Savimbi lost the presidential election. But the margin was so narrow, with 40 per cent of the national vote cast for Savimbi against 49 per cent for the MPLA's José Eduardo dos Santos, that a run-off ballot was scheduled under the electoral law.[1] It was an election that Savimbi should have walked – had he not succumbed long before-hand to messianic delusions and paranoia, and murdered his most able lieutenants, effectively eating his political seed corn.

Had people of the quality of Tito, Wilson, Jorge Sangumba, Mateus Katalayo and many others still been alive to campaign, they might have influenced the people of Luanda. As it was, votes in the capital city tipped the election towards the incumbent Dos Santos.

As the voting days approached, Savimbi had assumed that the nation wanted a strongman, and he became more and more bellicose. Dos Santos, by contrast, hired a Brazilian polling and media company that advised him to use pastel colours on his posters and brochures: the thinking was that after 30 years of conflict, people would be influenced by the idea of peace that the colours conveyed.

Human Rights Watch said it was told by one high-ranking MPLA government official, 'We didn't win those elections. Savimbi lost them.'

Revelations of Savimbi's atrocities tipped the balance in most of the big urban areas in the north towards the MPLA, with voters preferring 'the bandits we know to those we don't know'. Graffiti in Luanda prior to the election read, 'UNITA kills, MPLA (only) steals.' One cynical but realistic British diplomat told a reporter, 'The death of Tito must be put into an African context: your average man in the bush doesn't care, and in Luanda it only confirms everyone's long-held view that Savimbi is a bloodthirsty murderer. They will vote for the MPLA crooks instead.'[2]

Savimbi convinced himself that the 29–30 September poll had been rigged. He withdrew from the capital and ordered his forces to resume fighting. The vast little-known land, potentially the richest in Africa, slid once again into all-out conflict.

The UNITA military took over several towns outside Luanda, including Huambo and Cuito (the former Silva Porto), as well as the rich diamond fields of the northeast. By mid-1993, UNITA controlled about two-thirds of the country outside Luanda. Savimbi left many of his key officials in Luanda to negotiate with the MPLA. The human cost after fighting resumed was impossible to determine with accuracy, but the UN reported that some one thousand people were dying each day from conflict, starvation and disease – more than in any other conflict in the world at that time. If the human cost was staggering, so was the lack of international attention. Angola was labelled the 'forgotten war'. Angola's only experiment with democracy had failed.

Savimbi's strategy was to strangle the cities in the hope of provoking an eventual revolt against President Dos Santos. An estimated 30 000 people died in the battle for Cuito, which was dubbed 'the African Stalingrad'. Once perhaps the most exquisitely beautiful little city in Angola, it was reduced to a ruin: not a single building remained intact. People's yards became graveyards.

'The stench of dried blood, rotting corpses, filth and decay hung among the ruins,' wrote the first foreign correspondent to reach the destroyed city.[3] 'Half of the wounded had gangrene. Amputations were carried out without anaesthetics by nurses between lulls in the fighting. It was horrific … The middle class have fled. The remaining peasant population have no say over their fate. They are living wretched lives in mediaeval conditions: in rags, illiterate, unprotected against disease. A hoe and a *catana* (machete) is all their technology. When they meet 20th-century technology, chances are it is a rocket or a landmine.'

Elsewhere, an estimated 10 000 people, many of them civilians, died in the battle for Huambo. Regular flights of the United Nations Observer Mission in Angola were halted after UNITA shot down two UN aircraft, both Hercules C-130 transport planes, with the loss of more than twenty lives, many of them UN staff. 'It's the Wild West out there, and Savimbi is currently the deadliest sharpshooter,' Shawn McCormick told me after he visited Luanda and other MPLA strongholds in July 1999. 'He just wants to pulverise and punish the MPLA for the "lost" election. UNITA's struggle is now amounting to a gross, miserable waste of lives and resources.'

As for the MPLA and President José dos Santos, Shawn said that for them 'there's only one way to end all this: kill Savimbi'. And one of Savimbi's four children by his first wife, Vinona, turned up unexpectedly in Luanda at the end of 1999 and called for the killing of his own father. Breaking down in tears at a press conference, Arajau Domingos Sakaita accused Savimbi of murdering Vinona. The appearance of Arajau, who had been studying in West Africa, caused a sensation in the Angolan capital at a time when the MPLA was launching a huge land and air offensive against Savimbi's forces. 'UNITA is just Savimbi,' said his son. 'Without Savimbi there would be no war in Angola.'

In my original book, I wrote, on information from Tito, that Vinona Savimbi died in 1984 when lightning struck the hut in which she was sleeping. I subsequently heard from several informants that Vinona, a feisty, outspoken woman, had taken her own life, shooting herself in the head when Savimbi's treatment of her became intolerable.

As UNITA troops continued fighting their way into other towns beyond the capital, the MPLA turned on UNITA supporters in Luanda. Reuters' correspondent Judith Matloff was a witness to these events. Following Savimbi's announcement of his rejection of the election results, she wrote, 'Thousands of its (UNITA's) members were hunted down in the *musseques* (squatter camps) – chopped, shot, clubbed or sliced. People armed with kitchen knives, pistols, clubs, machetes went from door to door massacring anyone they suspected of belonging to UNITA.'[4]

UNITA's top brass in Luanda, the party's vice president, Jeremias Chitunda, and its chief negotiator, Elias Salupeta Pena, were murdered. Tito's successor as UNITA's foreign secretary, Abel Chivukuvuku, was badly wounded. Government 'WANTED' posters for Savimbi appeared on Luanda's streets, denouncing him as a war criminal and comparing him to Hitler, Idi Amin, Pol Pot and vampires. Several UNITA generals and brigadiers were taken prisoner as Savimbi took UNITA back to a war that lasted another ten years and which was more destructive in terms of lives lost and property and infrastructure destroyed than in all the earlier phases.

Savimbi was buoyed in the early stages of the resumed war by purchases of tanks, long-range artillery and other medium guns and rockets, purchased mainly through Ukraine and Bulgaria from the proceeds of the Cuango and Lucapa diamond mines UNITA controlled in northeast Angola. By some estimates, UNITA was earning up to US$700 million a year from the diamonds, which were fenced illegally through buying offices in Rwanda, Uganda and Zambia before ending up on open markets in Antwerp and Tel Aviv. Lebanese, South African, Nigerian and Portuguese dealers flew regularly into

UNITA territory to barter arms for diamonds.

The MPLA suffered a string of military defeats, and for a while Savimbi's forces controlled about 60 per cent of Angola's territory. But the MPLA gradually regrouped. It was able, unlike UNITA, to buy and transport arms through legal channels, financed from its increasingly lucrative oil fields. UNITA, sanctioned by the United Nations after the elections, had to pay substantial premiums on purchase prices and carrier costs of its arms.

By 1996, the MPLA had been officially recognised by the US as the legitimate government of Angola. It began to reorganise its army and gradually succeeded in regaining the upper hand, with substantial assistance of foreign advisers, including the CIA and Israeli intelligence, and mercenary reinforcements, largely from South Africa.[5] Savimbi, increasingly on the back foot with his reduced band of loyalists, began wandering through Angola's vast countryside and wilderness, further away from taking supreme power than when it all began in the 1960s. Government forces began nipping unceasingly at his heels. Before the end came, probably only about 200 soldiers remained in his column.

34

Savimbi: the end (2002)

The story of my relationship with Tito does not end with his death. In some ways, it has never ended, and never will. Many mysteries remain. Just why, for example, was Savimbi, who charmed so many people, so crazed as to feel compelled to kill Tito and scores of others who could have raised him to supreme power in Angola? What demons drove him to cast women and children on bonfires, to murder women with whom he had sex and who bore his many children?

Of course, if you behave as evilly as Savimbi did there comes eventually a time of retribution. UNITA Brigadier Geraldo Sachipengo Nunda was the man who proved to be Brutus to Savimbi's Caesar.

Nunda was one of Savimbi's finest commanders. I had trekked and canoed hundreds of kilometres across Angola with Nunda and his 2 000-strong UNITA battalion before the battle for Alto Chicapa.[1] Mild-mannered, quietly spoken and much loved by his soldiers, Nunda was called back from the northern front in early 1991 to become chief of staff of UNITA's army, second in the military hierarchy only to Savimbi himself.

Nunda, like Tito, to whom he was close and distantly related, believed that all Angolans deserved the opportunity to vote in multi-party elections, a possibility that had been denied them by the MPLA and its Cuban and Soviet backers. In 1992, after 17 years of post-independence MPLA-UNITA warfare, Nunda saw his ideal achieved when a peace deal was signed and parliamentary and presidential elections were held.

Nunda protested when Savimbi ordered a return to war after UNITA's narrow defeats in the presidential election and also the parliamentary contest.

'I told Savimbi that the decision to go back to war was a mistake,' Nunda told me. 'I said the people were exhausted and wanted peace, and it would be a long time before we got the opportunity again. I demanded a meeting of all UNITA's generals to discuss whether they agreed with Savimbi's decision to resume the war.'

Nunda by this time, in late 1992, was with his battalion in Huambo, 650 kilometres southeast of Luanda, one of the cities to which UNITA's forces had retreated. In Huambo, he said, he was told by his own personal bodyguards that Savimbi had given them money to kill their own commander.

'Most of my bodyguards had been with me for 17 years,' said Nunda. 'They were like brothers. They gave me Savimbi's 2 500 American dollars and said, "Take the money. The important thing is your survival and your honour. You must escape."'

Nunda had liaised closely with the MPLA in the two years of preparation for the multi-party elections. During that time, he had established friendships with two MPLA military officers. Following the fall of the Berlin Wall in November 1989, the MPLA did an ideological flip-flop and became a pro-Western capitalist party with a robber-baron flavour.

Nunda contacted one of his MPLA friends in Luanda, Army Chief of Staff João de Matos, by radio telephone and said Savimbi was planning to kill him. De Matos told him to gather his wife and daughter at a specific grid reference and an Alouette helicopter would arrive to evacuate them to the port of Lobito and then onwards to Angola's capital city.

The relief for Nunda was massive. His disillusion with Savimbi had been deepening for several years. Although his battalion operated in the far north, hundreds of kilometres away from Jamba and its pernicious internal traumas, he knew that Savimbi had been executing many of his outstanding top- and second-tier leaders. Earlier, when he was a very young officer and based in Jamba, Savimbi had also tried, unsuccessfully, to have sex with Nunda's wife.

'I concluded Savimbi was insane,' Nunda told me. 'Multi-party elections were what we fought for and now he was destroying all that. He was afraid of being an ordinary citizen. He wanted to be a presidential dictator.

'Until as late as 1989 I still thought UNITA was a big project of all the people. After that, as the killings accelerated of dissidents and of women who refused to sleep with Savimbi, I realised that he had turned the party into his own personal project. He knew how to manipulate people. Like a scientist, Savimbi was always experimenting to see how far he could go. I saw that he would advance to the very end, when everything would fall apart. There was no longer anything good he could do for the people.'

Nunda, immediately after his defection, was inducted into the national army as a special adviser on how to eliminate Savimbi. He was promoted rapidly to Deputy Chief of Staff, with the rank of general, responsible for training a special unit whose task was to track down and kill Savimbi.

With a special force formed around the national army's crack 16th Brigade – which Nunda had fought against with his UNITA men – Nunda launched from early 2000 onwards a scorched-earth campaign designed to flush out Savimbi from his central and southern Angola strongholds.

Supported by a flow of new equipment from Western and former Soviet bloc countries, Nunda's offensive gradually tightened the noose around his former leader's neck. UNITA communications were intercepted and passed to Nunda by the CIA – which transferred its support to the MPLA following the 1992 election. Israeli specialists set up a radar screen that made it impossible for Savimbi to bring in fresh weapons supplies by air. Lack of fuel paralysed UNITA's tank and truck units. A joint Israeli-MPLA team interrogated UNITA captives, the wounded, stragglers and deserters, as part of an intelligence gathering campaign.

According to some reports, former Israeli Defense Forces and Mossad international intelligence agency personnel arrived in Angola to help with the final entrapment of Savimbi.[2] The Israelis were supported by former South African soldiers who had once fought in support of Savimbi. They were hired through a private military company named Executive Outcomes, which was founded by Eeben Barlow, a former fighter with the crack Buffalo Battalion of the South African Defence Force. Barlow hired an estimated one thousand former South African soldiers to fight alongside MPLA forces. Executive Outcomes officers trained MPLA recruits at Cabo Ledo, a Cuban-built military base in western Angola.

In another blow to Savimbi, his diplomatic offices in Washington and Western Europe were closed down by host governments. Zambia's government, supportive for so many years, severed relations.

As Savimbi retreated, he ordered the execution of Ana Isabel Paulino, the woman Tito loved but who Savimbi stole to be his number-one official wife because of her beauty and sophistication. Citing accounts he gathered from people who had retreated with Savimbi, Eduardo Chingunji said, 'Ana's end was as brutal as that of Tito, her former fiancé. One day during the retreat by Savimbi from the pursuing Angolan Armed Forces, he called a small group to gather around him to witness something very important.' He sent one of his bodyguards to call Ana from a group of his wives and other women with instructions to bring her to a pit that was believed to be a wild animal's lair, possibly that of a hyena.

'When Ana asked where she was going, the bodyguard said he could not say and he insisted that she leave behind her personal belongings, including her habitual red purse. Savimbi was waiting. She was ordered to descend into the animal's lair and Savimbi watched as she was buried alive while begging for mercy.'

Eduardo said witnesses who spoke to him said Ana had been drinking heavily and showing signs of severe depression. Eduardo speculated that Savimbi, with disastrous defeat looming, believed that the desertion or capture of Ana would be a huge propaganda coup for the Angolan government. UNITA officers were deserting in significant numbers. 'The capture of Ana would finally and totally destroy his image and any remaining chance he had of fulfilling his lifelong ambition to become president of Angola.'

Ana's execution was confirmed by Linda Heywood, Professor of African American Studies at Boston University. Heywood, an Angola expert, quoted revelations by Savimbi's inner circle who said Savimbi feared Ana would 'reveal too much' if she fell into the MPLA's hands. Ana, Heywood, said, was buried alive in the lair while Savimbi 'watched it all from behind a small bush 100 metres away from the grave'.[3]

Finally, on 22 February 2002, Nunda's force trapped Savimbi and his remaining followers on the western bank of the Lweio River, a tributary of the Lungue Bungu River, which itself flows into the Zambezi. Savimbi was within 150 kilometres of the border with Zambia, which he may have been trying to reach, repeatedly criss-crossing rivers in his attempt to confuse his pursuers. With Nunda directing the operation from the nearby town of Luso, the Israelis, helping the MPLA attack force, deployed a radio-controlled drone fitted with a high-definition camera that flew a daily grid pattern. The drone spotted Savimbi eating his lunch on 22 February in a newly erected field tent, apparently confident he had deceived his followers. Nunda's troops surrounded the position and attacked from several directions. Savimbi ran through the back of his tent but was cut down in a withering hail of fire. According to one unconfirmed account, he was first hit with four or five bullets and begged on his knees for his life to be spared. But, in the fierceness and commotion of the assault, he was riddled with another ten bullets, two to the head.[4]

Savimbi was dead at the age of 67 along with more than twenty of his bodyguards. The circumstances of his final breath matched in many ways that of Che Guevara in Bolivia 35 years earlier.

Nunda walked into the clearing where Savimbi died, observed the body of his former leader and ordered that it be buried in a pauper's grave in the town of Luso, at the eastern end of the Benguela Railway.

Within days, a peace deal was signed between the MPLA and UNITA, ending more than 25 years of warfare that had laid waste to the country, caused countless deaths and left many more people maimed for life. Two generations of Angolans had grown up not knowing the nature of peace. Human Rights Watch estimated half a million people died in the post-election fighting or from a combination of starvation and disease. Few people knew any more what exactly the UNITA remnants were fighting about, except for Savimbi's increasingly deranged personal ambitions.

Nunda, who had organised the killing of the man he once admired and followed, told me, 'I had no regrets. He had tried to kill me, and he had killed a lot of other UNITA people who should never have died. He betrayed the very party he created and the people who had followed him so loyally. He eventually pursued objectives that were totally contrary to what he had once taught us. He had no remorse. He was a bad man. We felt we helped the country to find peace (by killing Savimbi).'

Eduardo Chingunji observed: 'For a man who dreamt of being Angola's president, Savimbi was in fact a remarkably short-sighted person. Nothing at the end remained of the dreams and principles my grandpa had when he initiated UNITA in 1965. He sought to have human rights, democracy and Africans' interests as cornerstones of the struggle. It was as if Savimbi was an agent of the MPLA, paid to destroy the fundamental founding ideas of UNITA that made millions of followers believe in it.'

Eduardo, inevitably and understandably, was outraged beyond all telling by Savimbi's excesses. 'In the end he could not be said to have any ideology,' Eduardo told me furiously. 'His only sincere belief was that he ought to be the president of Angola. He was just a selfish, sick, mentally deranged, psychopathic paedophile and murderer. This man burned to death and otherwise murdered children as young as two years old. Most of the positive things and successes of UNITA were a result of the thinking and sacrifices of people like my uncle, Tito, and others who he eventually eliminated to get the credit for himself. He killed all the members of my family, and when the Bicesse Peace Accords were signed in 1991, he thought he had won. But by September 1992, Savimbi had lost everything.'

'He dreamed of being Angola's and Africa's Redeemer, but, because he became detached from reality, his dream turned into a nightmare.'

Inge Lippman, an American foreign correspondent who worked frequently in Africa for *The New York Times*, introduced me to Savimbi back in 1975 and she also got to know Tito well. On hearing of his death, she wrote to me, saying, 'I adored Tito, who gave me a lot of encouragement on my various bushwalks. I can never forgive Savimbi for his murder. I do hope that if there is any justice in this world, which of course there isn't, the Devil will take care of Savimbi.'

It's curious: the dead Tito lives on vividly for his many friends in Angola and around the world, while the dead Savimbi is mourned by few and cursed by many. When you are no longer worthy, power and esteem just evaporate like morning dew. No one's death gives me pleasure, but Savimbi's removal had become essential if Angola was to have peace and a new beginning after three decades of largely futile war.

Tito was a noble, compassionate and humble man who gave his life to a cause that Savimbi ultimately destroyed.

I am honoured to say that Tito was, and remains, my brother.

EPILOGUE

I failed to save Tito's life after he entrusted me with the realities of UNITA under Jonas Savimbi. His death remains a profound and permanent sorrow. I miss him, but perhaps his courage in revealing the truth before his bleak and terrible end was necessary to save Angolans from electing a president on a cocktail of myths. Tito was an anachronism: an honourable man in what turned out ultimately to be a dishonourable and brutal liberation movement.

Savimbi's best-known characteristics for many years were his charisma, charm and brio: he convinced millions of peasant followers, and also international statesmen – and me – that he was Angola's best hope for a free and successful future.

Should his dark, paranoid, psychotic depths have been spotted earlier? The *Washington Post*'s Leon Dash, the Pulitzer Prize winner who completed two arduous treks with UNITA guerrillas, said he detected then none of Savimbi's underlying depravity and megalomania.[1] He did say, however, that Savimbi was an enigma, a man on whom many labels could be stuck: 'brilliant, charismatic, affable, unyielding, forgiving, temporising, Machiavellian, opportunistic, lying, nationalistic, Marxist, Maoist, pro-Western and socialist'.

But Leon only realised that 'mass murderer' should be added to the Savimbi label when he met and interviewed, in Washington in August 1990, the man who had been his personal bodyguard and interpreter in 1977 on his longer Angola trek. This was just over a year after Tito had revealed to me the truth about Savimbi.

George Chikoti, at the age of 21, had been selected by Tito Chingunji in 1976 to be a member of Savimbi's elite bodyguard. Chikoti defected in November 1988 when Tito was recalled to Jamba and severely tortured before being executed on Savimbi's orders in July 1991.

Chikoti told Dash that Savimbi had ordered many of his top officials, including Tito and Tito's parents, to be beaten to death, and had on at least two occasions burned women and their children to death. Dash said he trusted his informant, and wrote: 'Chikoti says Savimbi's targets were precisely those UNITA men and women who seemed most capable of challenging his dominance, then or in the future. Savimbi's targets for persecution were people with higher education and from influential families ... The killings in UNITA, Chikoti insists, began in the early 1970s.'[2]

Although reporters and statesmen failed to detect Savimbi's cruel and deadly instincts, they had been recognised by some of his own followers. The man revered publicly by Savimbi as UNITA's greatest hero, Samuel Kafundanga Chingunji, challenged the UNITA leader as early as 1970–1971 over the deaths of his brother, David Samwimbila Chingunji, and two other young recruits. The details were heard from his mother and others by Kafundanga's son, Eduardo, who related them to me.[3]

Two Angolans in their early twenties, Cesar Martins and Luciano Kasoma, who had both studied in the United States, trekked through the bush in 1969 to find UNITA and were recruited into the guerrilla army to fight the Portuguese. They disappeared some months later.

Kafundanga, posted to Zambia as UNITA's chief of staff[4] to ferry weapons and other supplies into Angola, received letters from Martins' mother, in Luanda, for delivery to her son in the bush. When she received no replies from her son she wrote to Kafundanga asking why. The reason, according to accounts Kafundanga heard from the bush, was because Savimbi had ordered Martins' execution after accusing him of being a CIA agent. Martins, a San Diego University graduate, was taken into the forest and was made to dig his own grave before being shot.

Kasoma, a mining engineer, was also accused by Savimbi of being a CIA agent. According to Kafundanga's informants, Kasoma was tied in a sack with a heavy rock before it was thrown into a river. Kasoma was never to be seen again.

'On one of his visits to guerrilla headquarters, rumours of the youths' deaths reached my dad's ears. He asked Savimbi about the whispers,' said Eduardo in his unpublished manuscript. 'Savimbi insisted that both Martins and Kasoma were alive and well, working at distant bases. He accused some people of trying to undermine his relationship with my dad in order to wreck UNITA's struggle against the Portuguese. He advised Dad not to listen to divisive falsehoods. Dad nevertheless stressed that it was important to show Martins' and Kasoma's families that their sons were still alive. Letters and photographs would be the best evidence. Savimbi agreed but never delivered.'

Kafundanga then had a furious argument with Savimbi when his younger brother, David Samwimbila Chingunji, was shot dead on 18 July 1970 during an ambush of a Portuguese military railcar on the Benguela Railway. Kafundanga was deeply shaken by Samwimbila's death and was convinced that Savimbi had ordered it. 'Samwimbila and my dad were not only brothers but very close friends. Samwimbila had already shared with Dad many misgivings he had begun to have about Savimbi,' said Eduardo. 'Samwimbila was an extremely popular commander. The more popular he became, the more Savimbi disliked it. He began painting Samwimbila as over-zealous and stubborn. People who liked both Samwimbila and my father later told Dad that his brother had been shot from behind, that no fire had been directed by Portuguese soldiers from the railcar and that no attempt had been made to retrieve Samwimbila's body. David was the only casualty in the attack.

'My father accused Savimbi to his face of organising Samwimbila's killing. Savimbi denied it, saying David was like a brother to him. My father did not believe him, but in order not to disrupt UNITA's cause, my father vowed to pursue a proper investigation only when the strug-gle against the Portuguese came to an end. Several people demanded the arrest of the people behind the plot to kill Samwimbila. Savimbi intervened and promised to conduct an official investigation into Samwimbila's death. He managed to convince my dad that the rumours about how Samwimbila died were fabrications and he also insisted that the failed attack was Samwimbila's fault.'

Kafundanga reached an understanding with Savimbi that the investigation would be carried out as soon as the war against the Por-tuguese came to an end. 'Calling witnesses at the time to testify against Savimbi would have been near-impossible,' Eduardo told me. 'Most would have been in fear for their lives. Dad might have been backed by a few commanders, but UNITA would probably have broken up there and then if an investigation had gone ahead.

'However, just when it was clear that Portuguese rule was about to end (in April 1974), my dad died on 24 January 1974, in the Zambian border town of Mongu shortly after he had returned from a meeting with Savimbi. UNITA said Kafundanga died of cerebral malaria. My mother, Grace, who was then living 600 kilometres from Mongu in the northwestern town of Solwezi, is convinced to this day that he was poisoned.'

The promised post-independence elections never took place and the issues of Samwimbila's and Kafundanga's deaths were not raised again after UNITA was driven from the towns in 1976 and began its bush war against the MPLA, Cubans and Soviets.

Grace Chingunji moved, after her husband died, from Solwezi to the Zambian capital, Lusaka, with her children and established various small businesses. She made enough money to buy a small house in the Lusaka suburb of Kamwala and to educate her children.

Eduardo, aged nine at the time of his father's death, was heart-broken. He had hero-worshipped his father and his reputation as a strong and dashing liberation movement leader. Eduardo wished to emulate him and, as he grew older, he longed to travel to Savimbi's bush headquarters to join UNITA's fight against the MPLA and its Cuban and Soviet allies.

Grace told her grieving son that she believed a Chokwe man named Chimwute had poisoned his father. Chimwute was a link man between Savimbi and Kafundanga. 'He travelled frequently with Dad on his missions into the bush,' Eduardo told me. Chimwute simply disappeared after Kafundanga's death and has not been heard of since.

Grace also told her son that Chimwute had been sent by a 'very powerful person' whom she did not name. 'She warned me it would be dangerous to talk about it. With the benefit of hindsight, I believe that Savimbi realised my dad was serious about establishing the truth about the deaths of his brother, Martins and Kasoma and decided the time had come to kill him.' With rumours of impending change in Portugal that would lead to independence, Eduardo speculates that Savimbi was further convinced that he could kill Kafundanga and get away with it: he just had to make sure it did not look too suspicious. Using a Chokwe as the assassin meant that any hostility could not be directed at Savimbi's own larger and more powerful Ovimbundu tribe.

Eduardo grew up still uncertain about the cause of his father's death but proud nevertheless of Kafundanga's reputation. He became determined to visit Jamba once he finished secondary school, lured by the romance of the guerrilla struggle. He told his mother he intended travelling to Jamba to meet Savimbi and relatives he had last seen a decade earlier. Grace was devastated. She cried throughout the night the day before he left in June 1986. 'My mother said, "Are you out of your mind? You won't last long once you get there. The people who have been killing our relations will kill you." She cried and cried, but in the end she accepted that it was my choice. She had done her best by insisting I got a good education: now it was up to me, at the age of 22, to decide my own future.

'I still did not believe that Savimbi himself could have been responsible for my father's death. Years had passed and most of the people who were upset by what happened to Dad were now staunch supporters of Savimbi. Meanwhile, Uncle Tito had moved up from being Savimbi's chief bodyguard to the post of foreign secretary. Surely, I thought, if all the rumours were true Tito also would be dead.'

Eduardo wrote to Tito, at a time when he was preparing to move from London to Washington, about the rumours. Tito's reply said Eduardo should put aside for the time being a search for a reason for the deaths. Tito said: 'UNITA's main objective is to find a solution to the conflict in Angola. Once that has been achieved, we can calmly find out who killed them.'

Eduardo was exhilarated by the warmth and enthusiasm with which Savimbi greeted him when he arrived in Jamba in 1986. Savimbi introduced him to others as the returning son of the great Kafundanga. Savimbi said UNITA was cash-rich, after receiving copious aid from the US and other Western countries, and therefore Eduardo would be given a scholarship to study civil engineering at New York's Columbia University. 'He was really nice to me,' Eduardo recalled. 'He showed no animosity towards me. When he said he would ensure that UNITA cared for Kafundanga's family, I was comforted and felt there was no way he could have been involved in the killing of my dad.'

Eduardo was greeted like a hero at a political studies institution named after his father – the Kafundanga Studies Centre – where UNITA leaders underwent courses on Savimbi's political philosophy.

Savimbi, however, delivered a lecture that horrified Eduardo. He began by paying glowing tributes to Kafundanga and Tito. According to copious notes that Eduardo scribbled, Savimbi said: 'We can be grateful today that Tito has helped us lessen the loss of Kafundanga. Without Tito, UNITA would not have managed to secure the support of Western powers and in particular the Americans.'

But Savimbi then launched into an anti-West rant that frightened Eduardo. 'Let me teach you how to deal with Western nations,' said Savimbi. 'First, you have to play their game. You have to pretend that you stand for everything they believe in – religion, democracy, freedom of speech, free movement of people, freedom of property, freedom of privacy and a free market economy. Once you claim these to be your fundamental values, all the doors of the Western powers will open to you.

'When I was in the United States I was given a form by one UNITA supporter which he asked me to sign confirming that I was a Christian. I obliged and the stupid man walked away happy that I was a Christian, and UNITA gained another valuable backer. But all of us in UNITA know that we do not believe in God or religion. We do not believe in any Western system, but to get their money we have had to lie – and today we have millions of dollars to support us as we go for power.'

Savimbi, said Eduardo, went on: 'At one time the Americans used to describe us as terrorists, but now that we are winning the war they call us freedom fighters. We will only use them until we seize power. Our contract with them will have finished and we shall turn our back on them. As for the MPLA, if they ever accept a peace deal and the forming of a transitional government, I, Savimbi, shall overthrow that government and take over. If, however, elections happen first, we will contest them, but if UNITA loses we have prepared contingencies to take over by force. We shall be in power whatever.'

Eduardo was stunned by Savimbi's cynicism and demagoguery. 'It was surreal, a total contrast to the image and beliefs of Savimbi projected to the outside world. He was playing a deceitful game, and here he was bragging about it.' He was appalled by Savimbi's attack on the MPLA. Tito and Wilson were the originators of the idea of opening dialogue with UNITA's opponents. Now Savimbi was dismissing the initiative as a sham.

Eduardo was also astounded by the passion and the enthusiasm with which the lecture was greeted by Savimbi's students. The standing ovation he received made it clear they adored the man.

Savimbi, following his lecture, took Eduardo north some 80 kilometres to Likua where, at a huge rally, he again showered praises on Kafundanga who, he said, had been cut down by cerebral malaria.

After the rally, Eduardo met his father's and Tito's youngest brother, Dinho, whom he had last met ten years earlier. Dinho was obviously nervous and did not know how to start. Eventually he told Eduardo: 'A lot has happened since we last met. Things for us here are no longer what our father and brothers had in mind when they cofounded UNITA. Things are not as rosy as you might have been feeling when Savimbi introduced you to the masses at the rallies.

'A catalogue of very disturbing things has happened to our family in your absence. The facts that we shall tell you can easily claim our lives ... During the next few days we are going to tell you everything that has happened to us here. It is very hurtful stuff and we would be grateful if you would keep your cool because this will distress you.'

Dinho said that back in the 1970s, the family was caught up in the independence euphoria, and as a result questions were not asked that should have been asked. 'Now we know the whole truth, but it is too late and it is impossible to get out of here … There is a group of people in UNITA who want to eliminate physically and completely the whole family of Jonatão Chingunji. Hopefully, your arrival might improve our situation.

'We know that your father and David and possibly Paulo were murdered and by whom. Please do not tell anyone here outside our family about what I have just said. God is the only being who knows how we have survived up to this point.'

Eduardo said that at first he just sat speechless. 'I felt really scared, wondering what kind of mess I had got myself into by ignoring my mother's warning not to travel to Jamba. I realised that all Mum's beliefs about my Dad's death in Zambia in 1974 were actually right. Now I was wondering how I was going to be able to get out of there.

'I confided in Dinho all the suspicions, events and anger from when Dad died, and said that Mum always believed he had been murdered but had not discovered the exact reason why he was killed and on whose orders.'

Dinho returned to see Eduardo a day later with Lulu. They had decided to risk telling Eduardo everything, he said. There were truths about the Chingunjis' fate that no one was allowed to talk about in Jamba, but the facts were known by many who kept silent out of fear for their lives. 'Dinho and Lulu warned me that our family was on the verge of extinction because of one man's hatred for what the family had done for Angola and for the position we had consolidated in society.

'For the first time, I was told the terrible truth about the deaths of my grandparents. Savimbi's propagandists, I was told, began agitating the masses by alleging that my father, Kafundanga, and my uncle, Samwimbila, were actually killed by Violeta herself to enhance her witchcraft powers. Savimbi had told the population it was a matter of life or death. Grandpa wanted to kill him and all he had done was to defend himself. From that point onwards Savimbi did not let the Chingunjis live in peace, except for Tito, who was performing miracles overseas. Following my grandparents' murders, the rest of the family had been in and out of Savimbi's concentration camps.'

During Eduardo's time in Jamba, preparations were being made for the holding in August of UNITA's 6th policy-making congress, which Tito and other overseas representatives were going to attend. 'By this time Tito was no longer naïve about Savimbi's motives or his wicked plans for our family,' said Eduardo.

Tito, Eduardo learned,[5] had been imprisoned by Savimbi in 1984 on one of his return trips to Jamba. Ostensibly Savimbi wanted to re-educate him about UNITA's fundamental Maoist beliefs and the hard realities faced by everyone living in the bush. 'Tito's imprisonment ended only when UNITA was faced by a huge government offensive. Savimbi realised that UNITA's diplomacy was suffering in Tito's absence abroad and that he desperately needed Tito to reinvigorate the diplomatic effort.'

Tito's wife, Raquel – prevented from joining Tito abroad – and his sisters urged him to avoid ever returning again to Jamba until a peace accord had been signed with the MPLA. 'Tito simply laughed off the idea,' said Eduardo. 'He said there was no way he would abandon his family to face Savimbi's vengeance or mercy without him.'

Savimbi summoned Raquel, who was pregnant with twins, to a private meeting just before Tito was due to leave for Washington. Eduardo said she was visibly shocked and physically drained when she returned from the rendezvous. Her normal thin frame looked further reduced. She called everyone into Tito's bedroom, where the family held its private meetings out of sight of the 'system's' prying eyes.

Raquel told them: 'Savimbi has flipped! You won't believe what he has just told me. It was the most bizarre and terrifying meeting I have ever had with him. I now believe that as long as the Chingunjis exist, he will not rest. The hatred and grudges he has towards you as a family are beyond anything you can imagine. He is talking about the total eradication of the "entire Chingunji family plague".'

As Eduardo listened to Raquel, he said he felt sickened by the twisted thinking of the man to whom he had been willing to give the benefit of the doubt. 'I realised he had reduced everything to almost biblical terms, saying the main war was between two 'royal' families, the Chingunjis and the Savimbis. He told Raquel he was no longer worried about the war against the MPLA because UNITA would be the victor.'

Savimbi told Raquel he was furious with her for failing in the mission he gave her to spy on Tito. He accused her of betrayal and being a sell-out, and warned that when 'the day of judgement' came he would not only eliminate all of the Chingunjis, but her also for being a traitor.

Raquel's news was devastating to the Chingunjis. For Tito, it further reinforced his belief that he must work hard to achieve dialogue to end the war and achieve peace as soon as possible. It was the only way to save the family. He said, however, that he did not believe Savimbi would go to extremes and blow his chances of ever becoming Angola's president.

'However, of all my family members who gathered in that room that day, I am the only one who was not subsequently killed on Savimbi's orders,' writes Eduardo. 'The others were all executed by 1991.'

Eduardo was eventually told to gather his possessions and board a South African Defence Force helicopter to take him to the outside world. He was given an envelope from Savimbi containing US$500, as a parting gift, and a Zairian passport in the fictitious name of Muko Kongolo. He presumed he was allowed to leave because of the iconic reputation of his dead father – Savimbi dared not curtail the life of the son of UNITA's great hero Kafundanga. Dinho regarded it as a 'great escape.'

Tito, by now in Washington, awaited Eduardo's arrival. But a message from Savimbi diverted Eduardo's civil engineering funds to a course at the University of London. Eduardo regarded this as a deliberate Savimbi ploy to keep the two Chingunjis apart, but they communicated regularly by phone. Together they decided that Tito needed to brief me in depth on what was really happening inside UNITA. When Tito decided in November 1988 to return to Jamba, on Savimbi's instructions, Eduardo pleaded with his uncle not to go. Savimbi would kill him, he said.

Tragically, he was right.

Geraldo Sachipengo Nunda, who plotted Savimbi's killing in 2002, told me that before he defected from UNITA in 1992, he had already detected Savimbi's dark side. Nunda said Savimbi imprisoned him briefly and tried to poison him to death in 1986.

Nunda at the time was commanding four UNITA battalions in the Lunda diamond fields hundreds of kilometres north of Jamba. From time to time, he was called back to Jamba for consultations.

'From 1979 onwards Savimbi's relations with his senior commanders were becoming more remote,' said Nunda. 'He created mistrust. Although he was still militarily sound, he was turning into a dictator who did not consult. There were constant changes in his personality which confused people. The collective leadership had collapsed and Savimbi had begun killing some of his own senior commanders.

'I protested about the 1983 witch burnings. I was the only one in the leadership who spoke out. I believe this tragedy was UNITA's worst mistake. It would mark UNITA and Jonas Savimbi for ever. I told him that neither his father nor my father, who was a Protestant pastor, believed you could advance our war effort through witchcraft. I said many of our people were Christians and that witchcraft practices were superstitious delusions.'

Savimbi punished Nunda by dropping him from a delegation due to visit the United States, but allowed him to return to his battalions. In August 1986, he wrote to Savimbi saying that while UNITA's military strategy remained largely correct, the UNITA leader himself had become too autocratic and that he was mistreating senior commanders. He had transformed into a leader of whom the people were afraid. Nunda, who also told Savimbi he was still too dependent on South Africa, was summoned to Jamba and imprisoned for three months.

'I was expecting to be executed,' said Nunda. 'The prison chief said, "I am sorry. No one leaves here alive." I knew my friend Brigadier Antonio Vakulukuta and another general, Chikossi, were among many people who had been killed there.'

Nunda became suspicious when, after 70 days, guards began bringing milk for him to drink instead of tea or coffee. 'I didn't trust it. I poured it away,' he said. 'I didn't get any additional food, so when they brought a rice pudding I was so hungry that I ate and swallowed a very small portion to test it. There was something strange about the rice, so I didn't eat any more. But within ten minutes I felt as though all my internal organs were dissolving. I was unable to stand up for the rest of the day. A young boy brought water for me containing salt and sugar. The prison chief thought I was dead when he saw me lying down. But when he saw me standing up the next morning he said, "You didn't die?!"'

Nunda was released and continued as a Unita brigadier and then general until Savimbi next tried to kill him, in early 1993, following UNITA's post-election retreat from Luanda.[6] Nunda survived the new assassination attempt, defected to the national army and plotted Savimbi's eventual death, which came on 22 February 2002.

Bela Malaquias, a former captain in UNITA's guerrilla army, also witnessed the enormity of Savimbi's deeds, including the witch burnings of 1983. But her testimony surfaced only in her 2020 book, *Heroínas Da Dignidade* (Dignified Heroines),[7] after she had escaped from UNITA in 1997. She recorded an extraordinary number of killings and abuses of human rights perpetrated by Savimbi, the scale of which is beyond this book's scope but which could be a start document for war crimes trials, either in Angola or internationally. Malaquias said her lists of victims were not exhaustive – there were countless other unknown victims she was unable to document. 'The list is long and difficult, if not impossible, to enumerate,' she wrote. 'There are names that have been lost in time. Savimbi was a cruel social predator, devoid of feelings of remorse and guilt, who left a long trail of destroyed lives. He wielded his power with no restraints whatsoever. He was psychosocially toxic. He was arrogant and thought he knew everything.'

Malaquias told the daily *Jornal de Angola*[8] after her escape: 'When we joined UNITA we were children. You looked up at the ideals. You do not see the future … People were dragged into it before we even knew what the real essence of Savimbi was. I was sixteen.' Bela was reprieved and released in 1983 and recaptured in 1992 before escaping again in 1997.

Asked why more people did not flee from Savimbi's territory, Malaquias said, 'This is harder to explain. People were very afraid and knew if they moved a single blade of grass (without permission) they could be shot. People were so frightened that they were not even willing to be shot in defence of their mother, wife, brother or child. There are people who walk around Luanda today who have seen their young children being shot, but the father remains fanatical about UNITA. It is a situation that cannot be explained.'

Savimbi, Malaquias wrote in *Heroínas Da Dignidade*, was a 'master psychopath' with 'an incomparable degree of mastery'. He knew how

271

to exploit people's weaknesses to consolidate his power. People were either 'bought' or eliminated mercilessly.

Decades in power can cause leaders to succumb to megalomania or paranoia. Savimbi clearly succumbed to both. His promotion of the cult of personality made it likely that he would make a disastrous mistake. The place in history Savimbi yearned for himself clearly went wrong. He was the cause of his own ultimate destruction. He was a highly complex man with endless contradictions, said Sousa Jamba, a prizewinning novelist, prolific journalist and former UNITA political commissar.

'He loved books and education, but killed many intellectuals who fell out with him. He projected himself as a democrat, but he brooked no criticism. This cult was fanned by eager sycophants who wanted to be in the good books of the leader.

'Savimbi was solely motivated by power and by absolute control. He was ready to sacrifice hundreds of lives for his cause. This desire for control attained pathological proportions. He was his own worst enemy.'

ACKNOWLEDGEMENTS

This book could not have been adequately written without the support and prodigious research of Eduardo Chingunji. I am more grateful for his help and friendship than I can tell him. Olga Mundombe was a constant fount of support. Geraldo Sachipengo Nunda is one of the finest men it has been my honour to know, both when I yomped with him across Angola when he was one of UNITA's top commanders, and later when he began a revolt that proved terminal against Jonas Savimbi and his excesses.

I am deeply grateful to Annie Olivier for commissioning this work. She is a fine and lovely person. Karin Schimke was patient, indulgent and hard-working in the course of a gruelling final edit.

My thanks are eternal to Kathryn Bridgland-Kane, who died in 2016 after a long illness. Kathryn understood and suffered the Angola story. She was much loved by Tito, and she loved him.

Sue Armstrong has lived with the Angola saga and me now for a very long time. Her love, indulgence and encouragement have been beyond value.

My daughters Annwen, Rebecca and Samantha were more neglected than they should have been because of the demands of my sometimes wild career and lifestyle. But they were always much loved, still are and always will be. I thank them for putting up with me.

Edinburgh, 17 June 2022

NOTES

Prologue

1   *The Cuban Intervention in Angola, 1965–1991: From Che Guevara to Cuito Cuanavale*, Edward George (Frank Cass Publishing, London, 2005).

2   The largely peaceful coup was christened the Carnation Revolution as young protestors placed red carnations in the gun barrels of soldiers on duty.

3   Full name Pedro Ngueve Jonatão 'Tito' Chingunji. He was born on 5 July 1955.

4   I've been asked a few times whether Tito believed it was the witch doctor's 'magic' that worked and saved him. I doubt it. I think he was being gently ironic. However, Tito, a sophisticated man brought up as a Christian, deeply understood the rural population's cultural beliefs in a host of different spirits.

5   Mao Zedong's famous Long March in southwest China lasted a year in 1934–1935 and covered some 6 500 kilometres, crossing 24 rivers and 18 mountain ranges, as Mao's Communist insurgent guerrillas fled from encirclement by Nationalist government forces. The Long March established Mao as the undisputed leader of the Chinese Communist Party. He took power in 1949, after the Chinese Nationalist Party was defeated, and he ruled China for 27 years until his death in 1976.

6   According to minutes of a declassified US National Security Council meeting as quoted by the Paris-based *Mondafrique*, 20 August 2021.

7   See Chapter 2.

1. How it began

1   The ZANU infighting followed the assassination in Lusaka of ZANU leader Herbert Chitepo. To this day, it is unclear who killed Chitepo.

2   The MPLA was backed by the Soviet Union and its stronghold was around Luanda, the capital, on the Atlantic coast. UNITA's strength was on the high central Angola plateau and in the south. It was initially supported by China. A third movement, the FNLA (the National Liberation Front of Angola), was based in the far north. It was the weakest of the three movements and was initially supported by both China and the American CIA.

3   See, for example, *My Life With Tiny: A Biography of Tiny Rowland*, Richard Hall (Faber and Faber, London, 1987); *Tiny Rowland: A Rebel Tycoon*, Tom Bower (William Heinemann, London, 1993).

4   Renamed Cuito after independence.

5   The Alvor Accords, signed on 15 January 1975 in the Portuguese coastal village of Alvor, gave Angola independence from 11 November 1975 onwards.

6   Polícia Internacional e de Defesa do Estado (International and State Defence Police).

7   *CNN Perspectives* series, episode 17, 9 January 1998.

8   Declassified US National Security Council minutes, as quoted by the Paris-based *Mondafrique*, 20 August 2021.

9   *In Search of Enemies: a CIA Story*, John Stockwell (WW Norton, New York, 1984).

10 *In Search of Enemies.*

2. Jonas Savimbi

1   Author interviews with Fernandes, 6 July 2006 and 18 June 1998.

2   Conversation between the author and Professor Rieben at the

European Research Centre, Lausanne University, 15 May 1984.

3   Savimbi at that time was a convinced Maoist and remained so even when he began later to accept help from Western counties and proclaim his belief in democracy.

4   Leon Dash, in a series of four articles, headlined 'The War in Angola', in the *Washington Post*, 23–26 December 1973.

3. A military coup in Portugal

1   The elections promised in the Alvor Accords would not be held for another 17 years.

2   *Zambia's Foreign Policy: Studies in Diplomacy and Dependence*, Douglas G. Anglin and Timothy M. Shaw (Westview Press, 1979). *The Times* of London, 7 January 1976, reported that Kaunda appealed to Ford 'to reverse what he considered to be a tide sweeping the MPLA to victory'.

4. Some surprise help for UNITA

1   *Portugal's War in Angola,* WS van der Waals (Protea, Pretoria, 2011).

2   South West Africa, bordering Angola, was a German colony from 1884 to 1915. Following the First World War it was ruled by South Africa under a League of Nations mandate. Although the mandate was abolished by the United Nations in 1966, South Africa continued to control the territory despite its illegality in international law. The territory became independent as the Republic of Namibia in 1990.

3   Michael Nicholson died in 1996 at the age of 79. His colleagues at Independent Television News described him as a 'true legend', and some of his many exploits were indeed legendary. While reporting from Sarajevo in 1992, at the height of the war in Bosnia, Mike found 200 orphans living in a shell-wrecked building. Four children had been killed. Nicholson smuggled one of the orphans, nine-year-old Natasha Mihaljcic, out of the country, claiming to officials that she was his daughter. Mike and his wife, Diana, adopted Natasha and raised her with their own other three children.

Natasha subsequently went to university and graduated with a degree in England. The 1997 Hollywood movie *Welcome to Sarajevo* was based upon Mike's and Natasha's story.

4   At no stage did the United States or other Western democracies send, or consider sending, troops to fight alongside UNITA. There would have been no public appetite for involvement, and after it became clear that apartheid South Africa had become UNITA's ally that reluctance inevitably hardened. However, this did not stop the Western democracies, in a game of smoke and mirrors, from secretly encouraging the South Africans to get involved. The West did not want the Soviets, the Cubans their MPLA client to succeed in Angola.

5. International scoop

1   *Les Rebelles – Contre L'Ordre du Monde,* Jean Ziegler (Éditions du Seuil, Paris, 1983). One of Ziegler's best-known aphorisms reads: 'A child who dies from hunger is a murdered child.'

2   *In Search of Enemies: A CIA Story,* John Stockwell (WW Norton, New York, 1984).

6. South Africa and the US pull back

1   See *In Search of Freedom: The Andreas Shipanga Story,* Andreas Shipanga, as told to Sue Armstrong (Ashanti Publishing, Gibraltar, 1989).

2   17 April 1978.

3   *CNN Perspectives* series, episode 17, 9 January 1998.

4   *Evening Standard,* London, 10 February 1976.

5   *High Noon in Southern Africa: Making Peace in a Rough Neighbourhood,* Chester Crocker (WW Norton, New York, 1992).

7. The young Cuban who never fired a shot

1   Luis Rodriguez, a former Luanda newspaperman and BBC correspondent.

2   See: 'Portrait of a Rebel', by Sousa Jamba. *BBC Focus on Africa,* April–June 2002.

3 This divide between Moscow and Beijing was happening at the height of the Sino-Soviet split. There was a serious break of political relations between the People's Republic of China and the Soviet Union caused by communist doctrinal divergences. The split between the world's two biggest communist states lasted for more than a decade, and they even fought a number of military border skirmishes in Manchuria.

4 When I got back to Silva Porto I met an American NBC-TV team who were as surly and self-important as only an American crew can sometimes be when frustrated in pursuit of an objective. They had been patrolling Silva Porto's streets one afternoon shooting atmospheric footage when a convoy of South African soldiers drove through the town centre. The South Africans waved cheerfully at the townspeople, who waved back. The NBC cameraman merged into the crowds and shot the scenes. Nobody bothered him, and the NBC people went to bed at the former governor's mansion delighted with their scoop. But at 4.30 am a squad of UNITA soldiers burst into their rooms and at gunpoint confiscated all their film. Mike Nicholson's ITN footage remained the only film of South African soldiers to emerge from UNITA territory.

9. All external support for Savimbi collapses

1 *The Times* of London, 7 January 1976.
2 Reuters, Lusaka, 6 February 1976. Text of President Kaunda's national broadcast, 28 January 1976, declaring a national state of emergency.
3 Savimbi, in conversation with author, 21 January 1980.

10. Fighting back

1 *The New York Times*, 3 June 1976.
2 *The First Dance of Freedom*, Martin Meredith (Hamish Hamilton, London, 1985); *Angola: A Country Study*, Irving Kaplan (American University, Washington, DC, 1985); Jim Hoagland writing in *The Washington Post*, 28 May 1978.
3 See Prologue.

4 *The Struggle for Africa: Conflict of the Great Powers*, Gérard Challiand (Macmillan, London, 1982).

5 *The Angolan Revolution, Volume 2: Exile Politics and Guerrilla Warfare, 1962–1976* (The MIT Press, Cambridge, Massachusetts, 1978).

6 *The Christian Science Monitor*, 31 May 1983.

7 The London *Guardian*, 11 May and 22 December 1978.

8 *The New York Times*, 8 November 1979; *Newsweek*, 12 November 1979.

9 See Epilogue.

10 The 1922 Committee is the parliamentary group of the Conservative Party in the United Kingdom's House of Commons. The committee, consisting of all Conservative backbench Members of Parliament, meets weekly while Parliament is in session and provides a way for backbenchers to coordinate and express their views independently of government ministers.

11 *Institute of Strategic Studies* communiqué, 7 July 1980; *The Times* of London, 7 July 1980; *The Sunday Times* of London, 13 July 1980.

12 UNITA communiqué No 15/80, 25 August 1980. The MPLA men killed were named as Sub-Lt Jose Maria; Sgt Kisua Jacinto; Sub-Lt Pedro Tiragem; Sub-Lt Chico Joao Belo; Sgt Augusto Daniel Seco Seco; Political Commissar Joao Sahinga; security official Mario Pinto Jaime; Sub-Lt Necas; Sgt Zenza Dipombo; Lt Domingos Pedro; Sgt Antonio N'Jila; Sgt Jose Ngongo; Sgt Bento Joao Domingos; Sgt Alberto Zange; Sgt Estavao Euardo.

11. Mavinga

1 'Savimbi Defends Links With South Africans,' Richard Harwood, *Washington Post*, 24 July 1981.

12. Soviet prisoners

1 Kolya and Chernietsky were released a year later.

14. Consequences

1 *Washington Post*, 25 July 1981.

15. UNITA and the South Africans thrust north

1 The London *Observer*, 6 April 1986.
2 *The Times* of London and the East London *Daily Dispatch*, 12 August 1982; *Newsweek*, 23 August 1982; *The Economist*, 11 September 1982.
3 Reuters despatch from Luanda, 17 December 1981.
4 *The New York Times*, 4 December 1981.
5 *The Observer*, London, 24 January 1982.
6 *Africa Analysis* report, South Africa, 25 November 1988.

16. Cangonga and the Benguela Railway

1 Some Portuguese who lived in Angola joined UNITA, and also the MPLA, after independence.

18. 'I can only tell you the things that happened as I saw them'

1 For one detailed government account of the Cangamba battle, see *The Cuban Intervention in Angola, 1965–1991: From Che Guevara to Cuito Cuanavale*, Edward George (Frank Cass Publishing, London, 2005).
2 *Mafeking Road*, Herman Charles Bosman (Human & Rousseau, Cape Town, 1974).
3 *Newsweek*, 19 September 1983; *Washington Post*, 6 October 1983.
4 Radio Prague International, 2 August 2011.
5 To my deep regret, I have been unable to find the address given to me by Mr Novostny. I am trying to trace him through the Prague media and the post-communist Czech Republic Embassy in London.

19. British captives

1 *Washington Post*, 6 October 1983; *Newsweek*, 10 October 1983; Godwin Matatu, reporting from Luanda for November 1983 edition 147 of *Africa* magazine.
2 London *Daily Telegraph*, 2 April 1984.
3 *The Times* of London, 17 May 1984.
4 *The Times* of London, 14 and 17 May 1984; *Daily Telegraph* of London, 2 April 1984.

5   TASS, Luanda, 21 April 1984; *Angola Press Agency* (Angop), 23 April 1984; *Granma*, Havana, 25 April 1984; UNITA Communiqué No. 10/84, 20 April 1984.

20. 'Only peace will allow us finally to realise who we are'

1   *Jonas Savimbi: A Key to Africa*, Fred Bridgland (Hodder and Stoughton, London, 1988).

22. Peace agreements

1   I wrote about these battles in my book *Cuito Cuanavale: 12 Months of War that Transformed a Continent*, published by Jonathan Ball in 2017. The book appeared under a different title, *The War for Africa: Twelve Months that Transformed a Continent*, in 2017 by Casemate Publishers, Philadelphia and Oxford.

2   Between 7 and 11 November 1989.

23. A shock game-changing revelation

1   For detailed account of the death of Eduardo, see Epilogue.

2   UNITA moved from Delta to its Jamba base in 1980. The Delta base was dismantled in 1990 by the new government of Namibia.

3   Isabel died of cancer in the 1950s. She was the mother of Joanatão's two oldest sons. Violeta was the mother of his other eight children.

4   The eruption of the witchcraft narrative took me aback, despite the fact that I had already learned to take seriously many African traditional beliefs in a spirit world that permeates aspects of people's lives, especially in rural areas. Savimbi used witchcraft allegations innumerable times to justify assassinations. He may have believed that by killing strong people he increased his own mental and physical strength, recharging batteries that were running down.

It is a sensitive subject, but it is accepted in many parts of 21st century Africa that everyone runs the risk, despite education and globalisation, of being harmed by a witch: sooner or later, the evil is likely to get you. An accusation of sorcery can lead to violent and sometimes lethal retribution by communities. Huge ranges of spirits that Westerners mock are real to many, but of course not all, Africans. The white Rhodesian Army attempted to undermine enemy morale by dropping pamphlets by air in guerrilla-held areas telling the fighters that their ancestral spirits were displeased with their resort to violence.

In 1995, I interviewed in Harare, Zimbabwe's capital, Father Oskar Wempter, a Jesuit missionary and anthropologist from Germany who has studied Zimbabwean culture for many decades. He said that spiritually many black Africans live in two worlds. In normal circumstances those who have embraced Christianity are happy to follow a Christian way of life but, under stress, they tend to return to older beliefs. 'Two ways of thinking exist, often in the same person,' Father Wempter said. 'When they are sick, or they have had an accident, or they fail their driving test, or they go bankrupt, or a relative dies, people don't ask *what* caused it, but *who?* – that is, what unsettled spirit was at work?'

Allegations of witchcraft are made surprisingly easily – just as they were in mediaeval Europe. So, I suspect, it was not difficult for Savimbi to convince the majority of his followers, mainly rural and little educated, of the need for cathartic 'witch hunts.'

My late friend Heidi Holland wrote an excellent book on African traditional beliefs, *African Magic* (Viking, London, 2021), which I highly recommend. In the course of my own reporting, I once consulted a witch doctor, Peter Sibanda, in Harare. I asked him on which continent my future lay after shuttling between Africa and Europe for 20 years. Dressed in leopard skins and a monkey-fur hat, he asked me to close my eyes and establish contact with the spirits of my dead ancestors. Mr Sibanda threw his 'bones' – shells of the marula tree nut marinated in traditional wine and exposed at length to good and bad spirits. Before long, Mr Sibanda, a smiling man with twinkling eyes, established contact with the spirit of my maternal grandmother. She approved of the way I had conducted my life, thank goodness. She said important decisions loomed and I would eventually return to Britain, but only after I had completed a number of remaining tasks in Africa.

Ten years later, I returned home to Scotland for good. Thanking Mr Sibanda, I settled my bill, the equivalent of ten English pounds – a bargain, I felt, when compared to Harley Street's fees! (Harley Street in Central London has been famous since the 19th century as the location of extremely high-fee private medical specialist practices, including plastic and cosmetic surgery.)

5 An account confirmed by Bela Malaquias in her autobiography *Heroínas Da Dignidade* (Dignified Heroines), Nellcorp Publishing, Luanda, 2020. See also *Jornal de Angola* (Luanda's leading daily newspaper), 12 November 2019, and also an Amnesty International report, dated 23 June 1992, with the title 'Arbitrary detention/fear of disappearance, Bela Malaquias, her sister Germana "Tita" Malaquias and her father, Nelson.'

24. The murder of Jorge Sangumba

1 See 'Portrait of a Rebel', by Sousa Jamba, *BBC Focus on Africa*, April–June 2002.

2 6 July 2006 and 18 June 1998, London. Fernandes defected from UNITA in 1992 and subsequently served as the Angolan government's ambassador in London and New Delhi.

3 In one of many email conversations between 2019 and 2022.

25. Witch burning and other atrocities

1 *Heroínas Da Dignidade* (Dignified Heroines), Florbela Catrina Malaquias (Nellcorp Publishing, Luanda, 2020).

2 Leon Dash quoted senior UNITA defector George Chikoti, a former member of Savimbi's bodyguard, as saying the UNITA leader justified murdering children by saying, 'The sons and daughters of witches are also witches.' *Washington Post*, 30 September 1990, 'Blood and Fire: Savimbi's War Against His UNITA Rivals.'

3 Leon Dash, in a series of four articles, headlined 'The War in Angola', in the *Washington Post*, 23–26 December 1973.

4 Interview with author, London, July 2006.

5 *The New York Times*, 10 March 1989, 'Ex-Allies Say Angola Rebels

Torture and Slay Dissenters', by Craig Whitney and Jill Jolliffe.
6   Bela twice escaped from UNITA's control. The first time she was recaptured before escaping again in 1998.

27. Death threats

1   See Epilogue.
2   *The New York Times*, 10 March 1989.
3   *Patriots*, Sousa Jamba (Penguin Books, London, 1992).
4   *The Spectator*, 18 March 1989.
5   'Portrait of a Rebel', by Sousa Jamba; *BBC Focus on Africa*, April–June 2002.
6   Interviews with author, London, 6 July 2006 and 18 June 1998. Fernandes defected from UNITA in 1992.

28. Show trial

1   Actually, a beautiful oxbow lake, alive with waterfowl, in the flood-plain of the Utembo River.
2   Author's phone calls with Vahekeny before and after November/December 1988.
3   Interview with author, London, 6 July 2006.
4   Eduardo Chingunji and others are the source for this. Eduardo, who lives in Luanda, has carried out years of detailed research on events inside UNITA. He hopes eventually to publish his own findings, possibly in four volumes and as evidence for the International Criminal Court on crimes committed against humanity by some UNITA leaders.

29. Dark times

1   I was hired by the *Sunday Telegraph*, where Frank Thompson was by far the finest foreign editor I ever worked for. Frank gave me permission to write also for *The Scotsman* and for the Japanese news magazine *Shinchosha* (Foresight).
2   Shawn clearly meant that whatever happened to Tito, the Washington political establishment, people would easily forget, as they did with Jorge Sangumba.

3 See Chapter 31.

4 'The Mystique of Savimbi', by Radek Sikorski in the *National Review*, New York, 18 August 1989.

5 As related to the author by Nancy Soderberg.

31. Tito is dead

1 6 July 2006, London.

2 'Angola's Savimbi brings bloody past to election', by Liz Sly in Luanda, *Chicago Tribune*, 29 September 1992.

3 Author interviews with Fernandes, 6 July 2006 and 18 June 1998.

4 Fernandes, 6 July 2006, and evidence gathered by Eduardo Chingunji from multiple sources.

5 *Mal Me Querem* (They Don't Want Me), Miguel N'Zau (Papiro Editora, Porto, 2011).

6 While it was Kamy Pena, as head of Savimbi's execution squad, who led Puna to the bodies, no one to this day has been identified as the person or persons who wielded the clubs or fired the guns that killed any member of the Chingunji family.

7 As quoted by a United Nations Situation Report on Relief Operations in Angola, 1 February–31 March 1992. *Rebels and Robbers in Post-Colonial Angola*, Assis Malaquias (Nordiska Afrikainstitutet, Uppsala, 2007).

8 For example, 'Deaths and Desertions Undermine Tenacious Angolan Rebel', by Christopher S Wren, *The New York Times*, 7 April 1992.

9 'Profile: Jonas Savimbi, UNITA's local boy', by Chris Simpson, 29 January 1999. Simpson was the broadcaster's Angola correspondent in the 1990s. He died following a heart attack aged 53 in October 2016.

32. Death by chameleon

1 Fred Bridgland, 'Angola's Secret Bloodbath', *Washington Post*, 29 March 1992.

2 US Senate report, 7 May 1992.

3 Savimbi said in his response to Baker that Tito and Wilson and

their families had been killed on 12 and 13 November 1991. In fact, Puna and others confirmed, they were executed much earlier, on 5 July 1991.

4   Liz Sly, *Chicago Tribune*, 29 September 1992.
5   As told to Leon Dash, *Washington Post*, 30 September 1990.

33. The peace collapses and war resumes

1   On a 91.30 per cent voter turnout, the MPLA won 129 seats in the 220-member National Assembly and UNITA won 70.
2   Scott Peterson reporting for the *Sunday Telegraph*, 21 June 1992.
3   Mercedes Sayagues, *Mail & Guardian*, South Africa, 26 February 1999.
4   Judith Matloff, *Fragments of a Forgotten War* (Penguin, London, 1997).
5   A private South African 'security consultant' firm, Executive Outcomes provided armed personnel to assist government forces. Executive Outcomes had a multi-million dollar contract with the Luanda government. A leading Israeli military security company, Levdan, founded by retired senior generals, began training government soldiers and providing other services.

34. Savimbi: the end

1   See Chapter 18. As well as yomping with Nunda and his UNITA battalion in 1983, I interviewed him in depth in Luanda in September 1995 and twice in London in late 2021 after he became Angola's Ambassador to the United Kingdom.
2   See 'Sudden-Death Overtime: The Last Days of Jonas Savimbi and the End of the Angolan Civil War', 15 February 2003, by American journalist Sunni Khalid on kenyatalk.com: https://www.kenyatalk.com/index.php?threads/slow-sunday-the-last-days-of-jonas-savimbi-a-very-long-posting.70196/
3   'Angola and the Violent Years 1975–2008', by Linda M Heywood in the *Portuguese Studies Review*, January–July 2011.
4   *Seminario Angolense*, Luanda, 22 February 2022.

Epilogue

1 Interview, 30 May 2022.
2 'Blood and Fire: Savimbi's War Against His UNITA Rivals', by Leon Dash, *Washington Post*, 30 September 1990.
3 Recorded in a manuscript by Eduardo Chingunji. Eduardo, whose research sources are multiple, widespread and collated over many years, intends publishing the memoir as a book. His sources include his mother and close relatives, before they were murdered, and many defectors and survivors of Savimbi's purges.
4 Effectively deputy leader of UNITA.
5 And I also learned for the first time from Eduardo.
6 See Chapter 34.
7 Full title *Heroínas Da Dignidade: Memórias de Guerra, Um Invulgar Testemunho de Um Feminicídio e da Desmistificação da Figura Idolatrada de Jonas Savimbi* (Dignified Heroines: Memories of War. The Extraordinary Testimony of a Woman Liberation Fighter and the Demystification of the Idolised Figure of Jonas Savimbi), by Bela Malaquias (Nellcorp Publishing, Luanda, 2020).
8 *Jornal de Angola,* 12 November 2019, '5th Grade women were Jonas Savimbi's preferred targets', by Bela Malaquias.

INDEX

Page numbers in italics indicate photo captions.

ABOUT THE AUTHOR

FRED BRIDGLAND is a veteran British foreign correspondent and author. He reported on the Angolan civil war and the Border War for Reuters as the agency's Central Africa correspondent in the 1970s and then from South Africa for the *Sunday Telegraph* and *The Scotsman* in the 1980s and 1990s.

In 1975, he revealed the secret invasion of Angola by the South African Defence Force in support of the UNITA rebel forces.

Bridgland has written several books, including *Cuito Cuanavale: 12 Months of War that Transformed a Continent* (2017) and *Truth, Lies and Alibis: A Winnie Mandela Story* (2018).

www.ingramcontent.com/pod-product-compliance
Lightning Source LLC
Chambersburg PA
CBHW062043080426
42734CB00012B/2549